Skiing Tales Of Terror

T0163641

William Nealy

MENASHA RIDGE PRESS
Your Guide to the Outdoors Since 1982
an imprint of AdventureKEEN

Skiing Tales of Terror

Printed in the United States of America

Published by
MENASHA RIDGE PRESS
Your Guide to the Outdoors Since 1982
an imprint of AdventureKEEN

2204 First Ave. S., Ste. 102
Birmingham, Alabama 35233
800-678-7006, FAX 877-374-9016
adventurewithkeen.com

ISBN 978-1-63404-370-0 (pbk); ISBN 978-1-63404-371-7 (ebook)

PUBLISHER'S NOTE

What you hold in your hands is a book of William Nealy's art, pulled from the gnarliest Class VI rapids of time . . . almost lost forever.

But now Nealy's zany illustrations have been bound and bandaged together in a new monumental collection, including books and cartoons long out of print. Nealy's full-speed downhill no-holds-barred art has been reset and brought back to life like never before.

This is the craziest collection of cartoons since Nealy first put paddle to water and pen to paper. The result is a hilarious slice of the outdoor community as extreme and cutting as Nealy was himself.

Many of the illustrations have not been seen since they were first published. Now they're back and will certainly delight old and new Nealy fans alike. We've taken care to make sure the flow of Nealy's stories and illustrations work just as well in this new format as they did when they were first published years ago.

We are proud at Menasha Ridge Press and AdventureKEEN to help return Nealy's art and irreverent illustrations to the bookshelf. Nealy had a gift for teaching, storytelling, and capturing the beauty of the rivers he sketched and the people he loved. His humorous approach to telling the twisted tales of paddlers, mountain bikers, hikers, campers, inline skaters, and skiers everywhere is a gift to all participating in the weird, wonderful world of outdoor sports.

You can learn more about William, his art, and his many books at thewilliamnealy.com.

SINCERELY,
THE MENASHA RIDGE
PRESS TEAM

This book is dedicated to
Holly *
My permanent girlfriend *and main editor

Sherman

* She says "Watch
it, ski bunnies !!"

Dedication!
me?
Oh goody!

Harold

Acknowledgments

For their significant contributions to ski humor, special thanks to: Bob Sehlinger, Joe Cotton, Ed Chauner, James and Madison Torrence, Doug Tims, Henry & Donna Unger, Mark Zwick, Dan Cotton, Virginia Chambers, J.T. Lemmons, Marty Newley, John Barbour, Milo Asay, Aurelia Kennedy, Vera Novak, Sherri & Little Joe Cotton, Keith Griffall and Gordon Wade! Thanks, Dudes!!

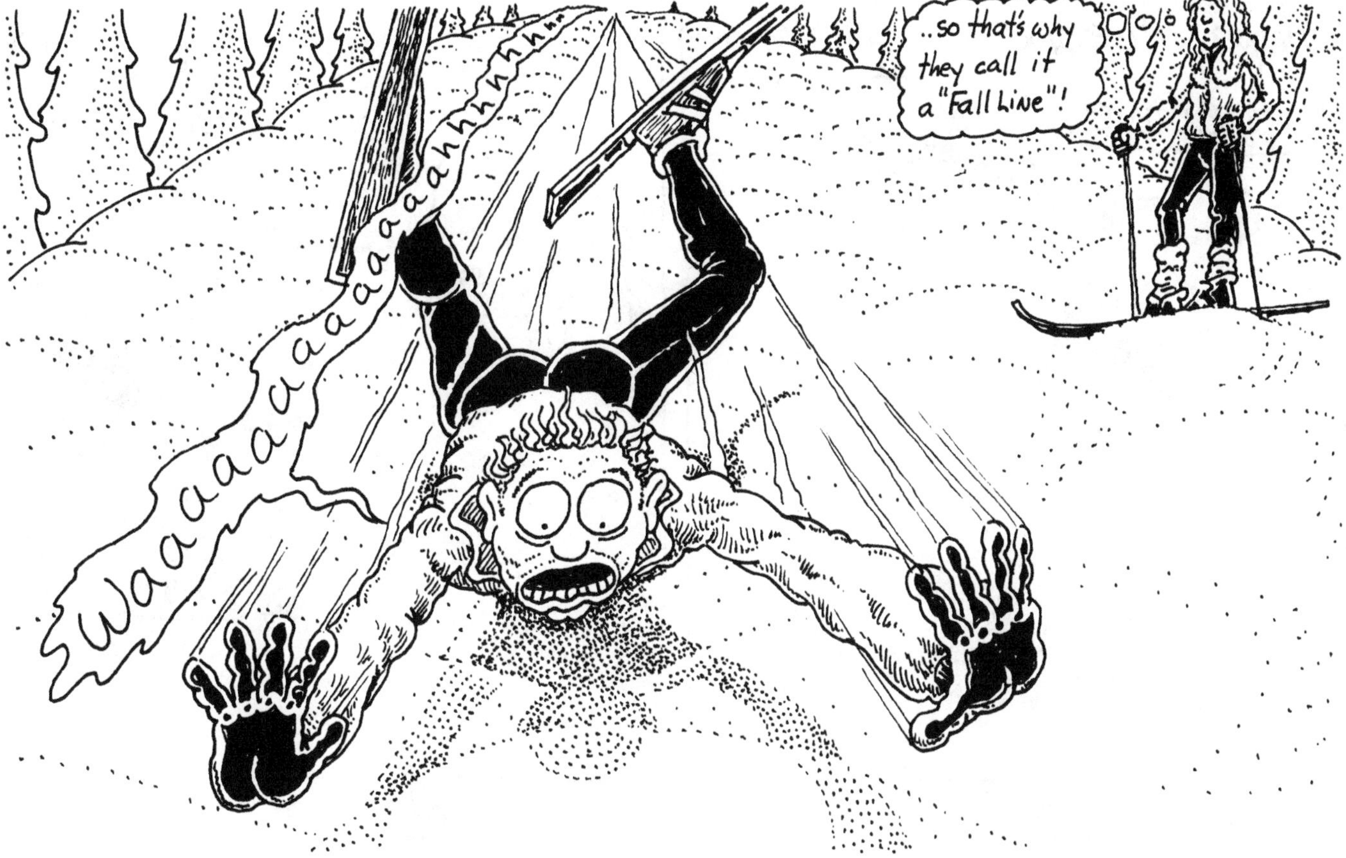
Waaaaaaaaaaaaaaaaaaahhhhhhhhhhhh
..so that's why they call it a "Fall Line"!

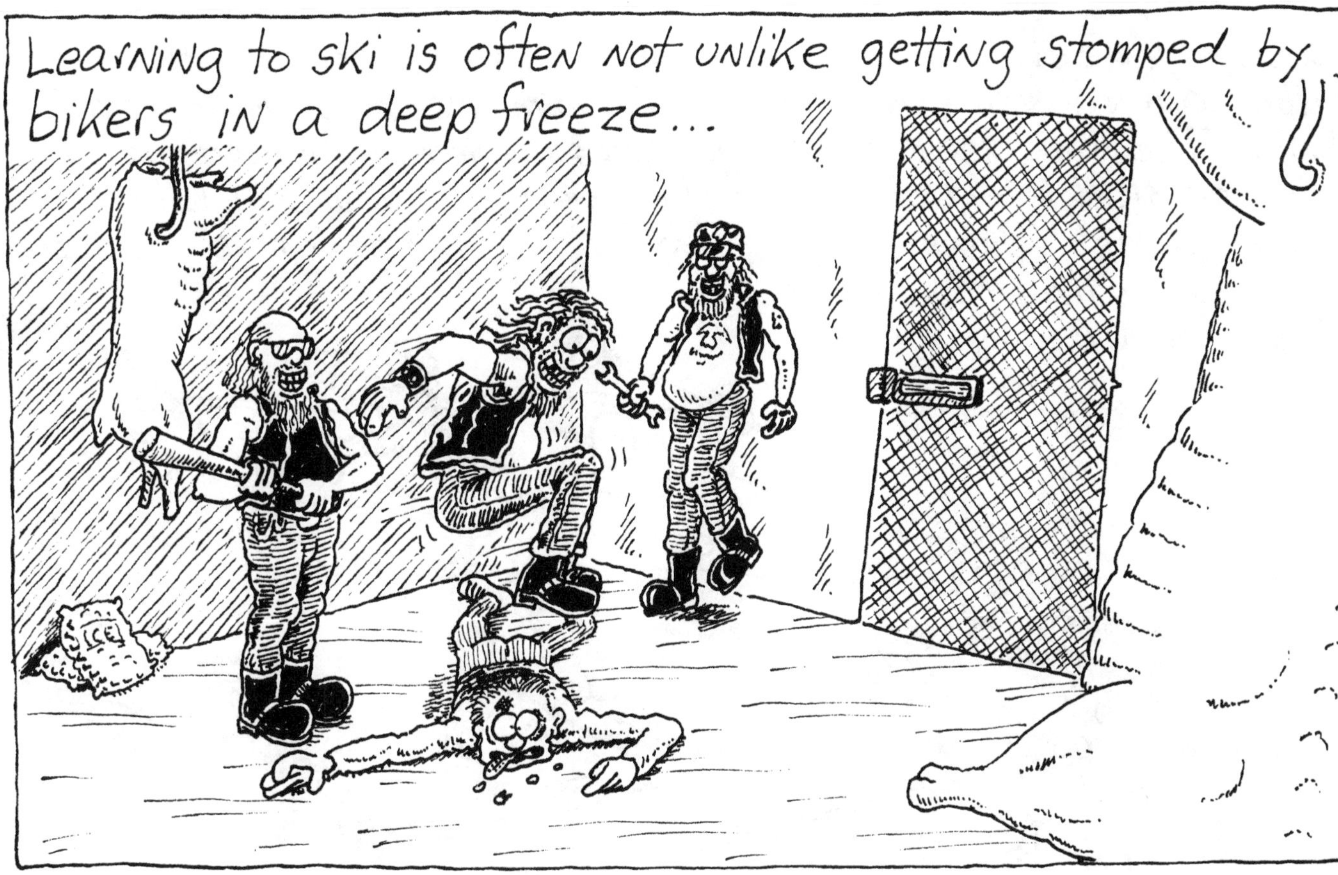
Learning to ski is often not unlike getting stomped by bikers in a deep freeze...
ICE

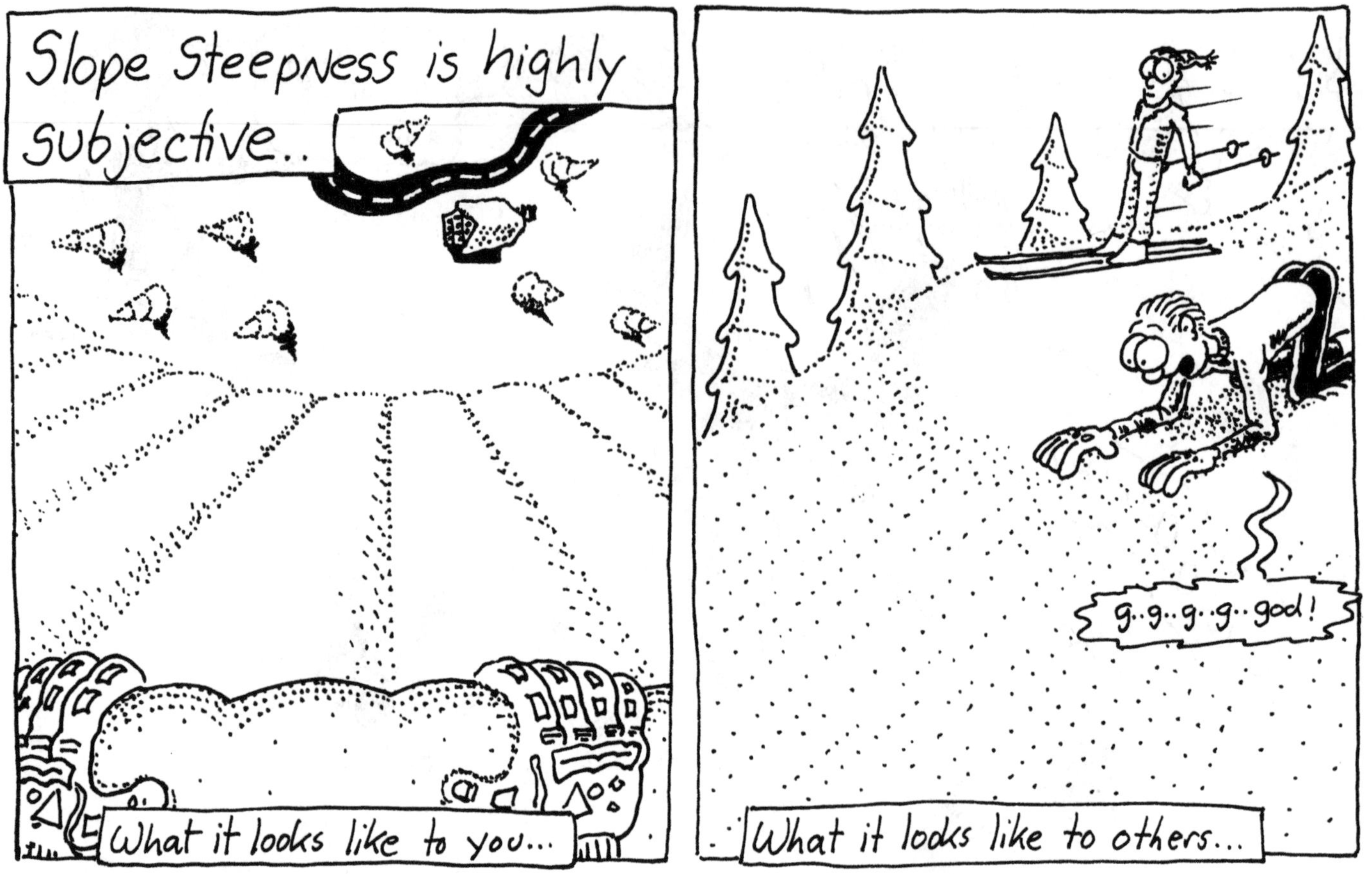
Slope Steepness is highly subjective...
What it looks like to you...
g..g..g..g..god!
What it looks like to others...

Geek (gēēk) N.- Generic term for beginner skiers. Also describes daring-yet-exceptionally-awkward skiers of higher skill levels. The true geek skier's gameness is inversely proportional to his/her skill level (or lack-of-skill level!). Variations include: "dork", "dweeb", "Barney", "gork", Freddie", etc. The geek motto: "It's better to be lucky than good!".
Geeky (adj.). Geekily (adv.)

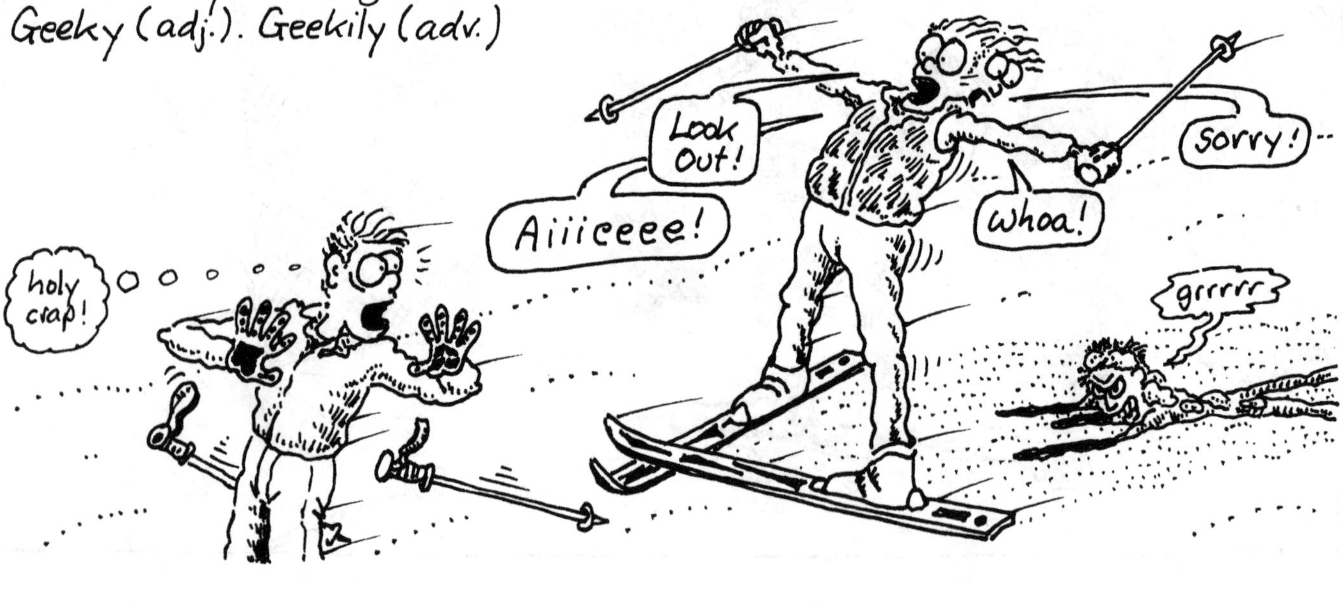
holy crap!
Aiiiceee!
Look Out!
whoa!
Sorry!
grrrrr

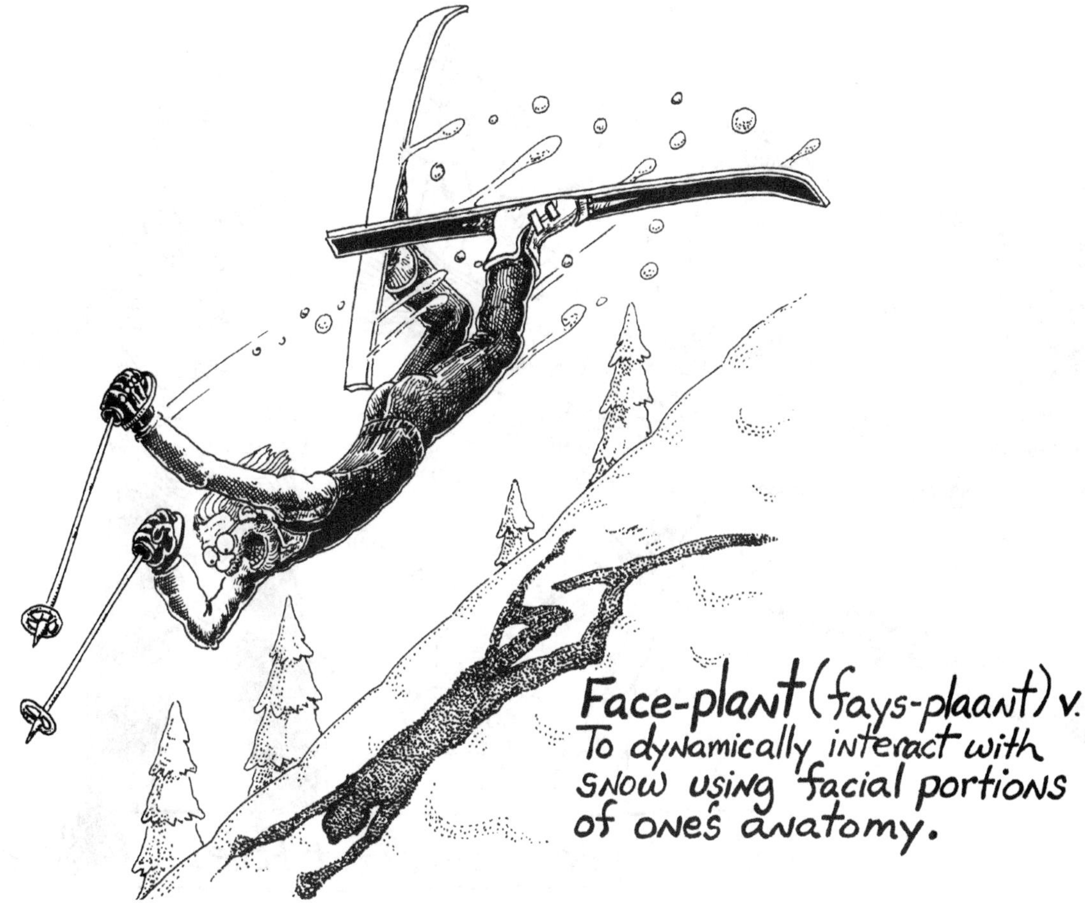
Face-plant (fays-plaant) v.
To dynamically interact with snow using facial portions of one's anatomy.

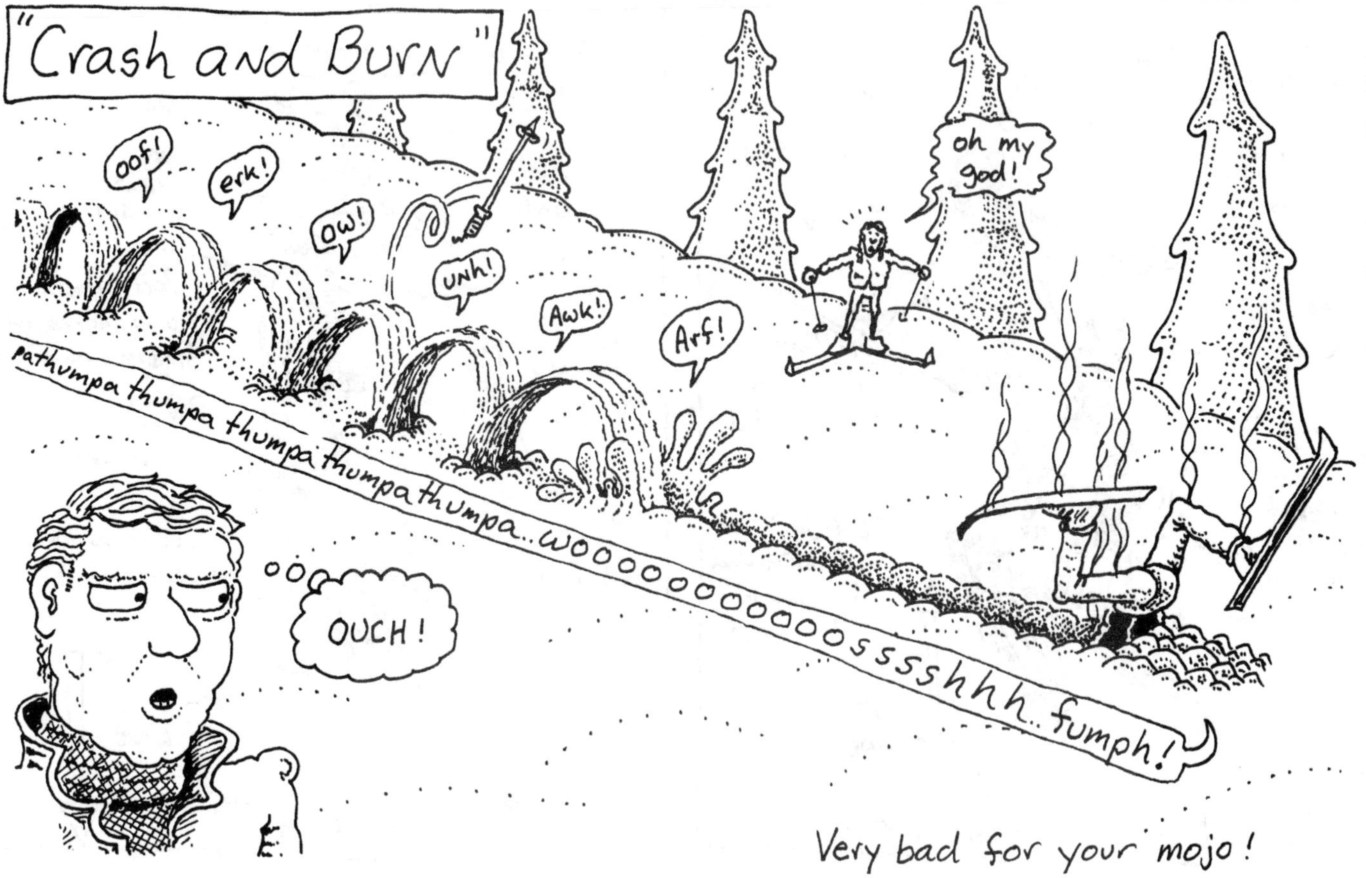
"Crash and Burn"
oof!
erk!
OW!
unh!
Awk!
Arf!
oh my god!
pathumpa thumpa thumpa thumpa thumpa thumpa..wooooooooooooosssshhh..fumph!
OUCH!
Very bad for your mojo!

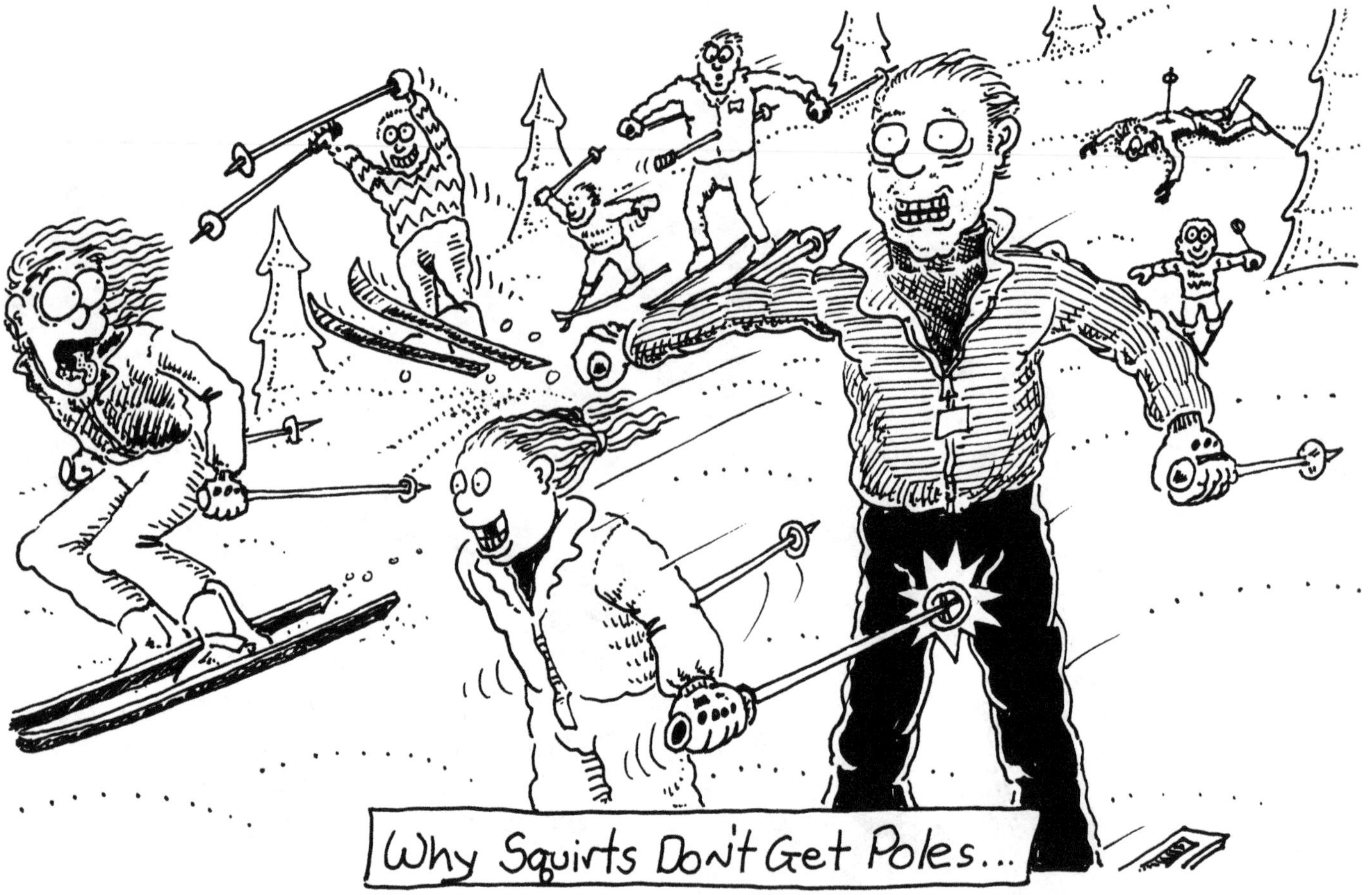

Why Squirts Don't Get Poles...

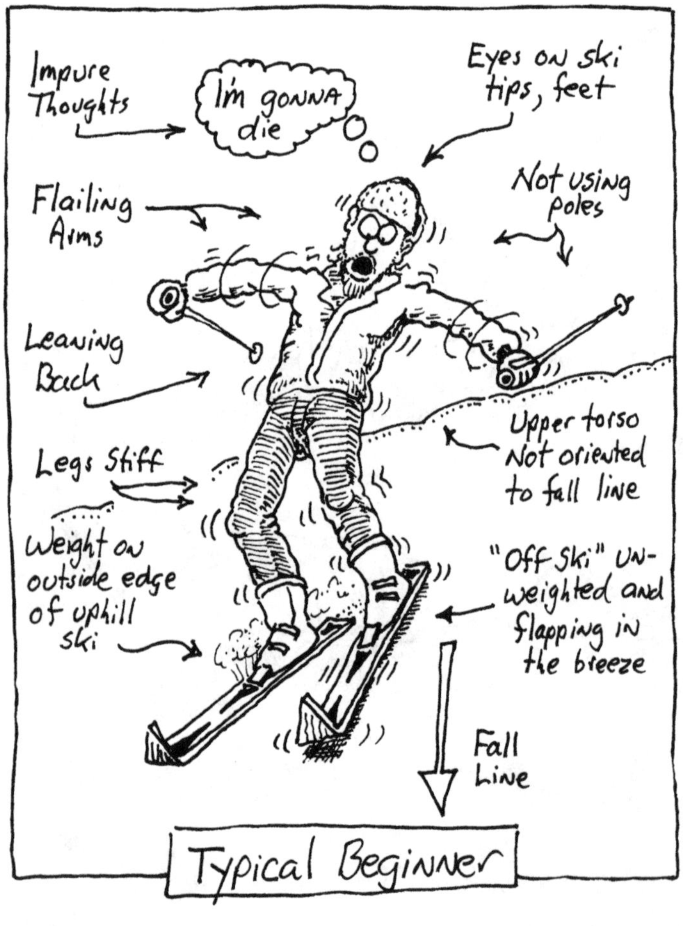
Impure Thoughts
I'm gonna die
Eyes on ski tips, feet
Flailing Arms
Not using poles
Leaning Back
Upper torso Not oriented to fall line
Legs Stiff
Weight on outside edge of uphill ski
"Off Ski" un-weighted and flapping in the breeze
Fall Line

Typical Beginner

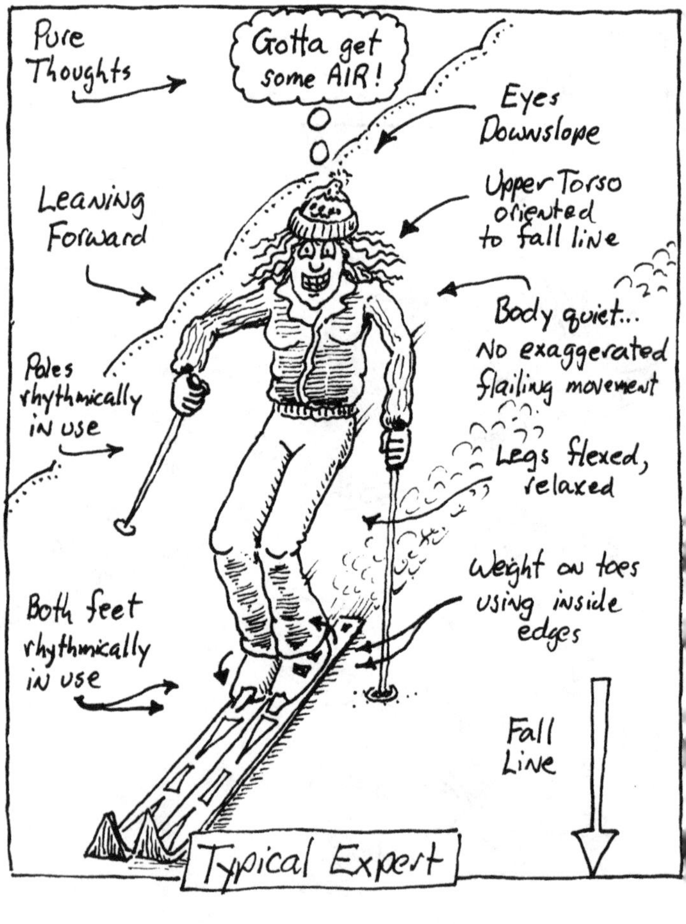
Pure Thoughts
Gotta get some AIR!
Eyes Downslope
Leaning Forward
Upper Torso oriented to fall line
Body quiet... No exaggerated flailing movement
Poles rhythmically in use
Legs flexed, relaxed
Weight on toes using inside edges
Both feet rhythmically in use
Fall Line

Typical Expert

Learning To Fall

Since you'll be wiping out every few seconds as a beginner it is very important to learn how to fall safely and stylishly. The Basic Fall protocol is as follows: the moment your neurons perceive a fall-in-progress you relax your body and sort of collapse into a laid-out sitting position to either side of your skis. Avoid fighting a fall by thrashing wildly* in the vain hope of stopping the fall... injury will ultimately result. Just relax and fall then get up and do it again. And again. Once you've learned to fall in a relaxed manner, it's almost fun!

* See "Flailing Fall"

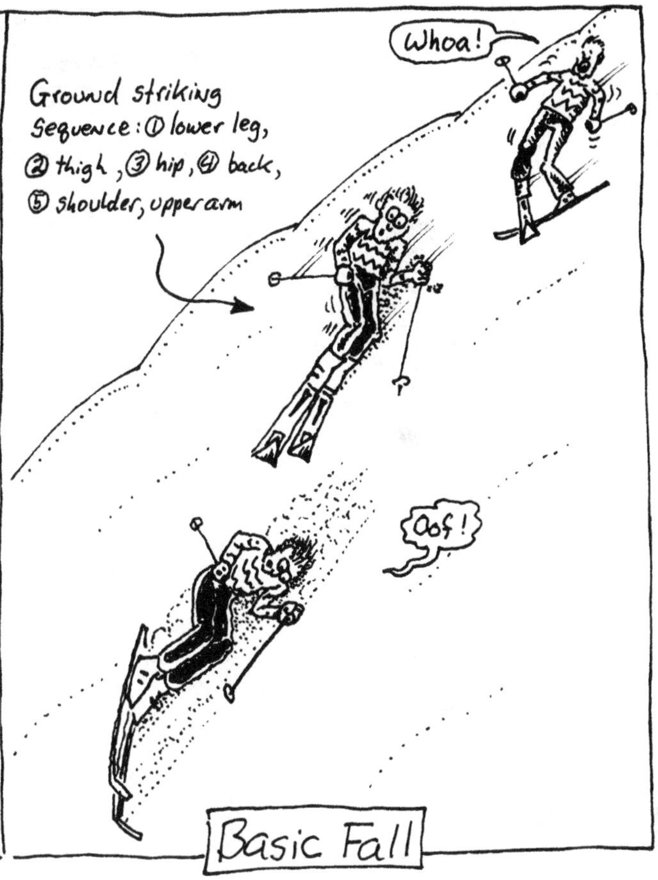
Whoa!
Ground striking sequence: ① lower leg, ② thigh, ③ hip, ④ back, ⑤ shoulder, upper arm
Oof!
Basic Fall

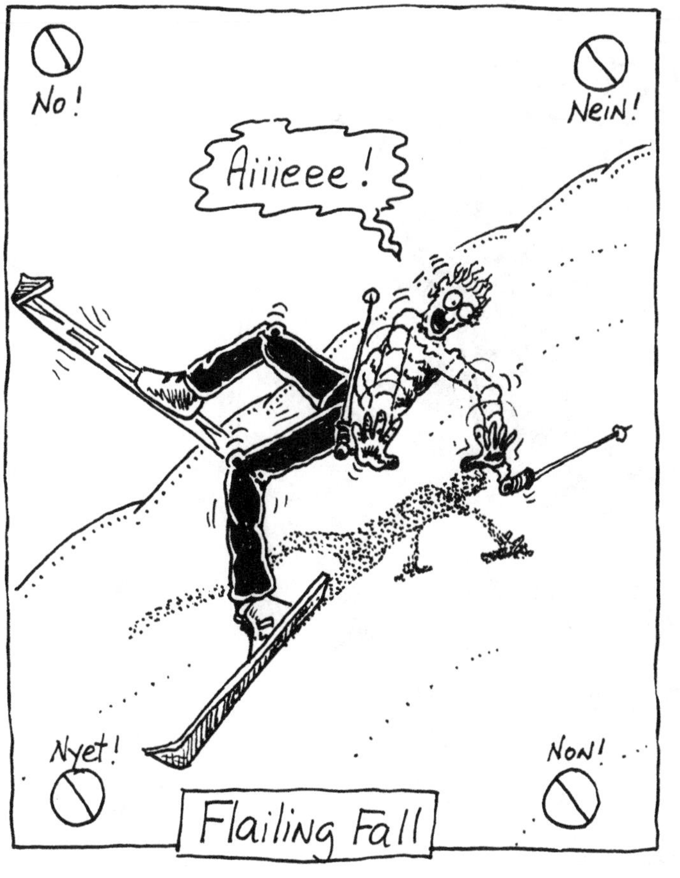
No!
Nein!
Aiiieee!
Nyet!
Non!
Flailing Fall

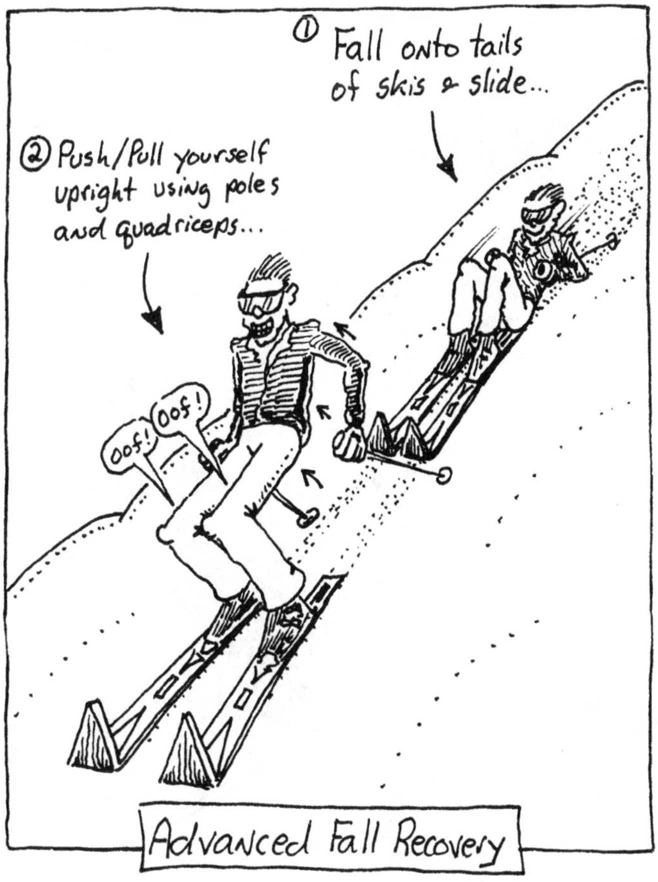
① Fall onto tails of skis & slide...
② Push/Pull yourself upright using poles and quadriceps...
Oof!
Oof!
Advanced Fall Recovery

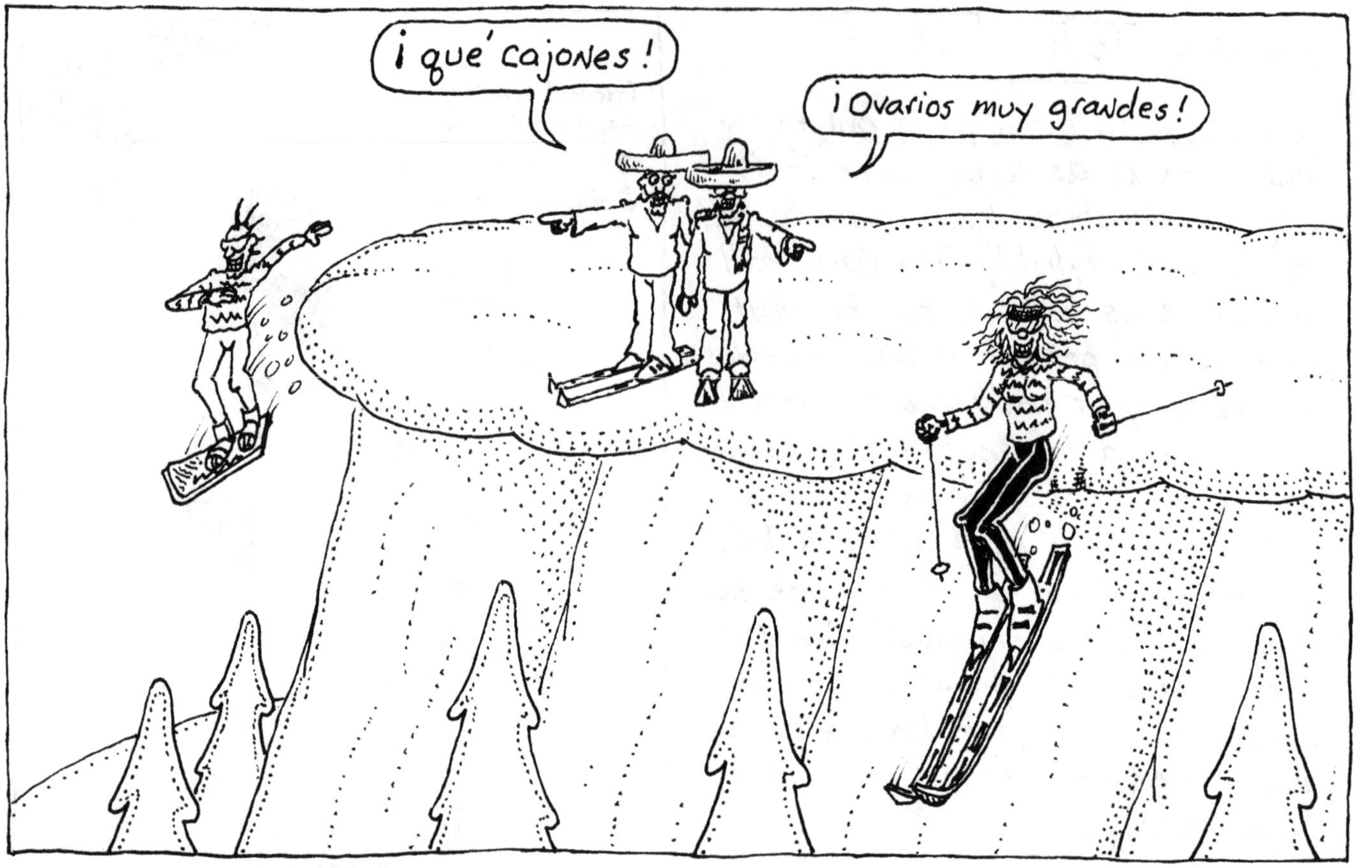
¡ que' cajones !
¡ Ovarios muy grandes !

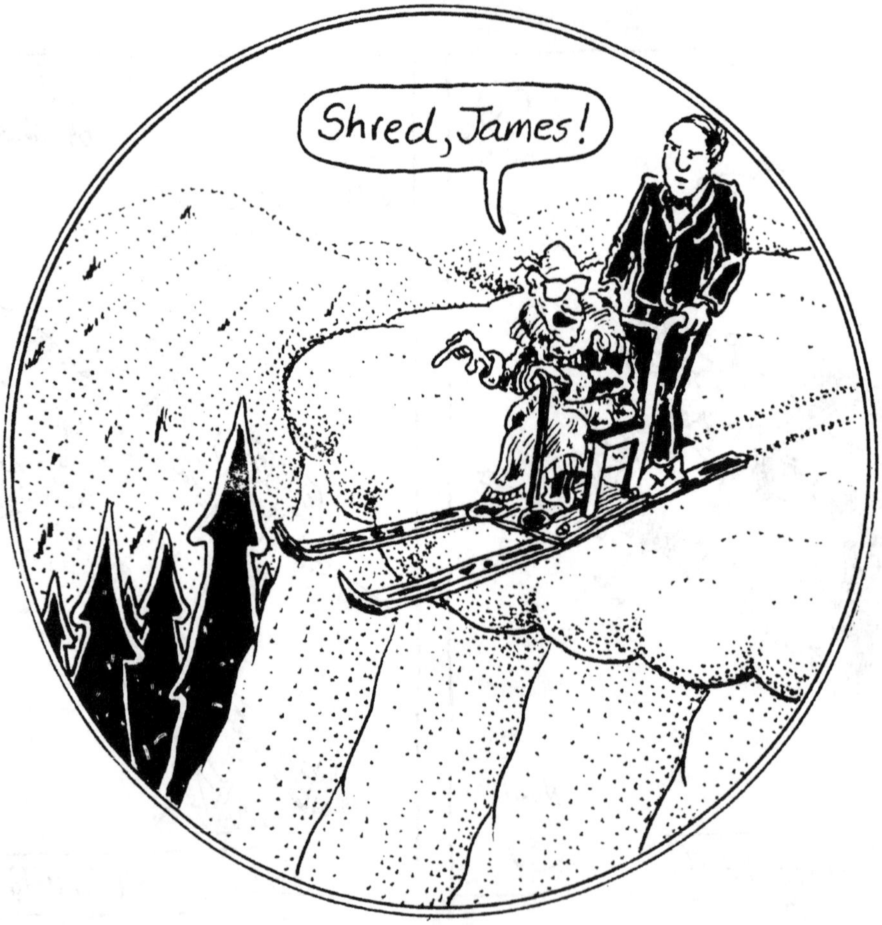
Shred, James !

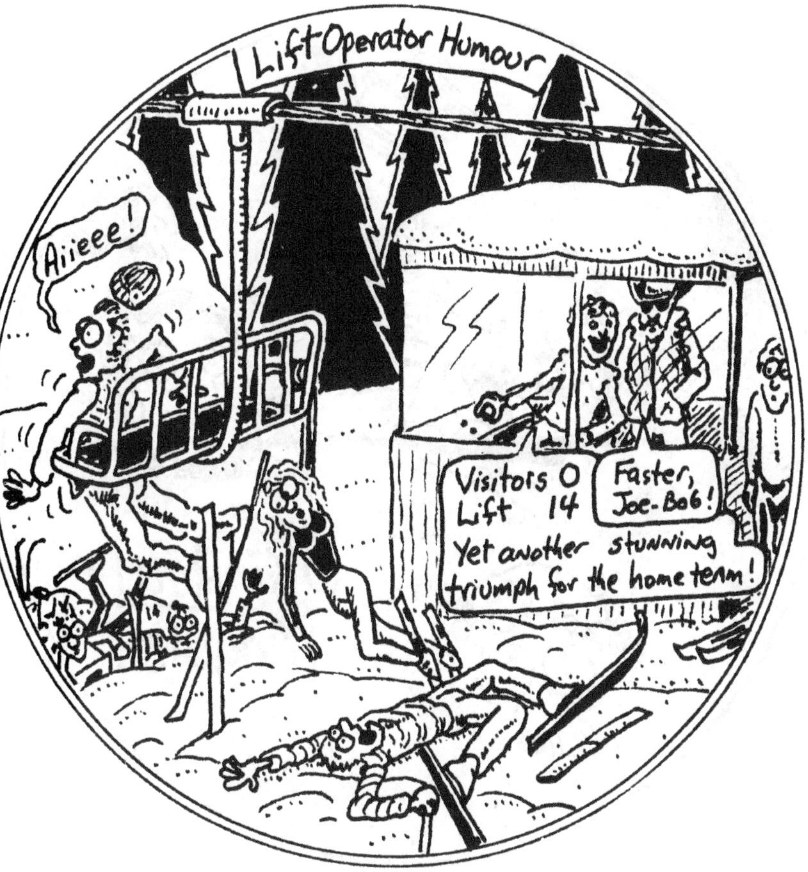
Lift Operator Humour
Aiieee!
Visitors 0
Lift 14
Faster, Joe-Bob!
Yet another stunning triumph for the home team!

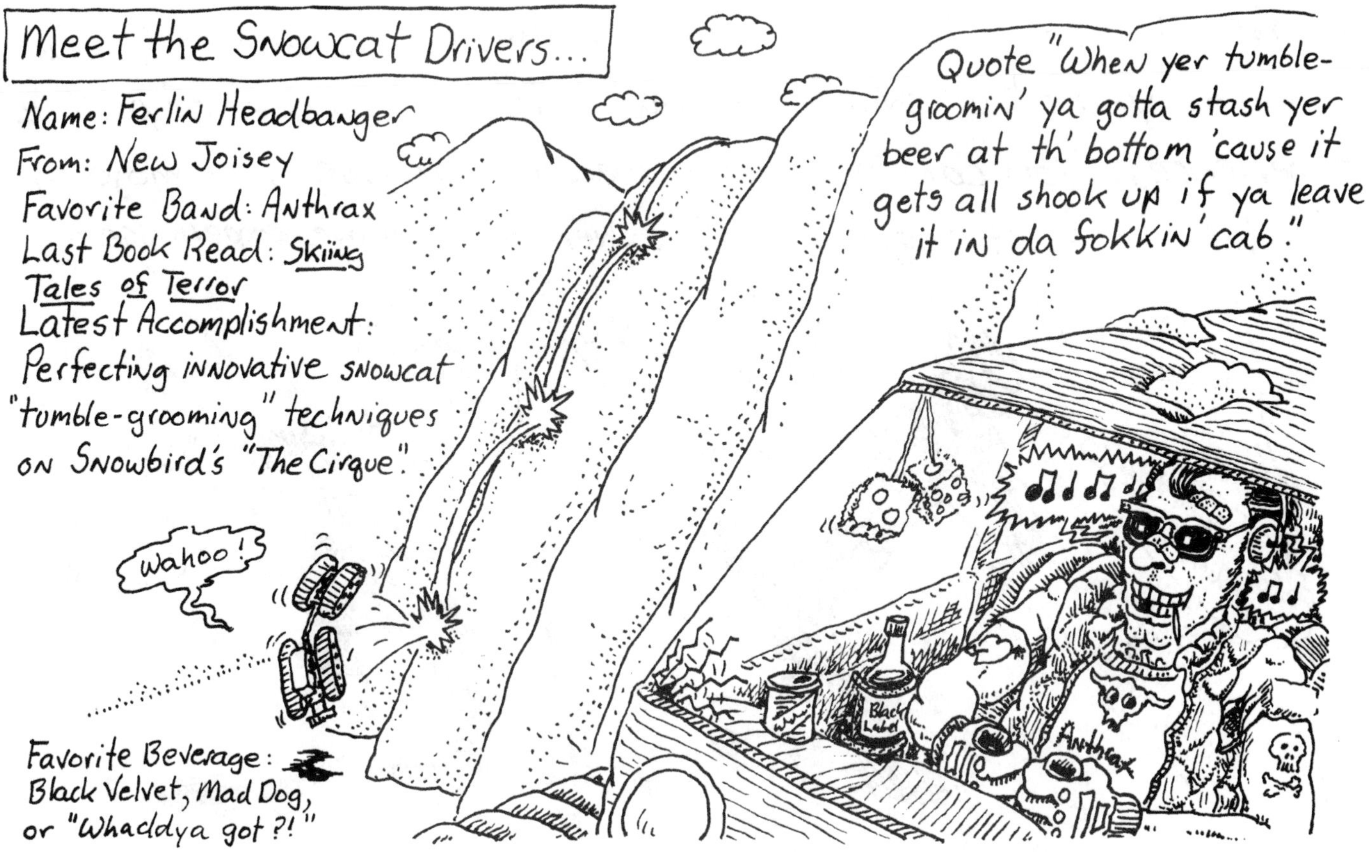
Meet the Snowcat Drivers...
Name: Ferlin Headbanger
From: New Joisey
Favorite Band: Anthrax
Last Book Read: Skiing Tales of Terror
Latest Accomplishment: Perfecting innovative snowcat "tumble-grooming" techniques on Snowbird's "The Cirque".
Quote "When yer tumble-groomin' ya gotta stash yer beer at th' bottom 'cause it gets all shook up if ya leave it in da fokkin' cab."
Wahoo!
Black Label
Anthrax
Favorite Beverage: Black Velvet, Mad Dog, or "Whaddya got?!"

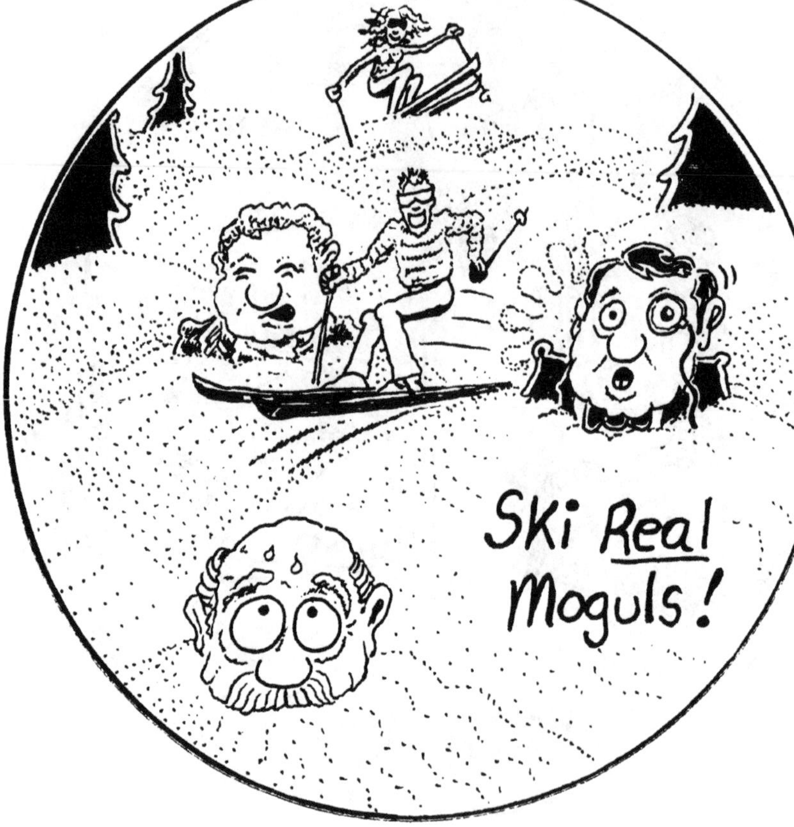
Ski Real Moguls!

Mojo (mṓ-jō) N. Nerve; positive psychic attunement. A linear condition you attain over time via a long sequence of positive experiences. You can drastically weaken or lose your mojo by a relatively short sequence of extremely negative experience.

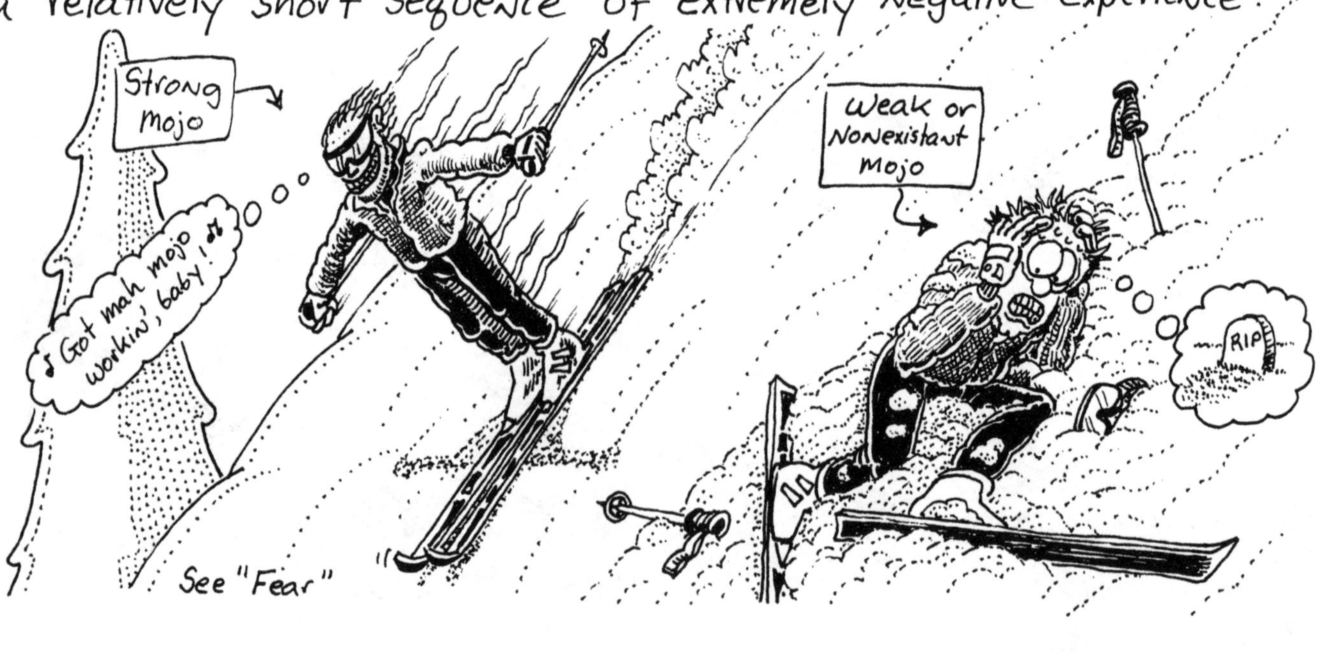
Strong mojo
♪ Got mah mojo workin', baby! ♫
Weak or Nonexistant Mojo
RIP
See "Fear"

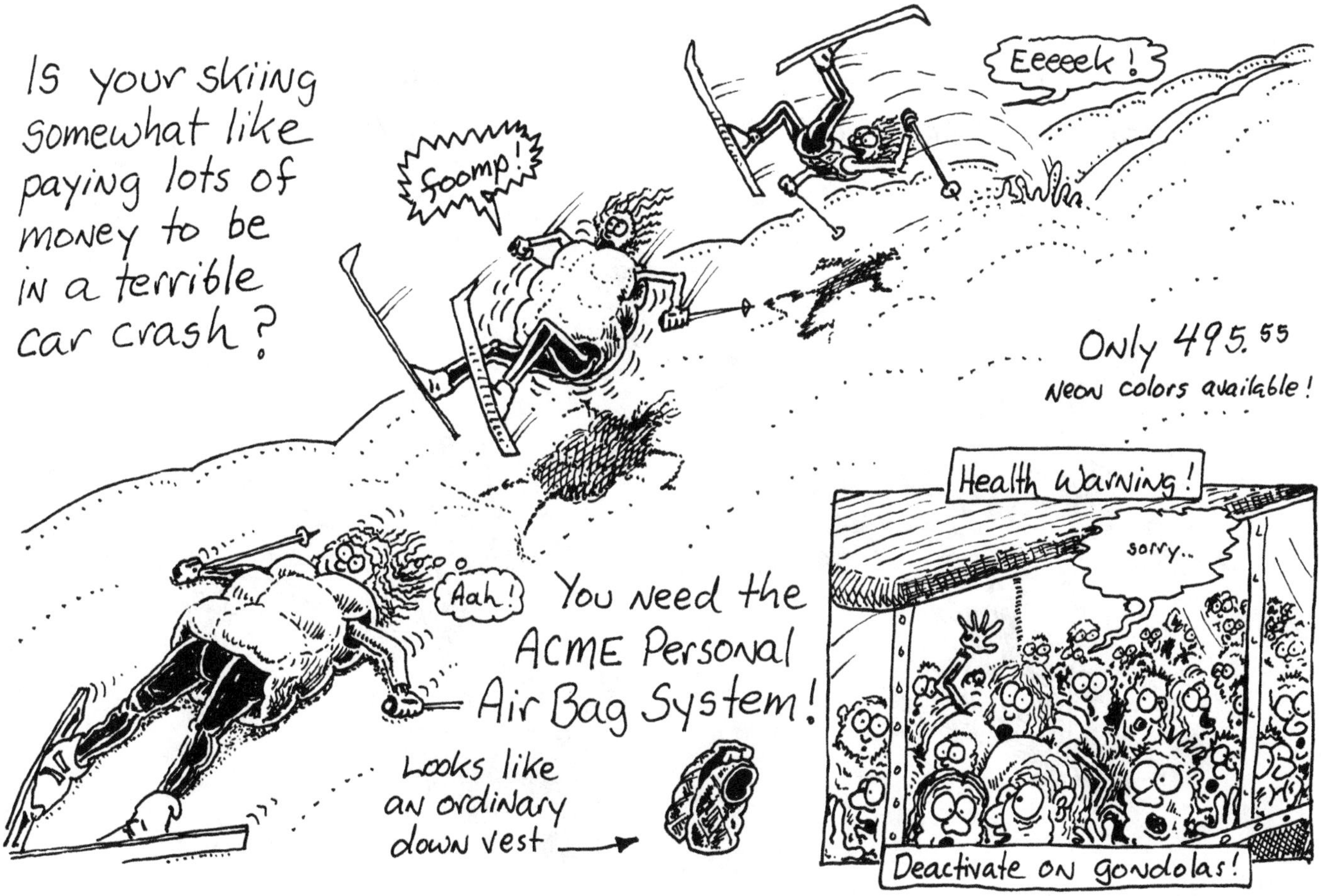

Is your skiing somewhat like paying lots of money to be in a terrible car crash?
Foomp!
Eeeeek!
Only 495.55
Neon colors available!
Aah!
You need the ACME Personal Air Bag System!
Looks like an ordinary down vest
Health Warning!
sorry..
Deactivate on gondolas!

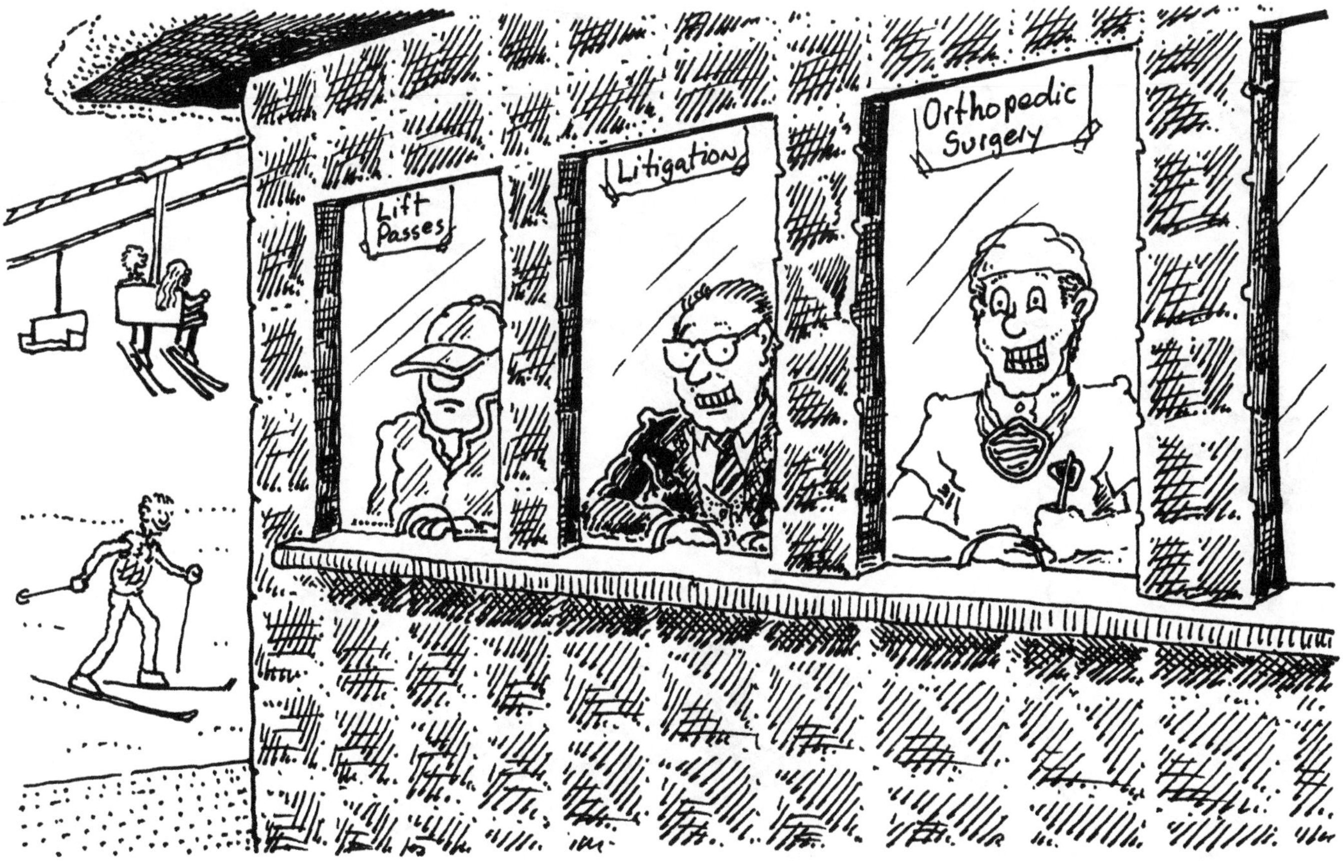

Lift Passes
Litigation
Orthopedic Surgery

Screamer (skrēm•r) N. A particularly intense pitch on a slope or a particularly distraught skier...

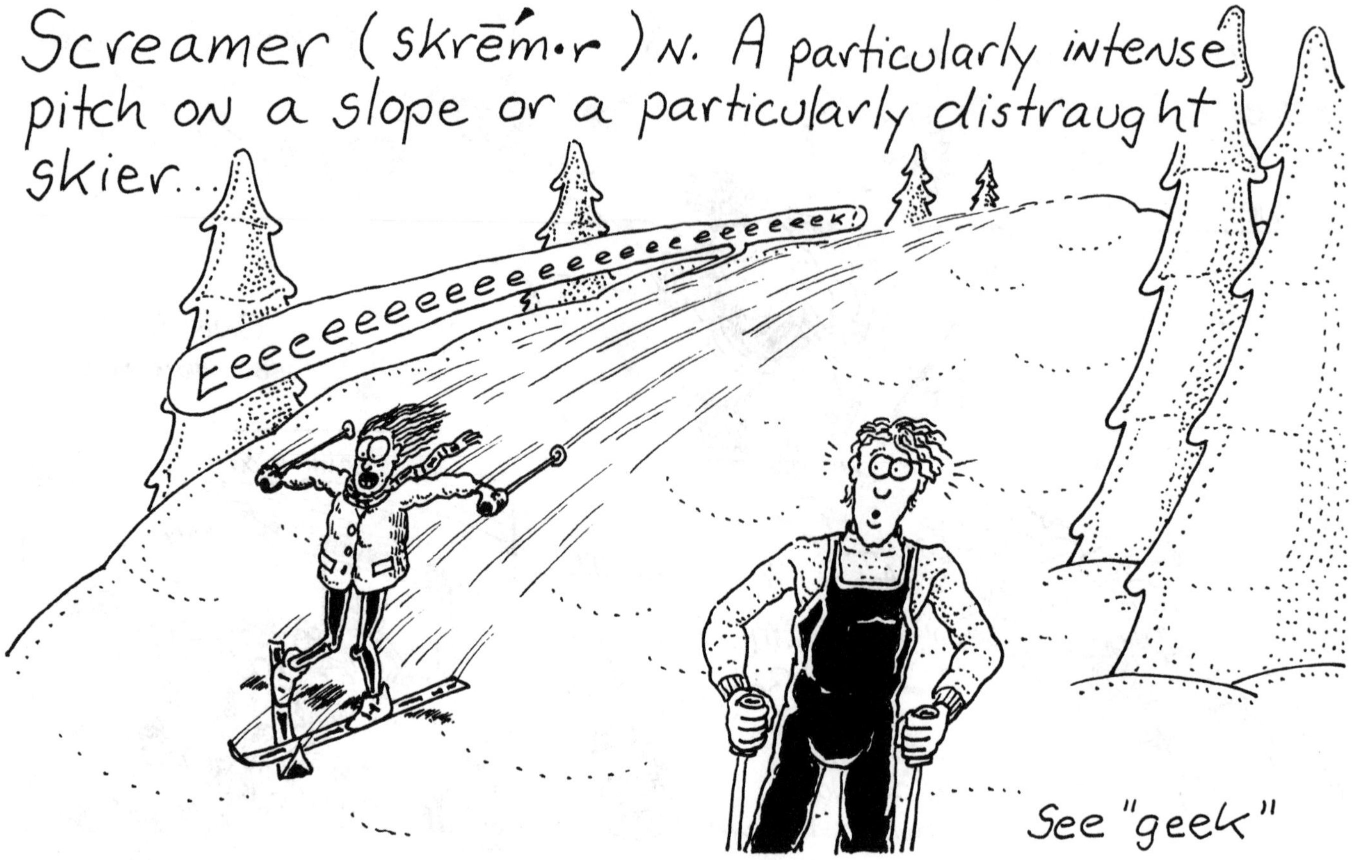
Eeeeeeeeeeeeeeeeeeeeeeeeeeeeek!
See "geek"

The Intrinsic Hazards of **Bungi Boarding**...

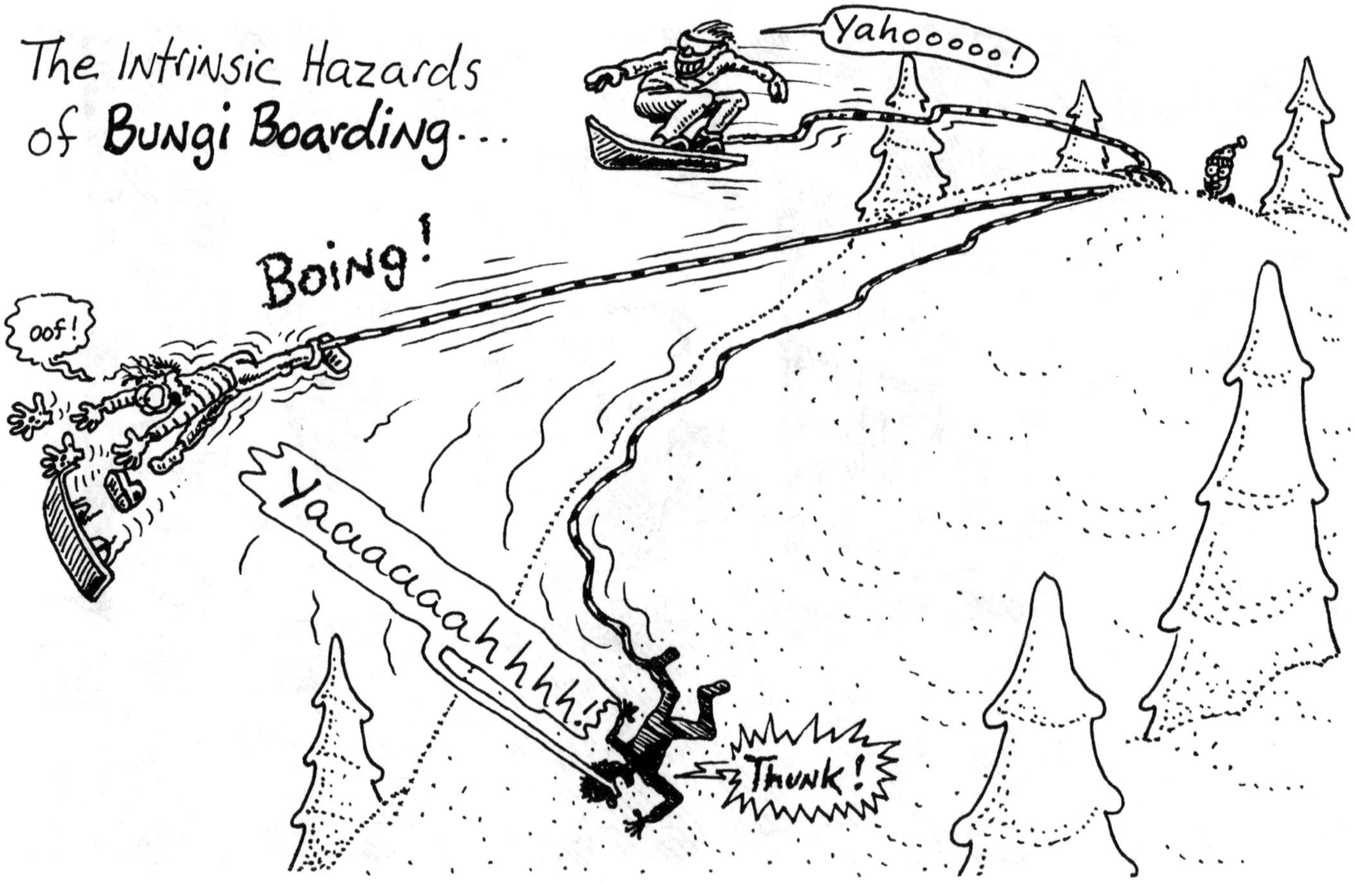
Yahoooooo!
Boing!
oof!
Yaaaaaaahhhh!
Thunk!

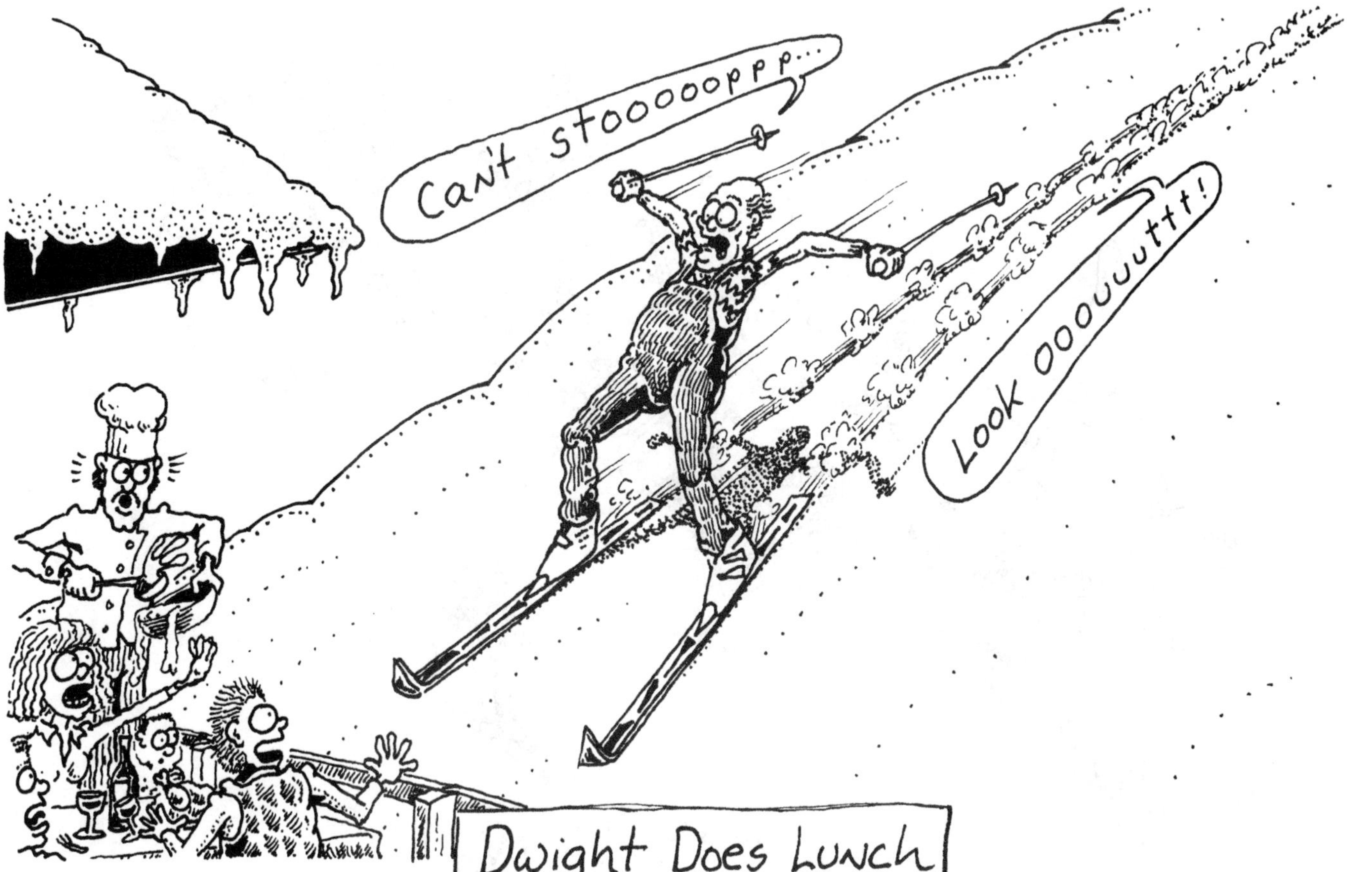
Can't stoooooppp...
Look oooouuuttt!

Dwight Does Lunch

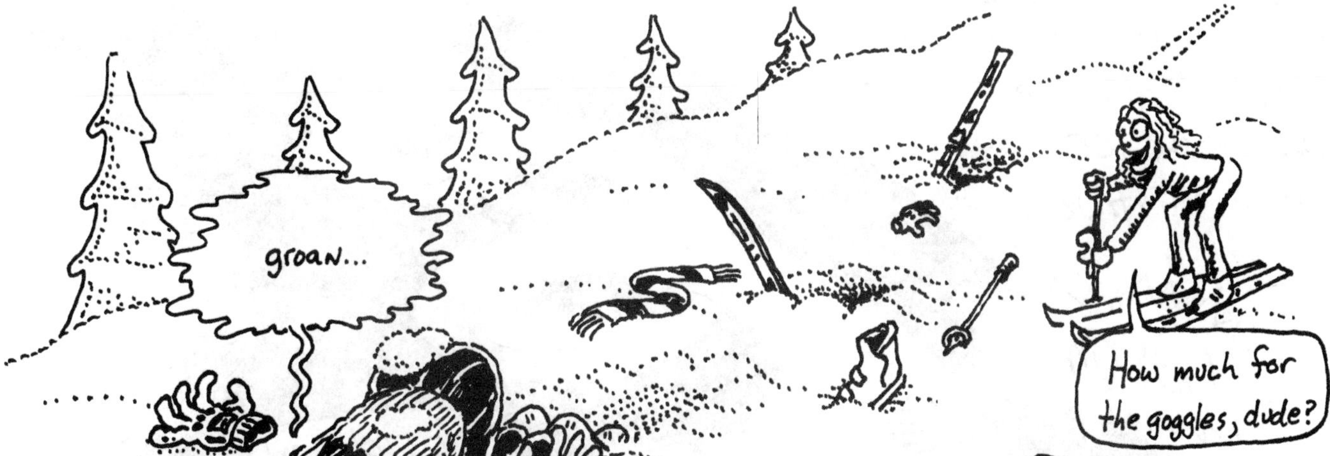
groan...
How much for the goggles, dude?

"Yard Sale" Crash

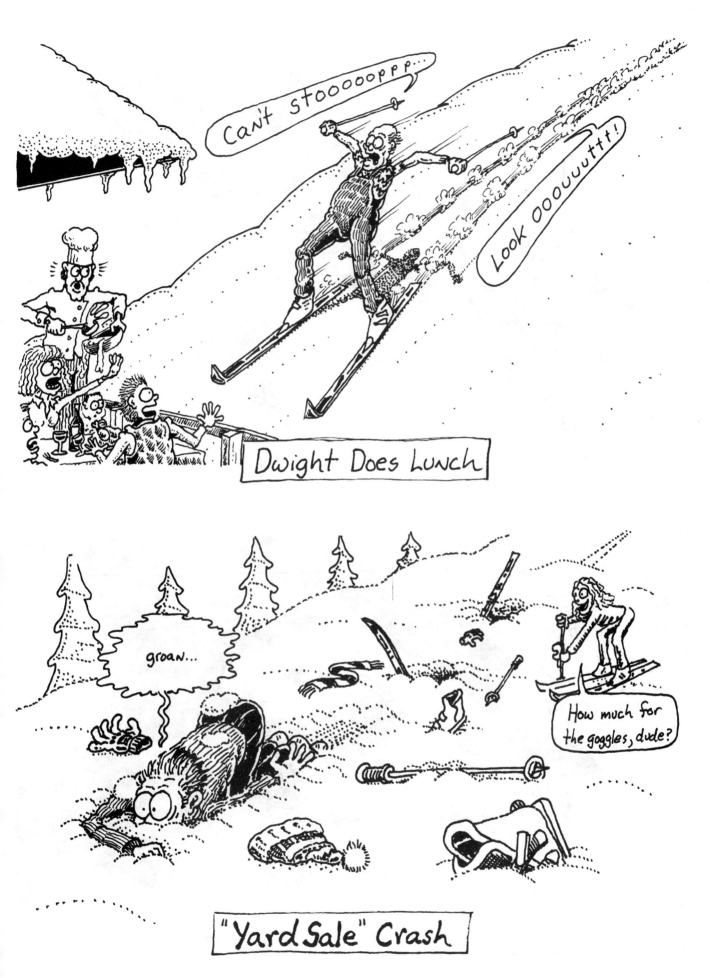

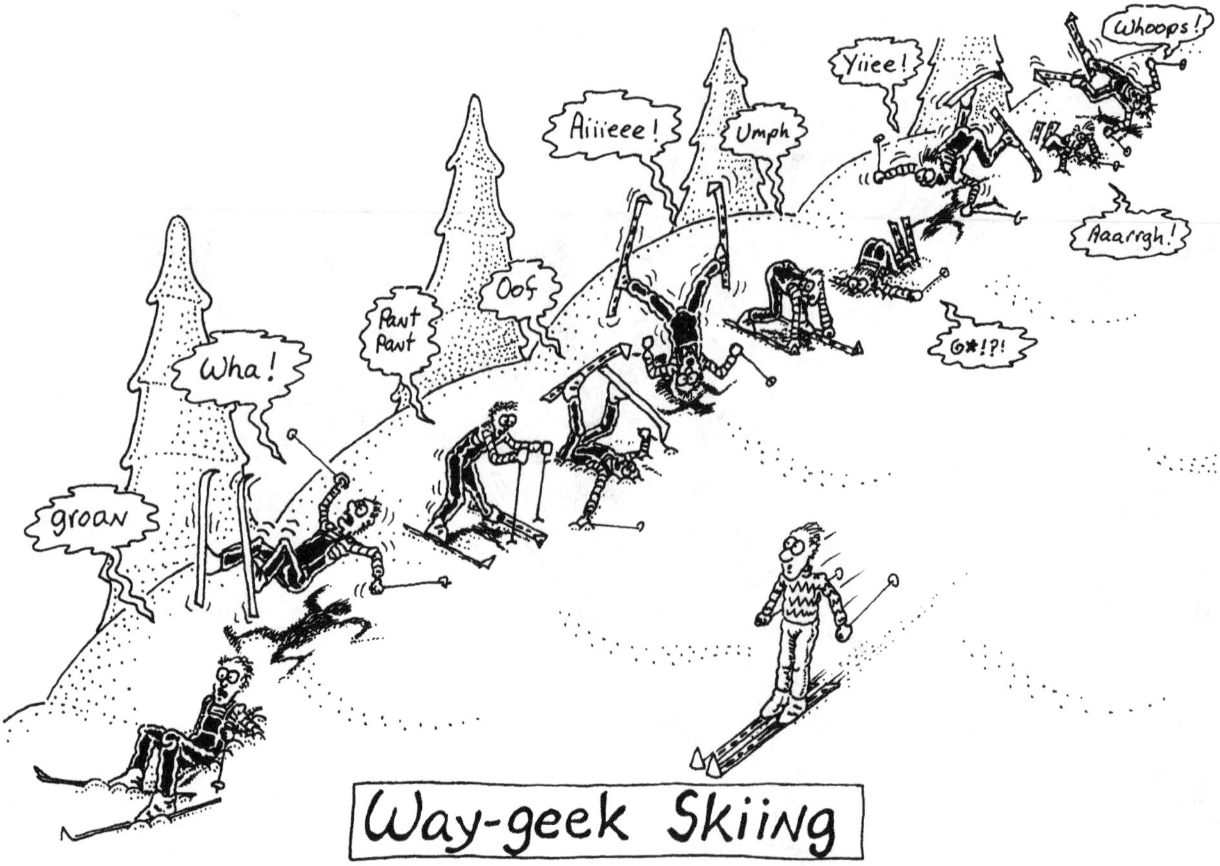
groan
Wha!
Pant Pant
Oof
Aiiieee!
Umph
Yiiee!
Whoops!
Aaarrgh!
G*!?!

Way-geek Skiing

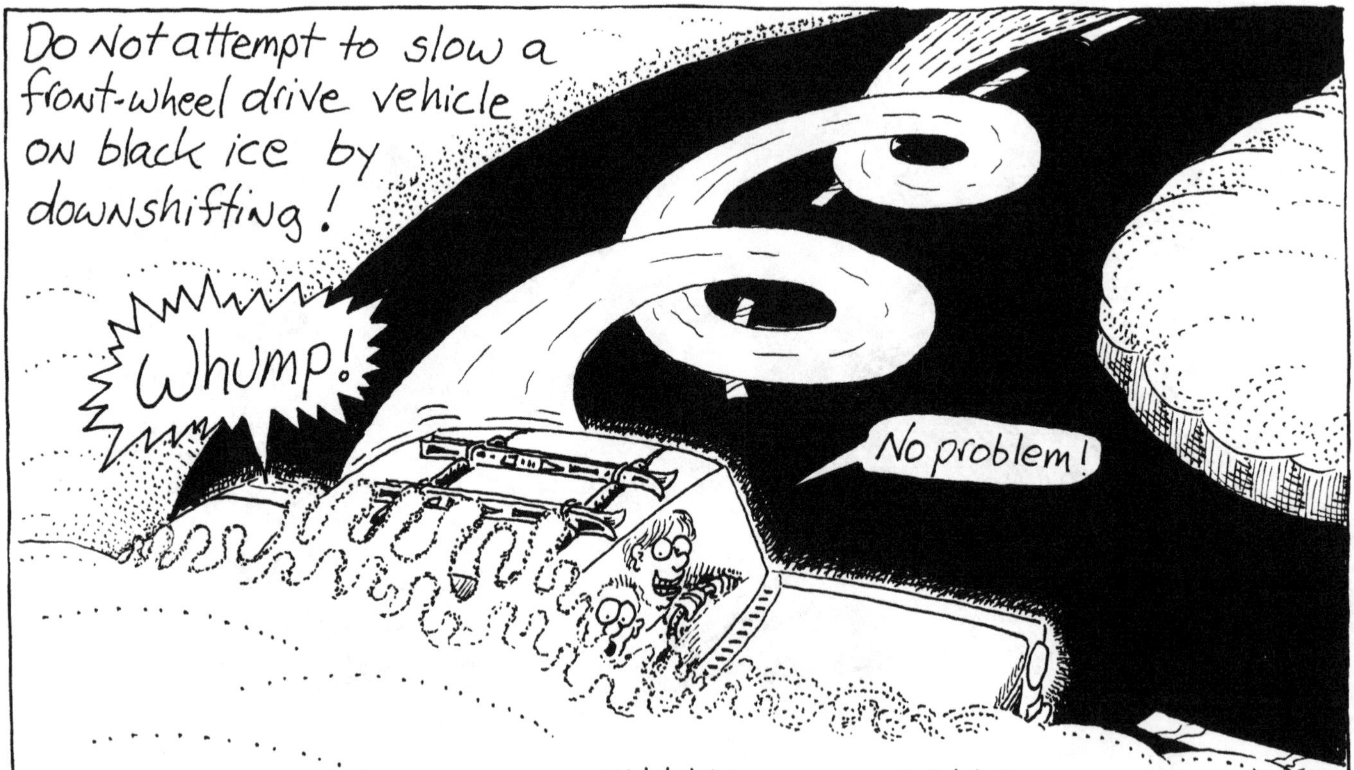
Do Not attempt to slow a front-wheel drive vehicle on black ice by downshifting!
Whump!
No problem!
...unless its a rental car!

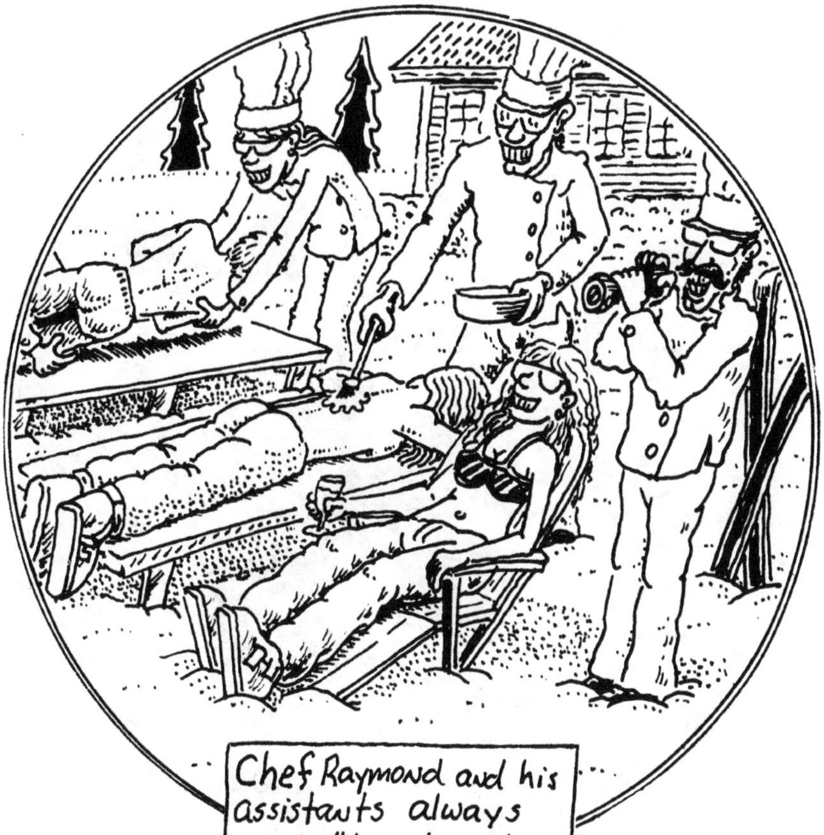

Chef Raymond and his assistants always enjoy "beach duty"!

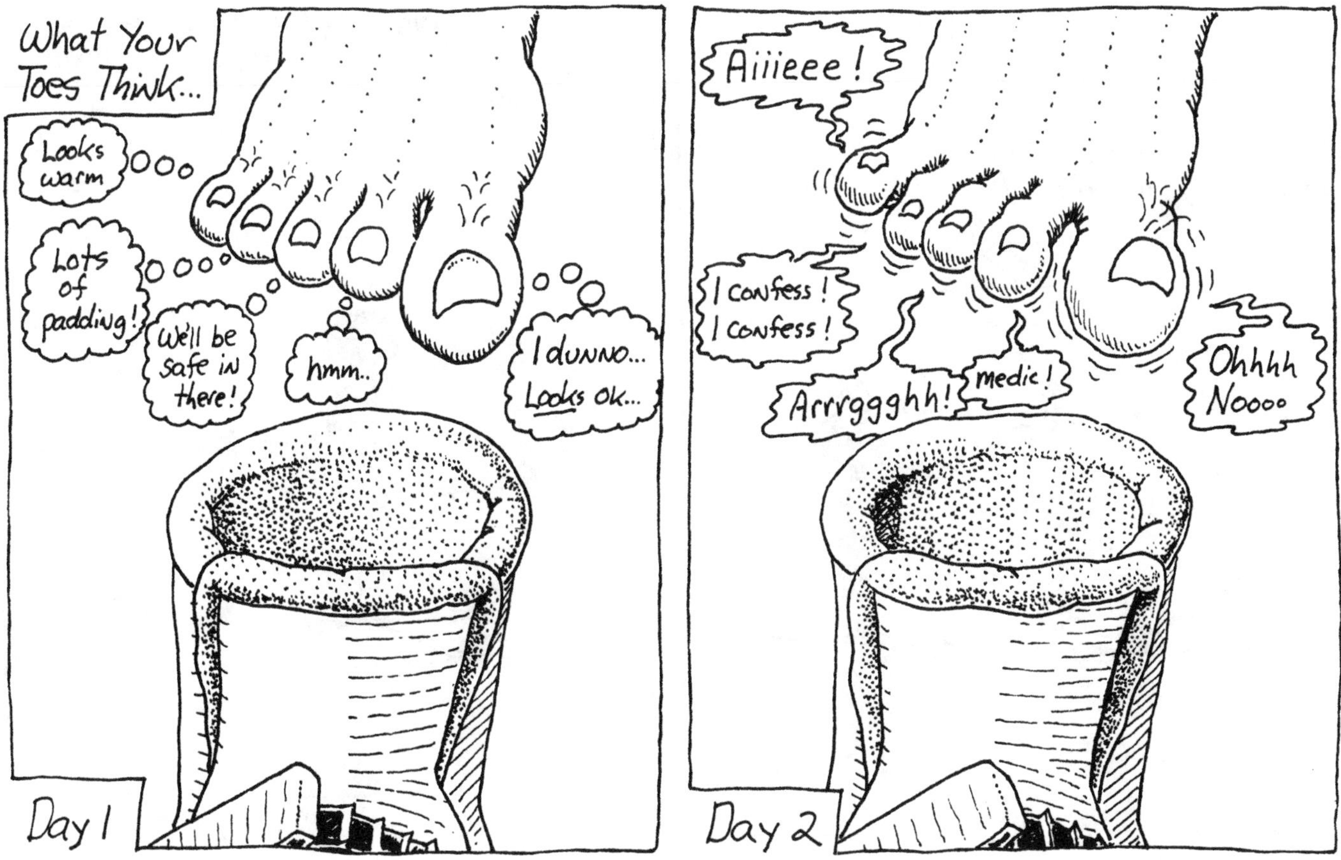
What Your Toes Think...
Looks warm
Lots of padding!
We'll be safe in there!
hmm..
I dunno... Looks ok...
Day 1
Aiiieee!
I confess! I confess!
Arrrggghh!
medic!
Ohhhh Noooo
Day 2

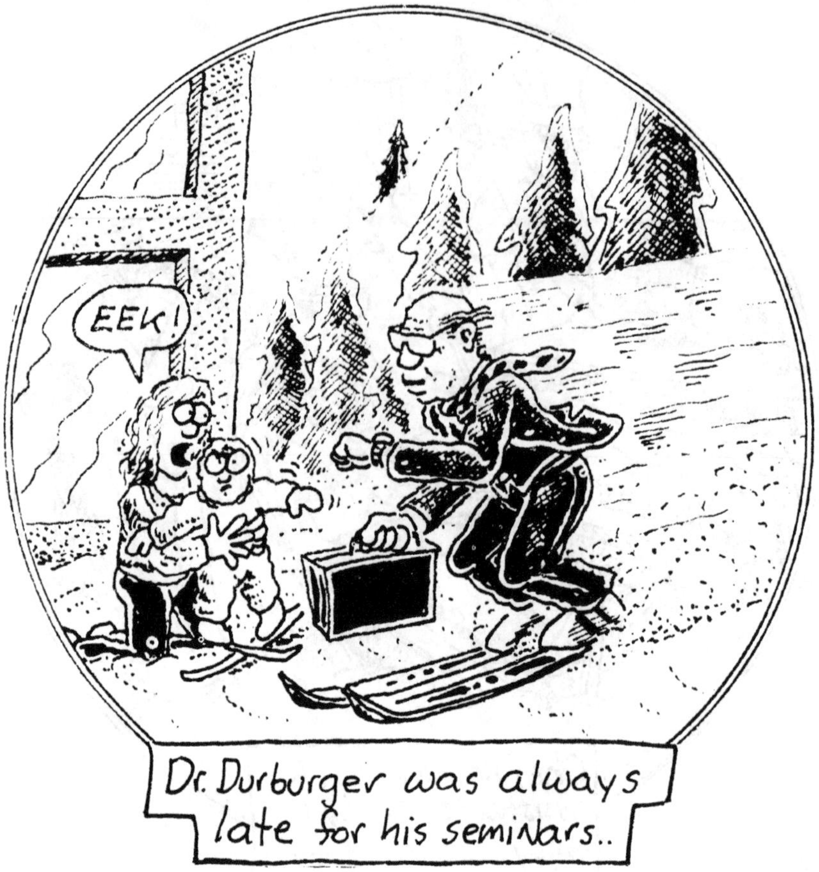
EEK!
Dr. Durburger was always late for his seminars..

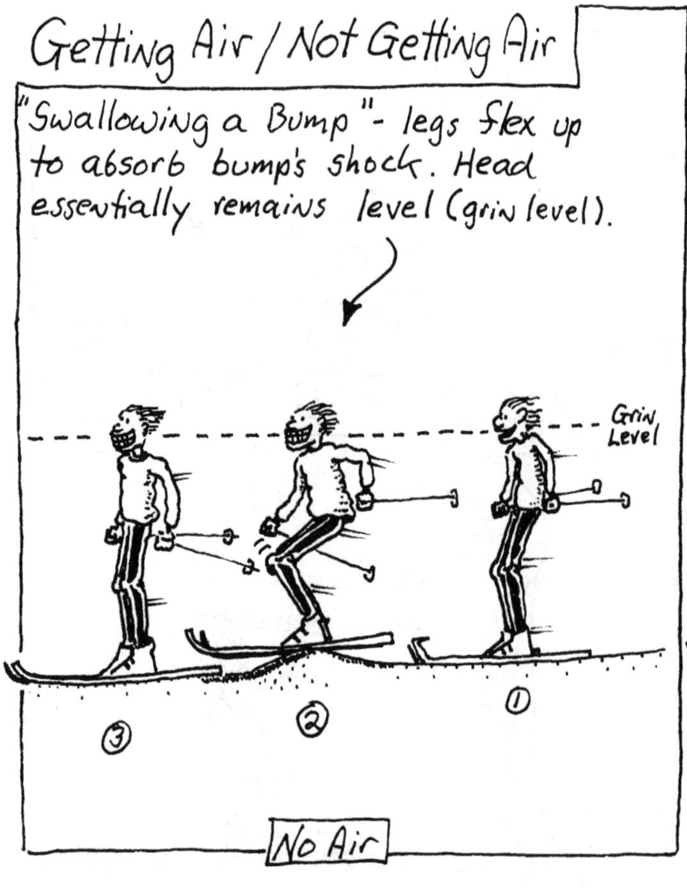
Getting Air / Not Getting Air
"Swallowing a Bump" - legs flex up to absorb bump's shock. Head essentially remains level (grin level).
Grin Level
③
②
①
No Air

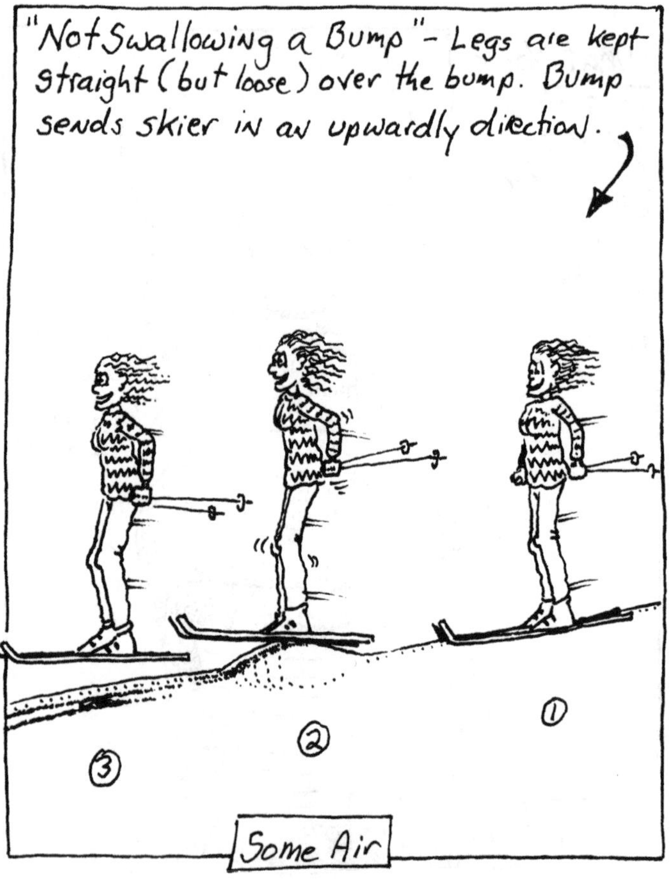
"Not Swallowing a Bump" - Legs are kept straight (but loose) over the bump. Bump sends skier in an upwardly direction.
③
②
①
Some Air

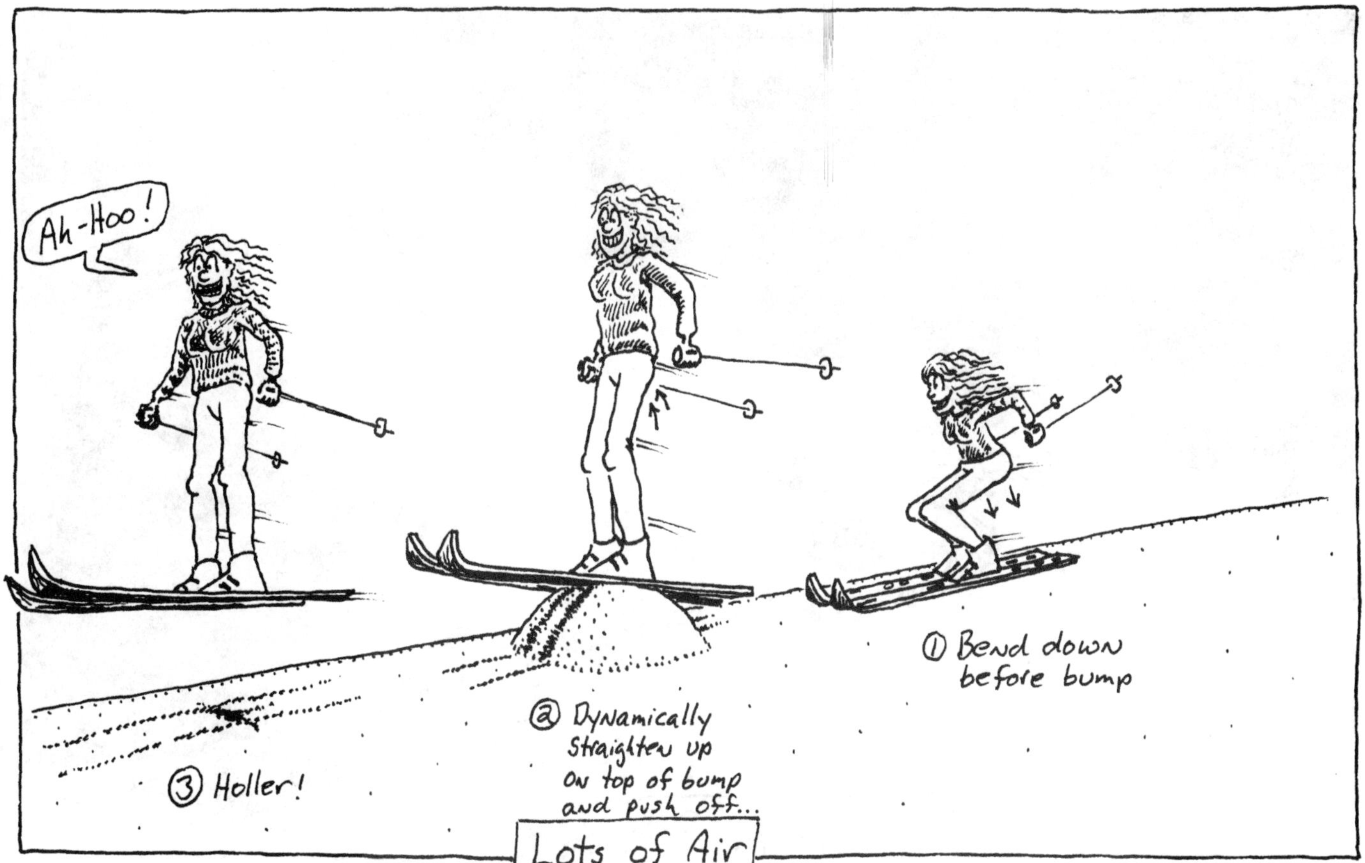
Ah-Hoo!
① Bend down before bump
② Dynamically straighten up on top of bump and push off...
③ Holler!

Lots of Air

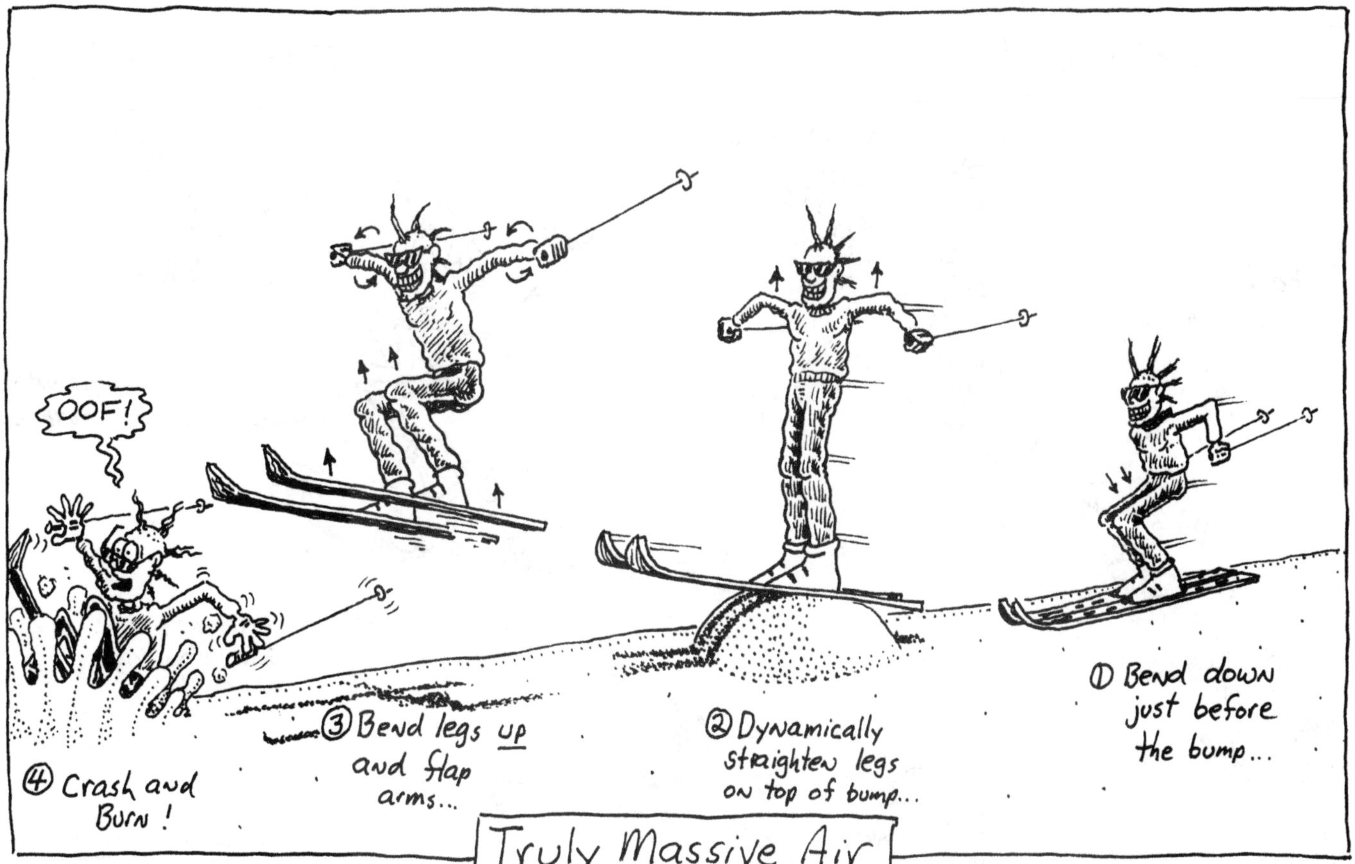
OOF!
① Bend down just before the bump...
② Dynamically straighten legs on top of bump...
③ Bend legs up and flap arms...
④ Crash and Burn!

Truly Massive Air

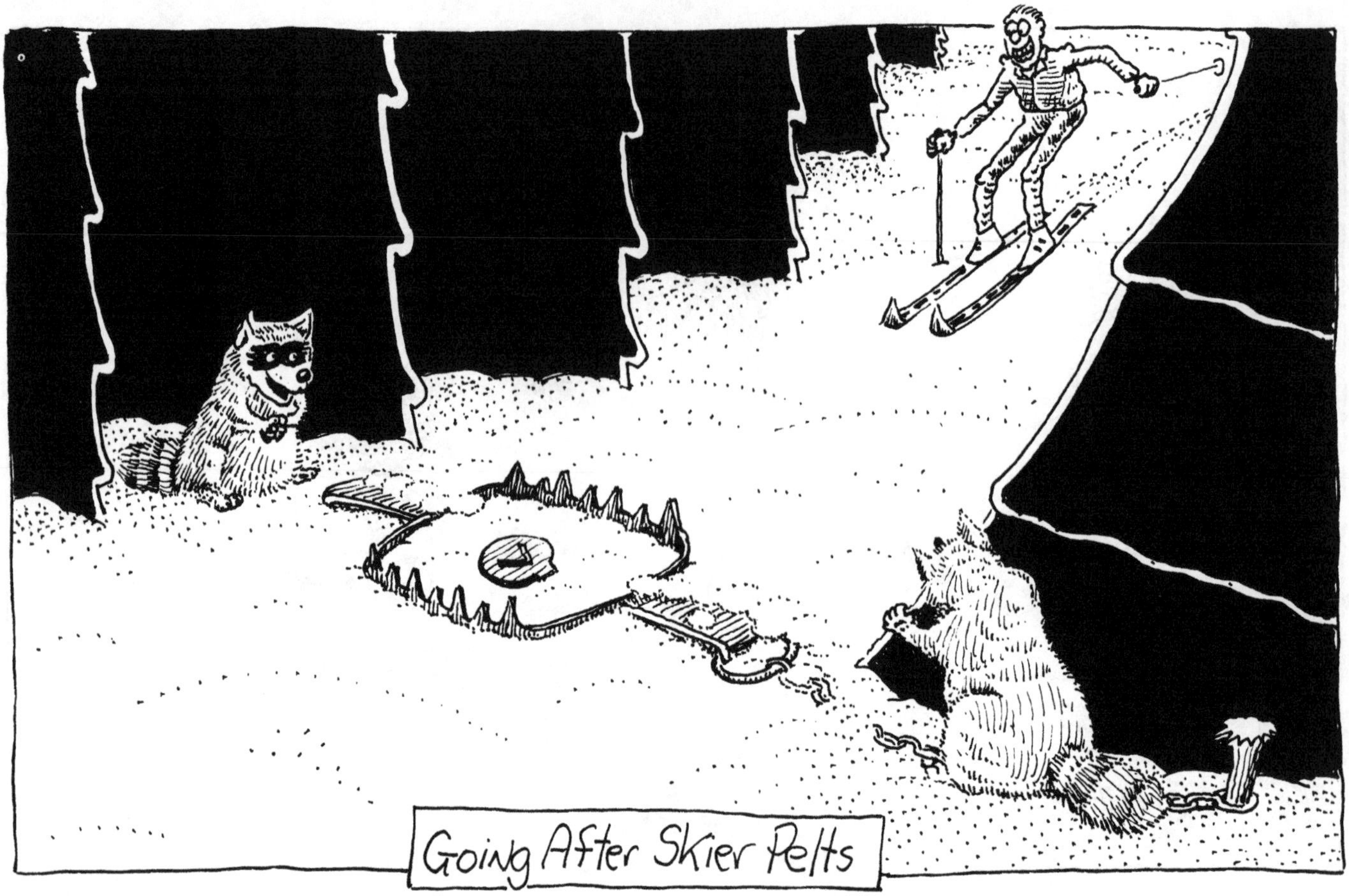
Going After Skier Pelts

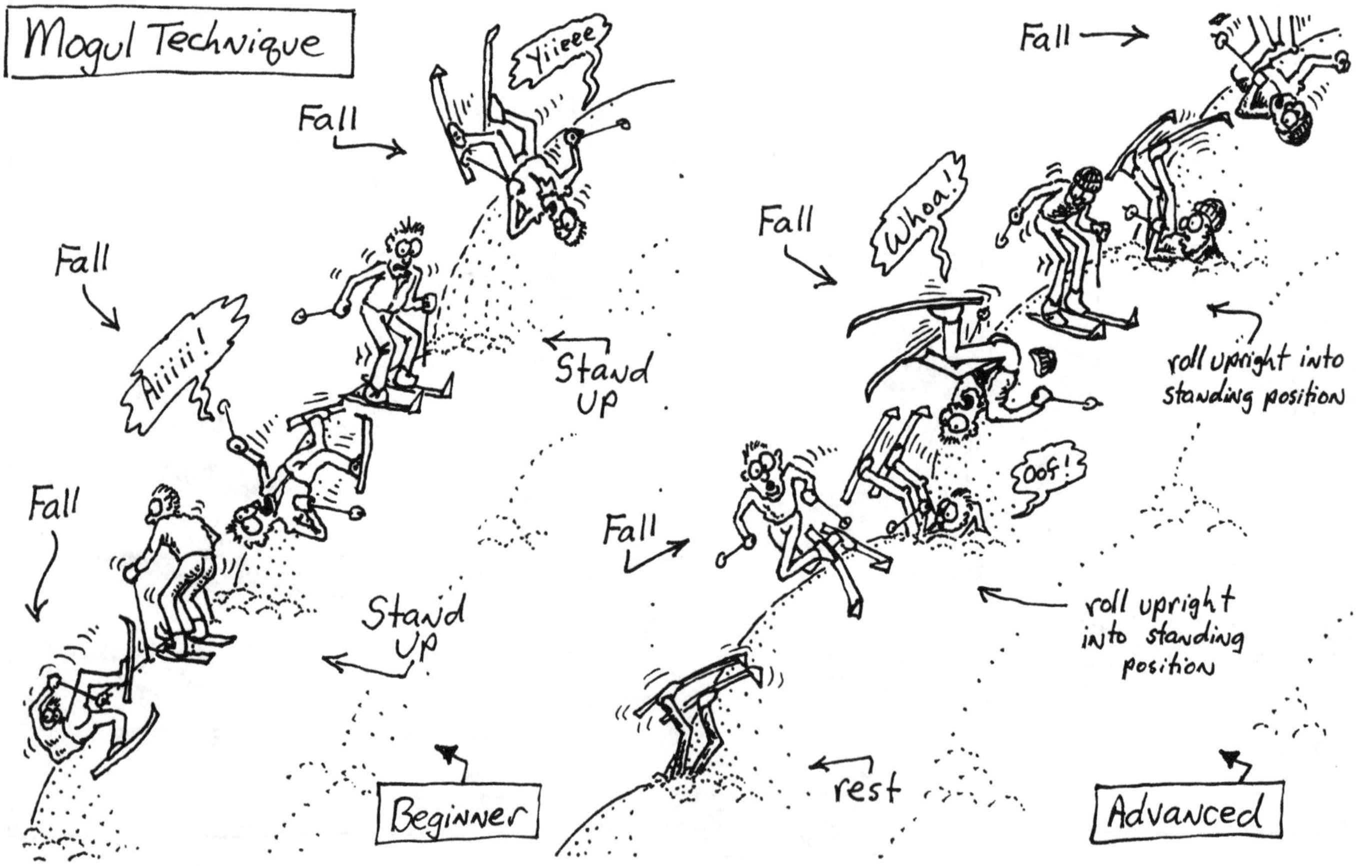
Mogul Technique
Fall
Yiieee
Fall
Fall
Aiiiii!
Stand up
Fall
Stand up
Beginner
Fall
Fall
Whoa!
roll upright into standing position
Oof!
Fall
roll upright into standing position
rest
Advanced

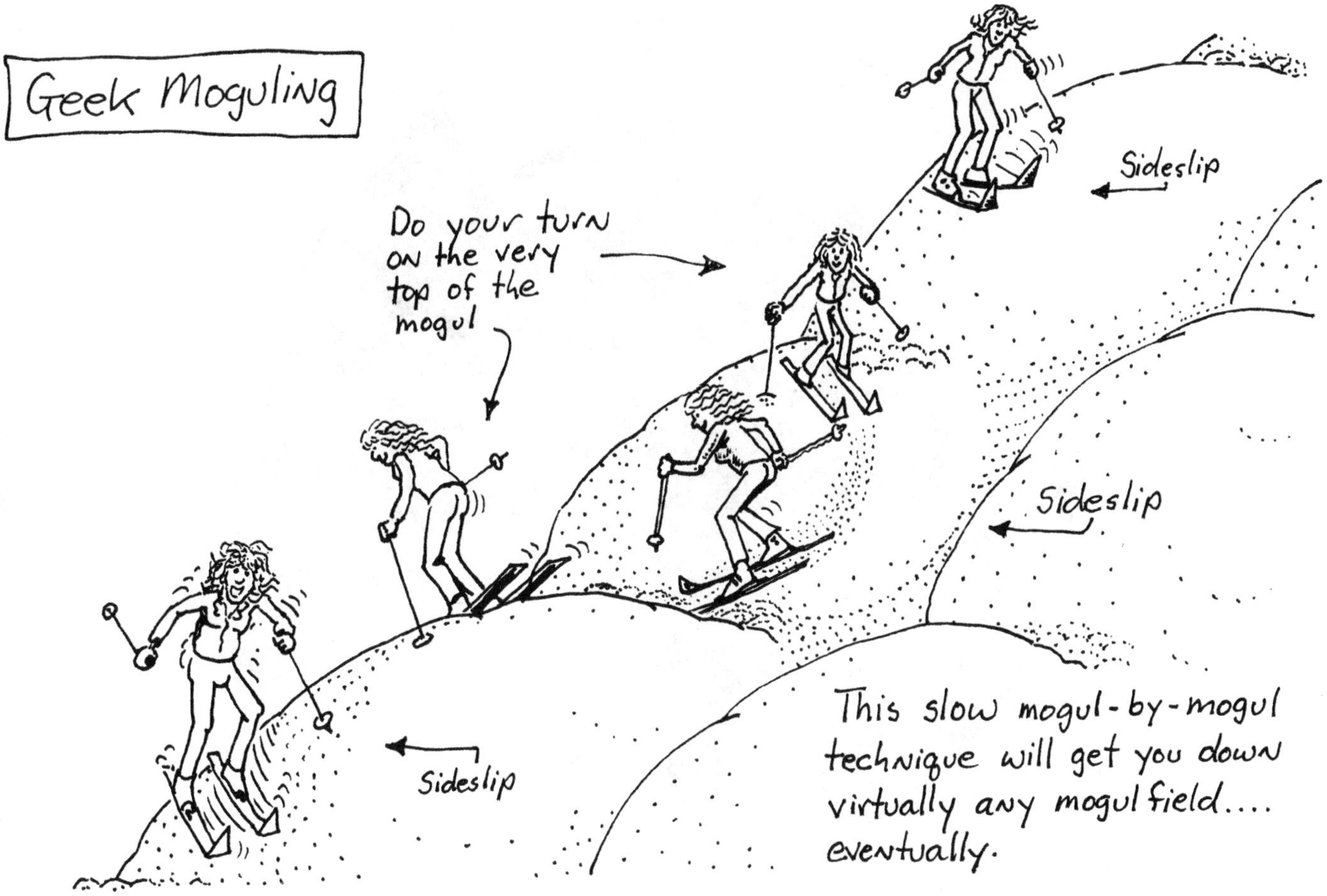
Geek Moguling
Do your turn on the very top of the mogul
Sideslip
Sideslip
Sideslip
This slow mogul-by-mogul technique will get you down virtually any mogul field.... eventually.

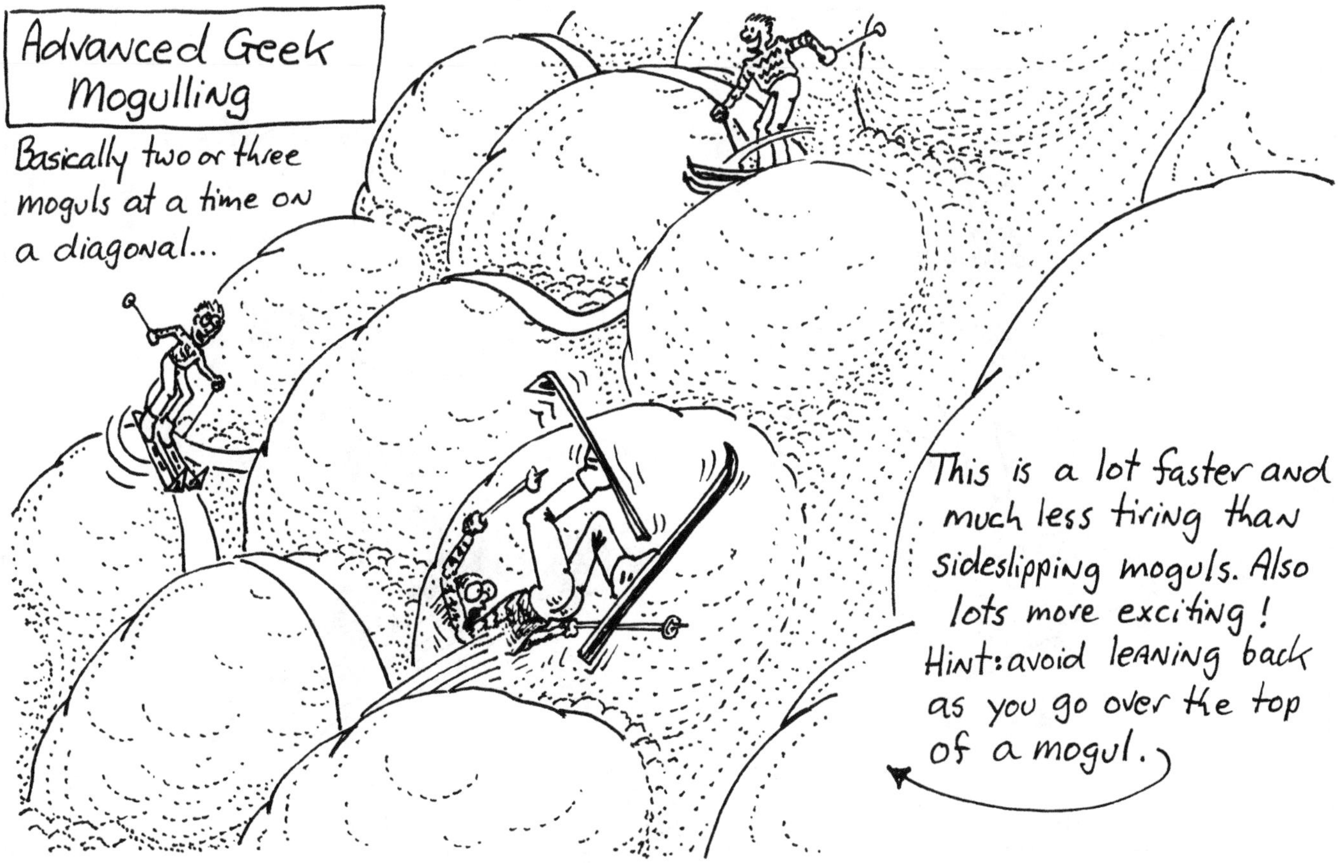
Advanced Geek Mogulling
Basically two or three moguls at a time on a diagonal...
This is a lot faster and much less tiring than sideslipping moguls. Also lots more exciting! Hint: avoid leaning back as you go over the top of a mogul.

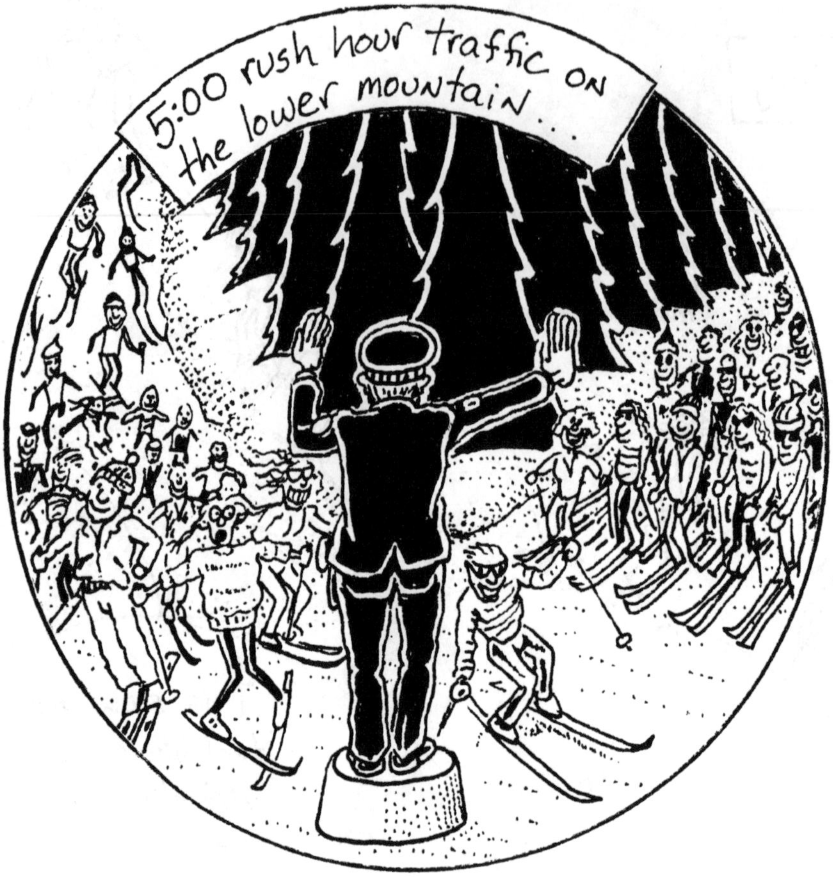
5:00 rush hour traffic on the lower mountain...

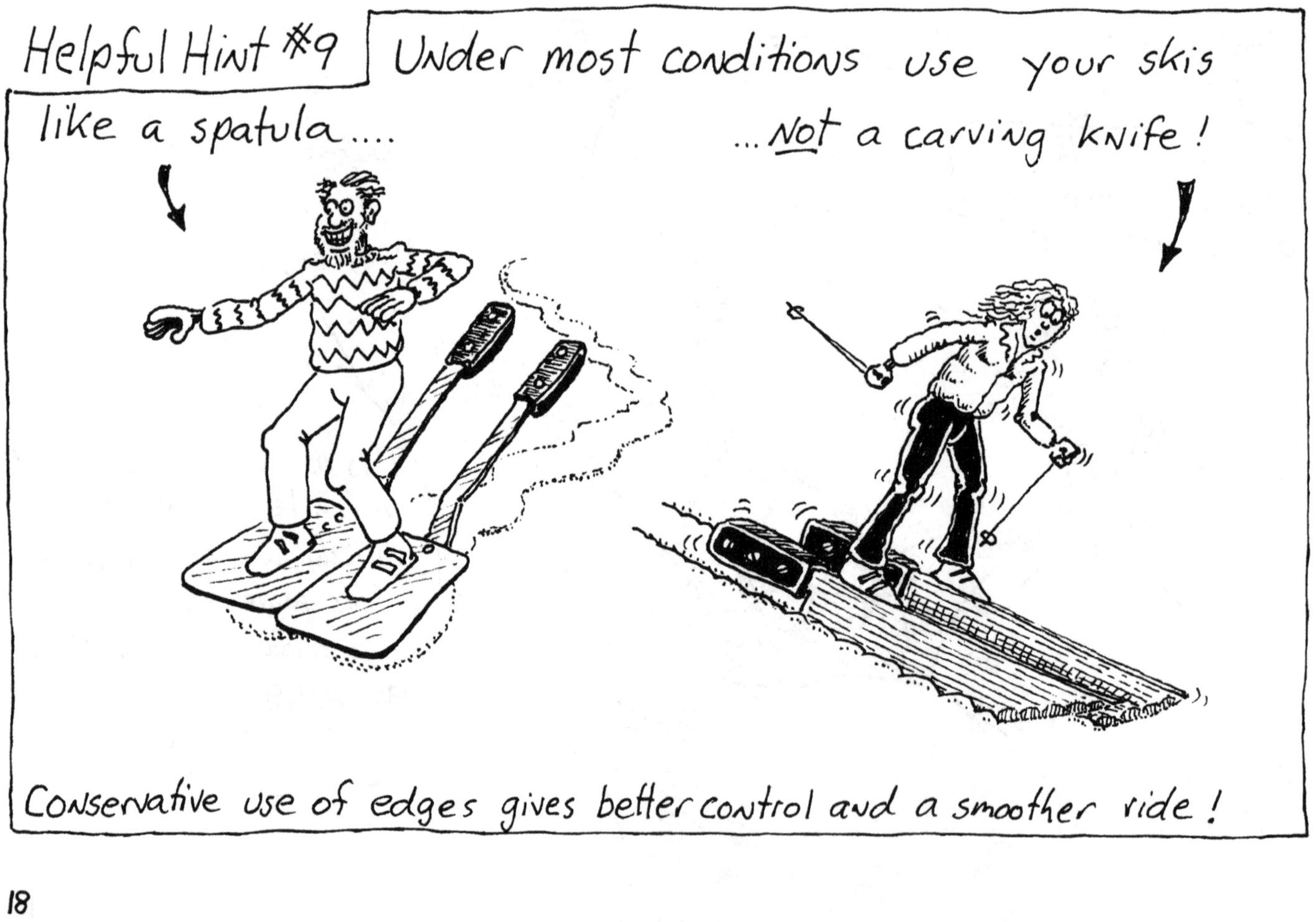
Helpful Hint #9
Under most conditions use your skis like a spatula....
...Not a carving knife!
Conservative use of edges gives better control and a smoother ride!

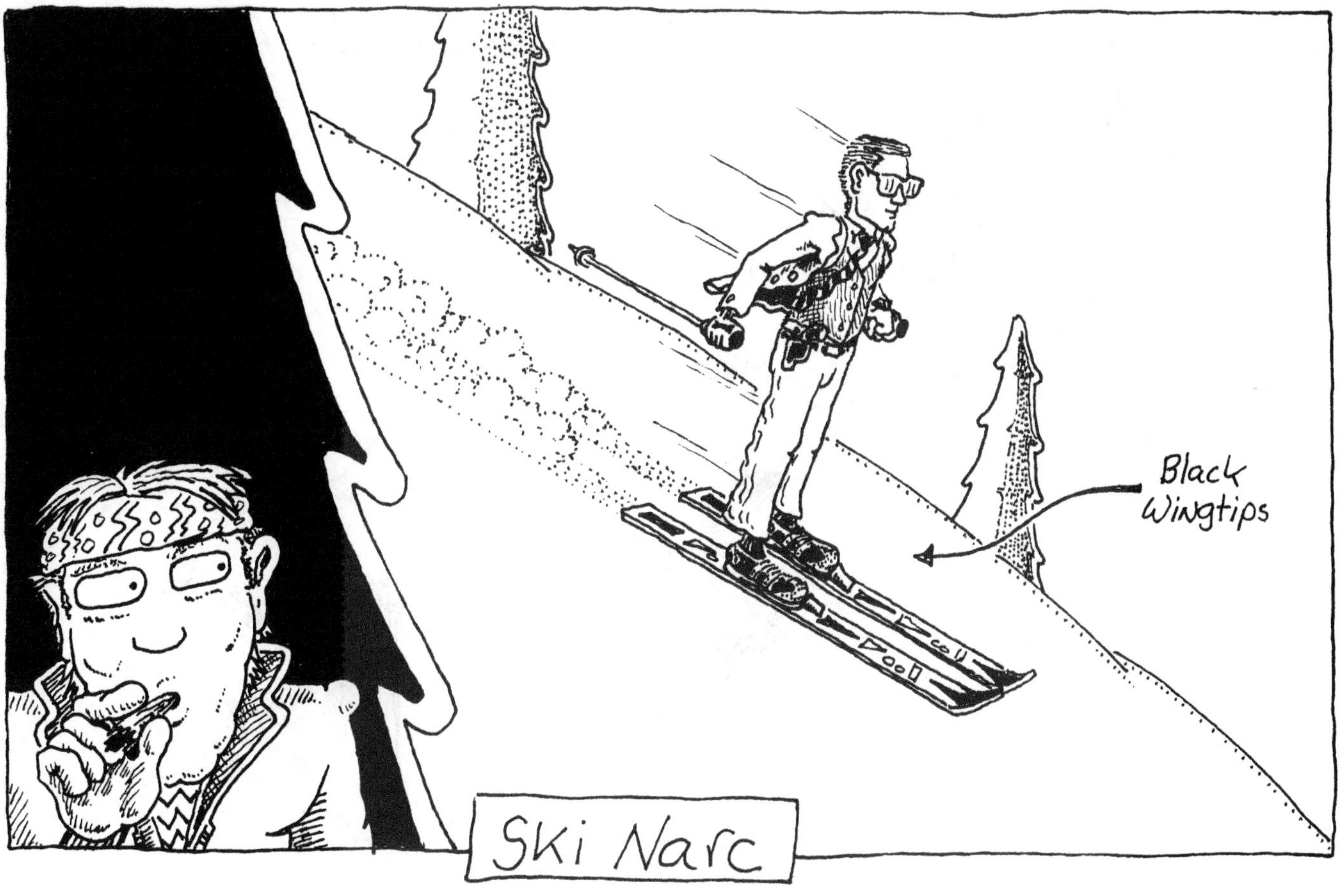
Black
Wingtips
Ski Narc

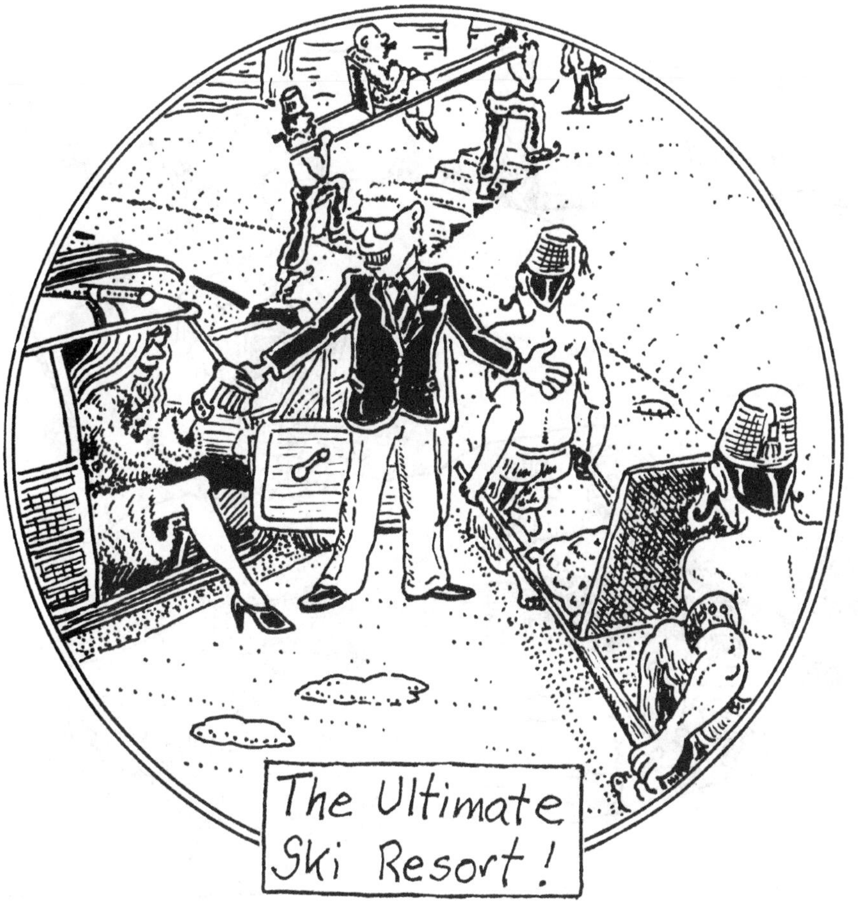
The Ultimate
Ski Resort!

Short Swing (shôrt swēng) [a.k.a. "dynoturn"] An abrupt carving turn that bleeds off speed. By flexing your knees and increasing your edge angles you can virtually stop at the end of each short turn.

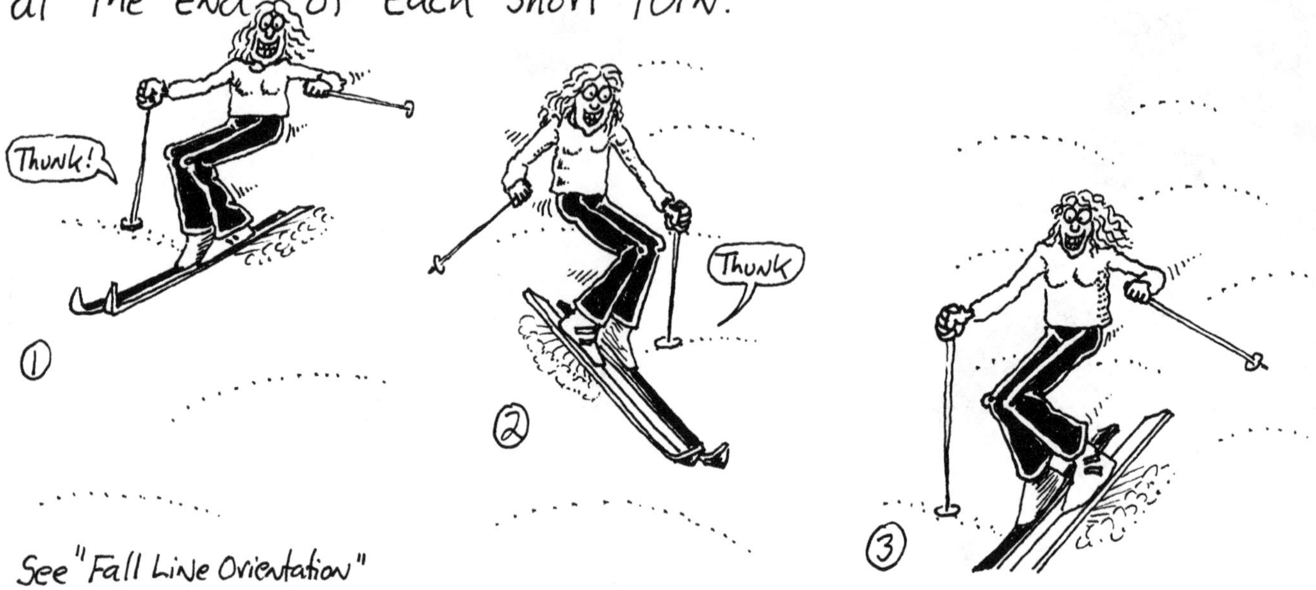
Thunk!
Thunk
①
②
③

See "Fall Line Orientation"

The Snowboarder From Hell goes hot-tubbing...

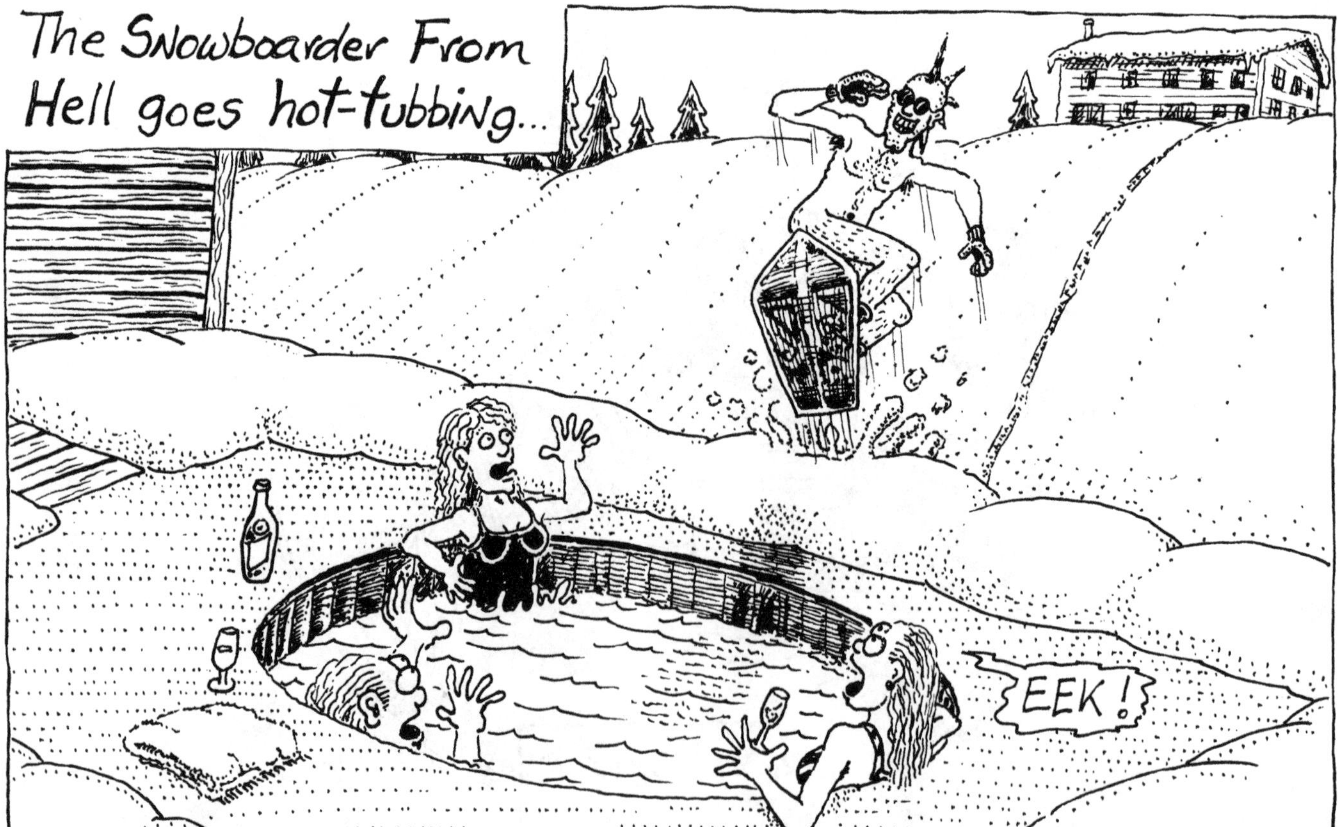
EEK!

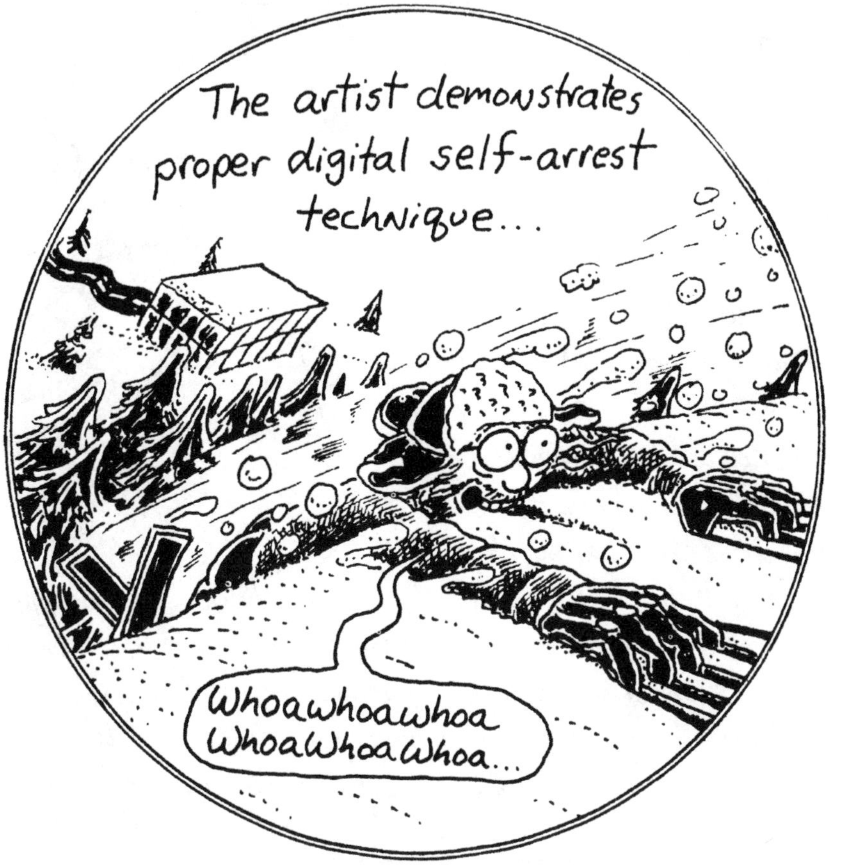
The artist demonstrates proper digital self-arrest technique...
Whoawhoawhoa WhoaWhoaWhoa...

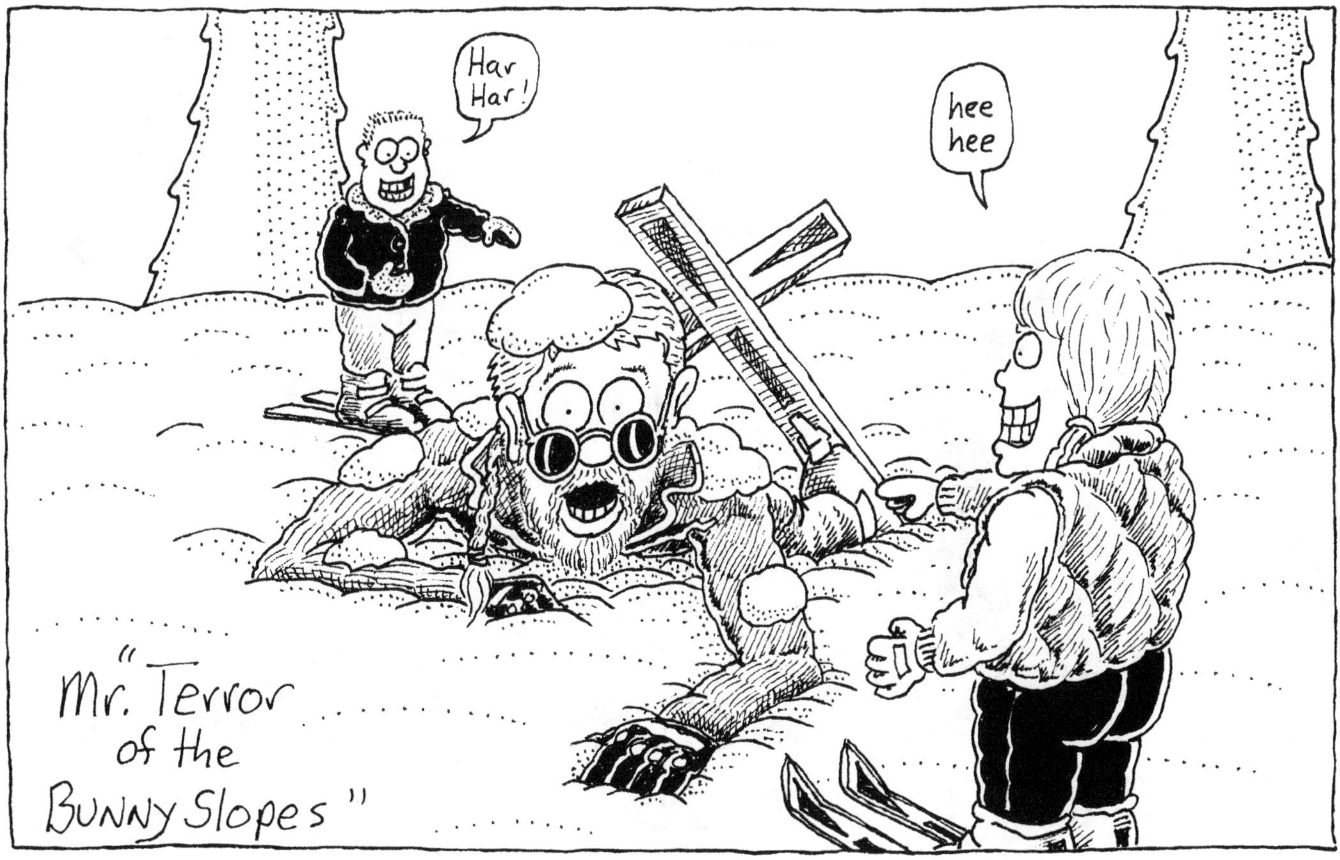
Har Har!
hee hee
"Mr. Terror of the Bunny Slopes"

All About Catwalks...

Catwalks allow us geeks to descend difficult/steep slopes by a series of switchbacking traverses. Catwalks are psychically challenging for beginners because of the exposure factor....you seem to be skiing along the edge of a cliff all the way down (see "Exposure","Fear") On really narrow catwalks snowplowing is next to impossible, adding to the fear factor. The best way to deal with a narrow catwalk from hell is to ski slowly but continuously (stopping makes it worse!) and bleed off speed by sideslipping and edging. If snowplowing is out of the question try "stemming," a kind of micro-snowplow with skis nearly parallel and weight exerted on the inside edges pushing out. Relax and keep in mind you can always stop by bodyslamming into the uphill side (see "forearm self-arrest") and finishing your descent by butt glissading the actual slope (see "butt glissade")!

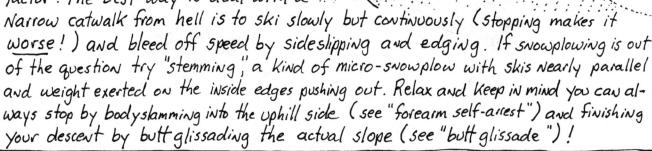

See "Forearm Self-arrest"

Catwalk

Cat Track

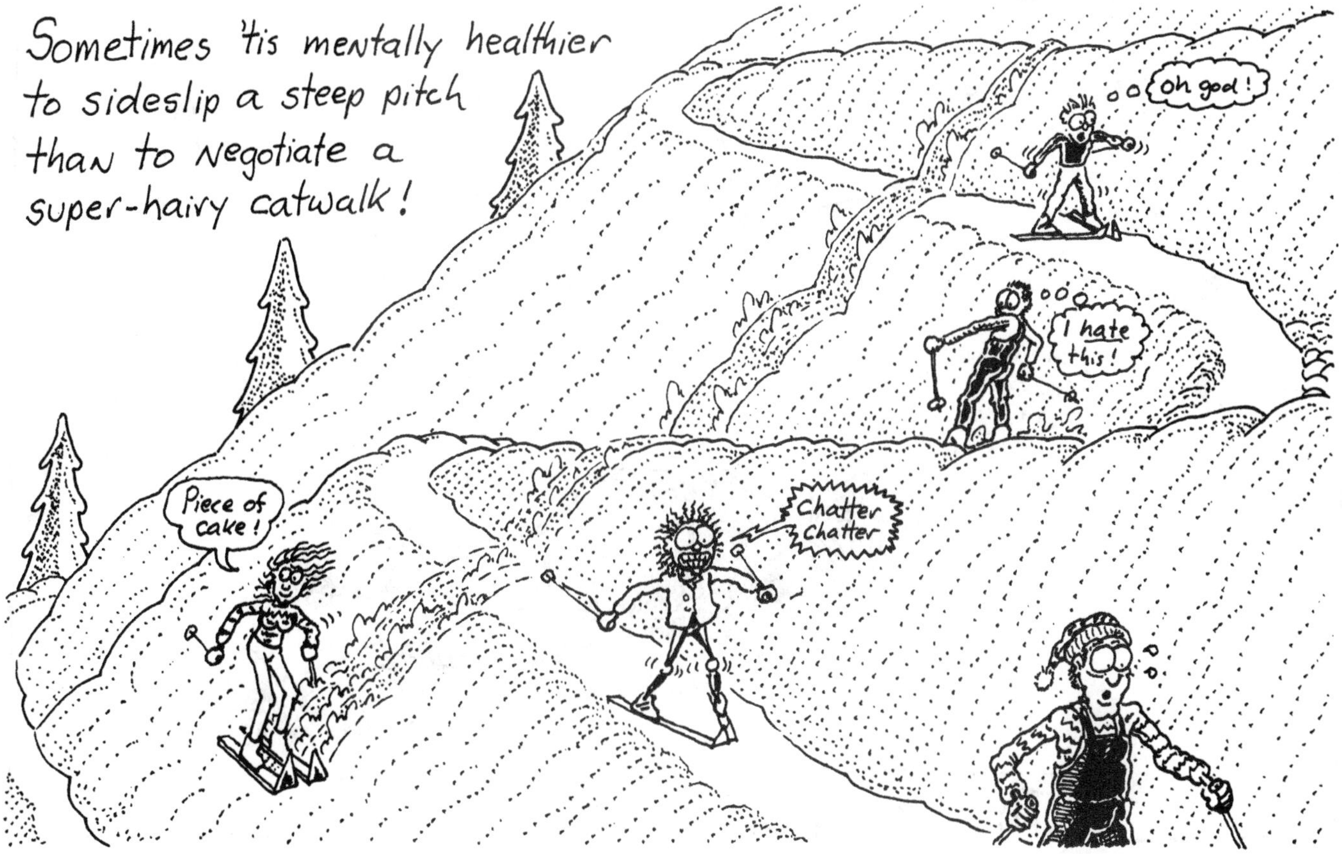
Sometimes 'tis mentally healthier to sideslip a steep pitch than to negotiate a super-hairy catwalk!
oh god!
I hate this!
Piece of cake!
Chatter Chatter

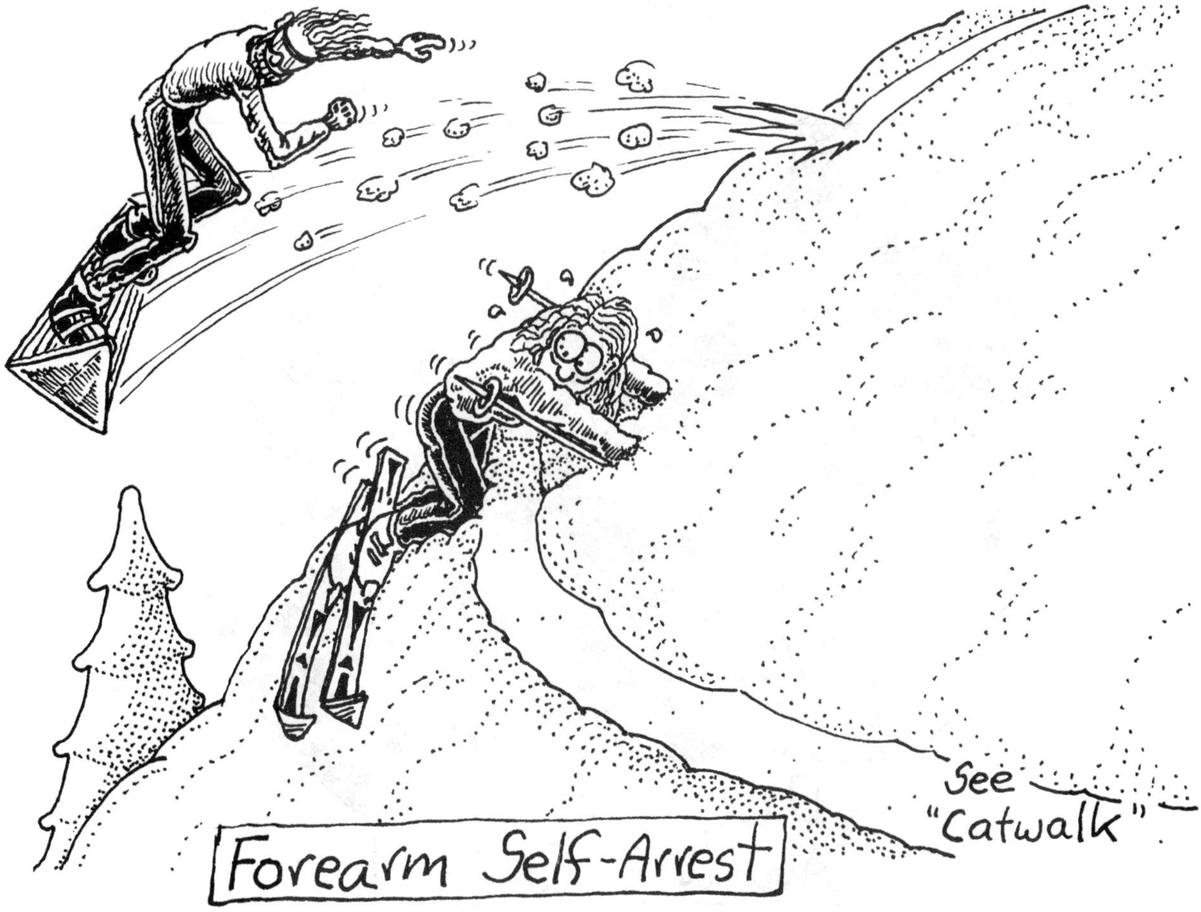

See "Catwalk"

Forearm Self-Arrest

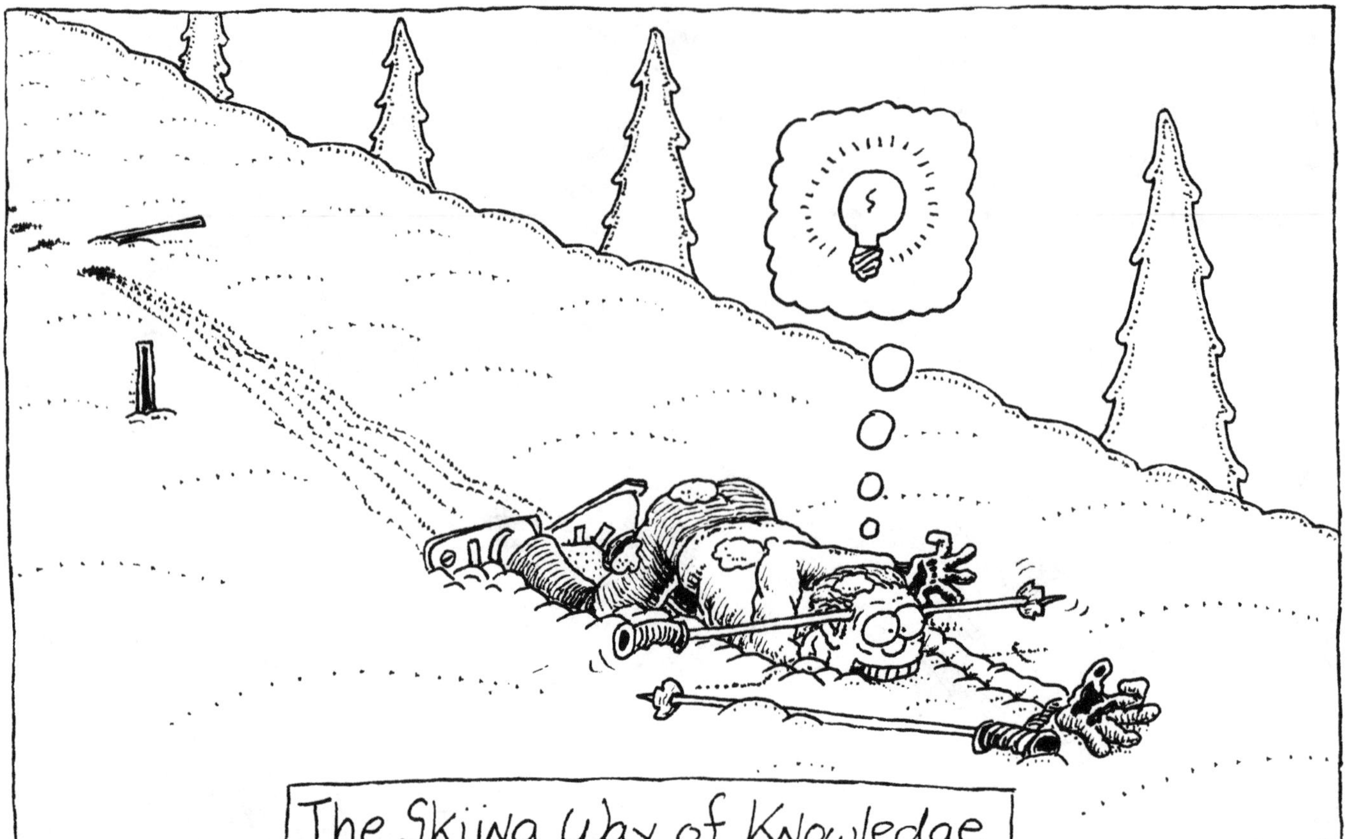

The Skiing Way of Knowledge

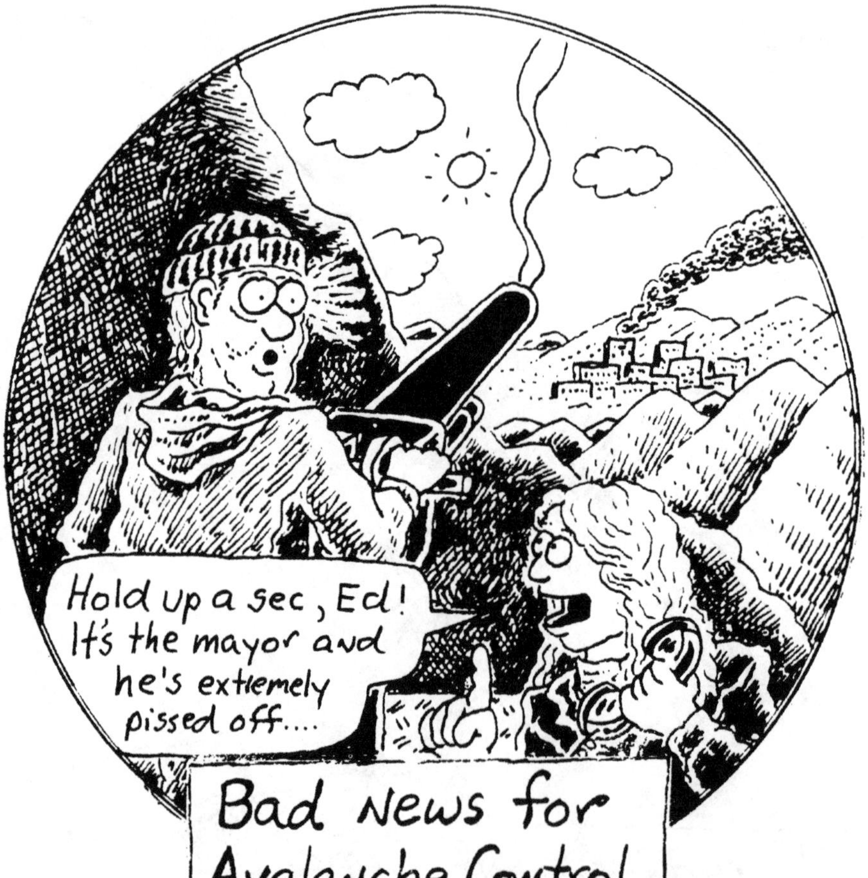
Hold up a sec, Ed! It's the mayor and he's extremely pissed off....

Bad News for Avalanche Control.

Hockey Stop (hôk·ē stôp) Super-dynamic ending in an abrupt stop. Mucho funo!

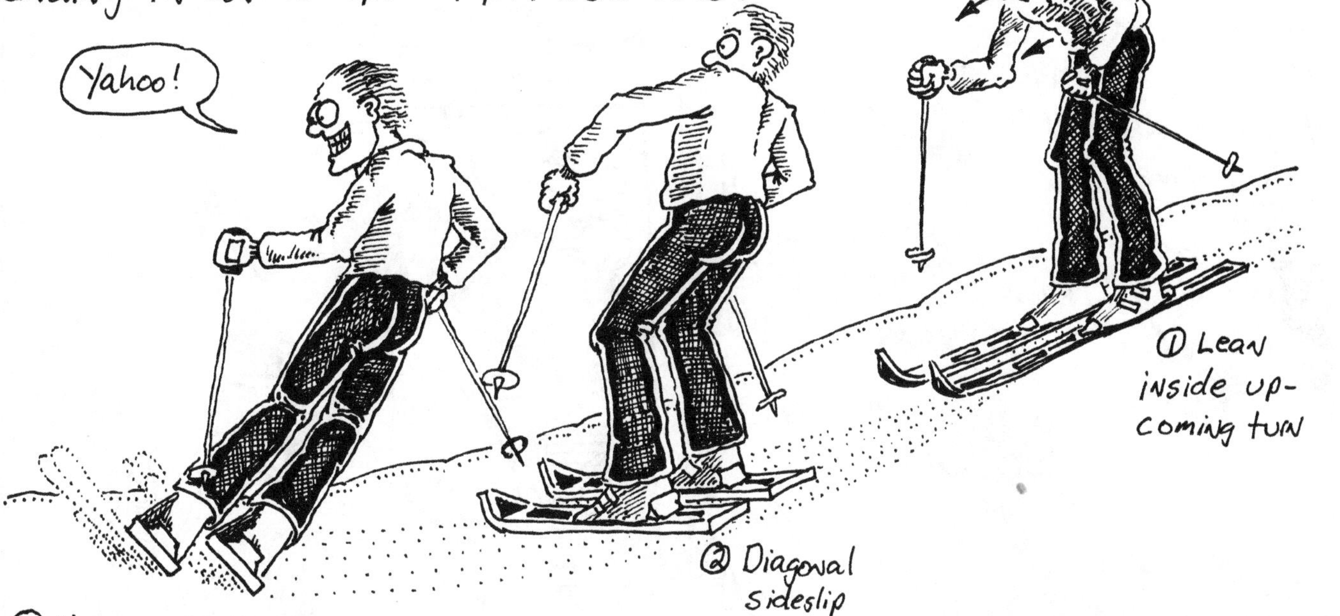

sideslip
Yahoo!
① Lean inside up-coming turn
② Diagonal sideslip

③ Using ankle torque, dig in uphill edges...

Once you've mastered hockey stops you can begin working on "short swings", a continuous series of semi-hockey stops.

Fun With Hockey Stops..

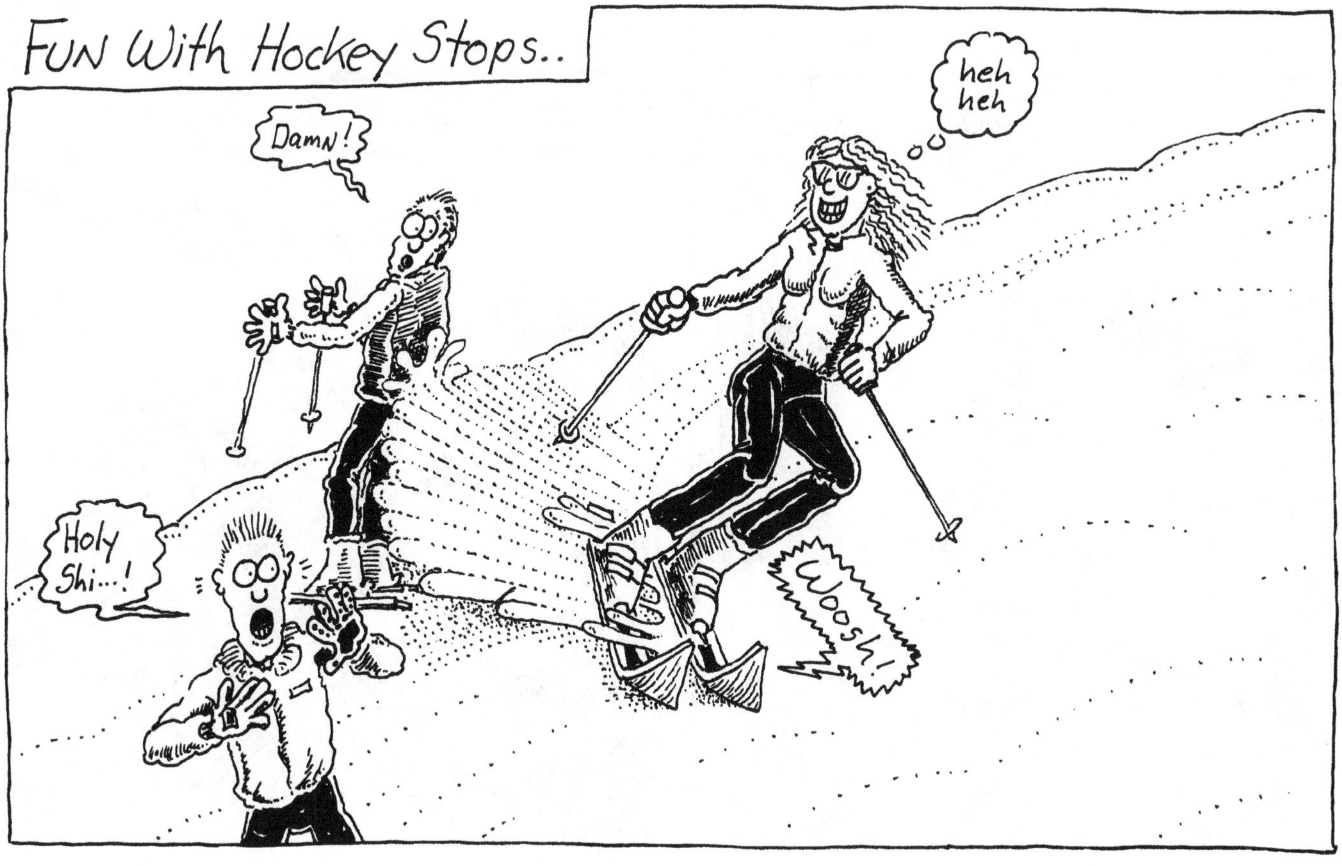

Damn!
heh heh
Holy Shi...!
Woosh!

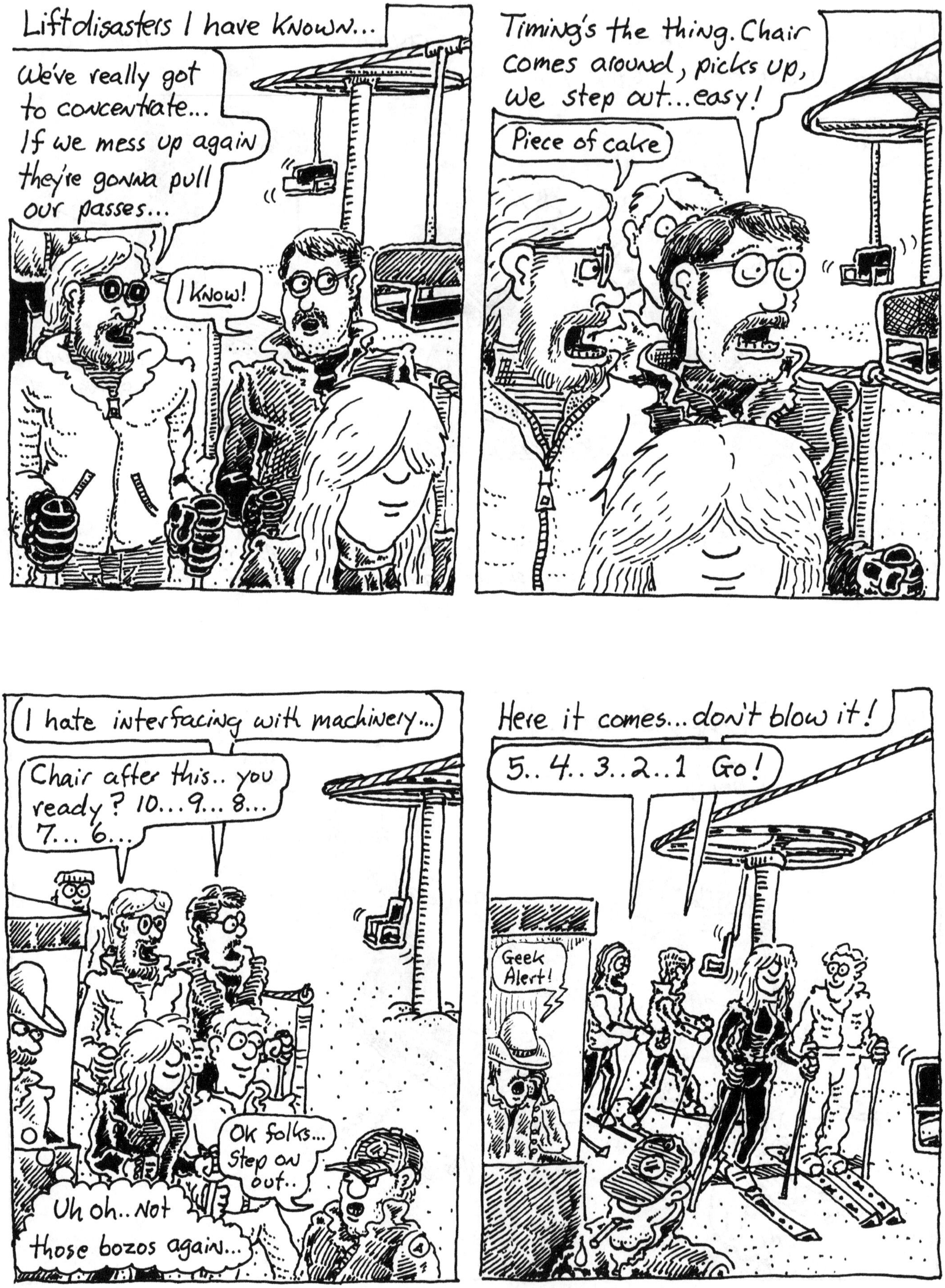

Liftdisasters I have known...
We've really got to concentrate... If we mess up again they're gonna pull our passes...
I know!
Timing's the thing. Chair comes around, picks up, we step out...easy!
Piece of cake
I hate interfacing with machinery...
Chair after this.. you ready? 10...9...8... 7... 6...
Uh oh.. Not those bozos again...
Ok folks... Step on out..
Here it comes...don't blow it!
5..4..3..2..1 Go!
Geek Alert!

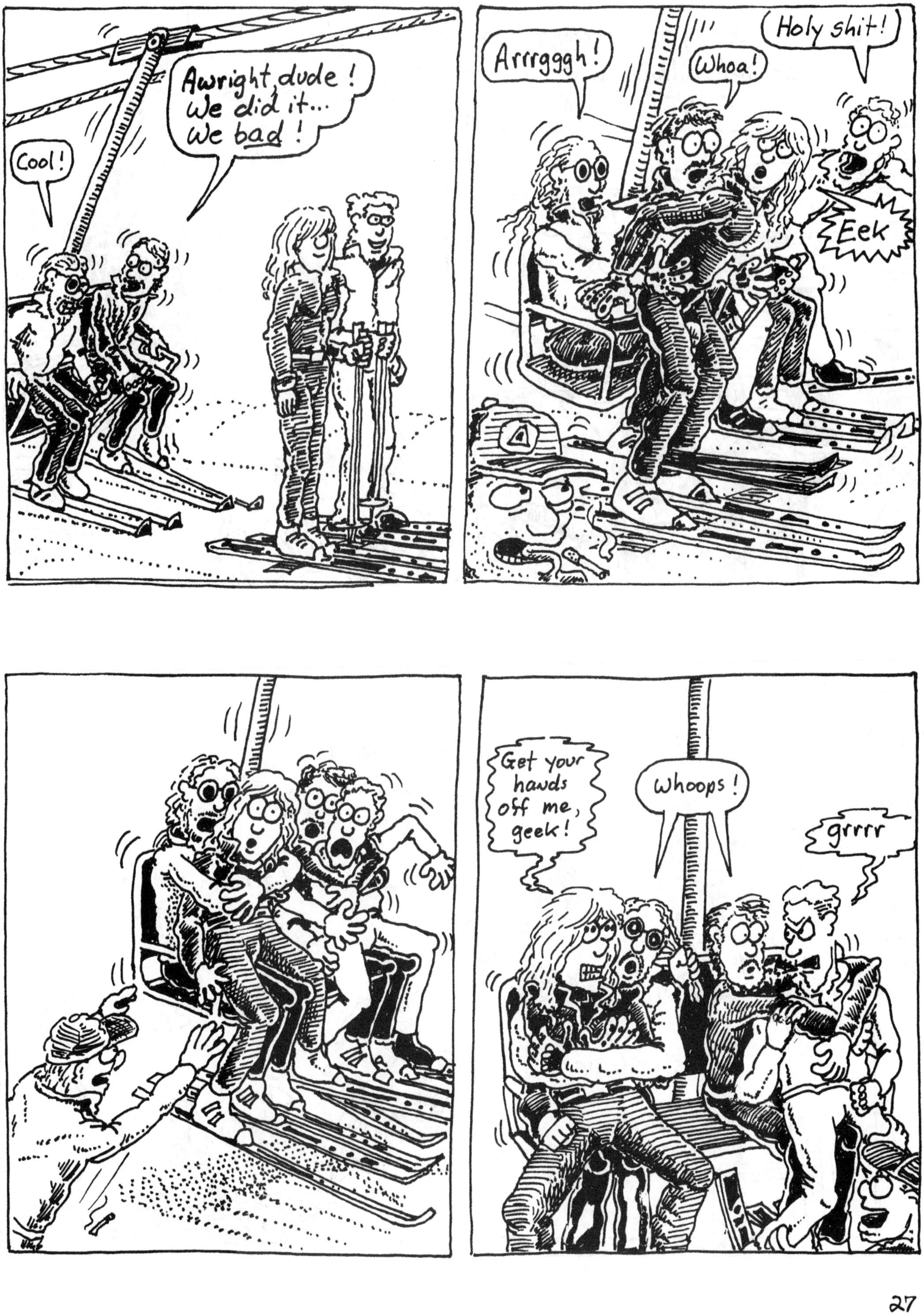
Awright, dude! We did it... We bad!
Cool!
Arrrgggh!
Whoa!
Holy shit!
Eek
Get your hands off me, geek!
Whoops!
grrrr

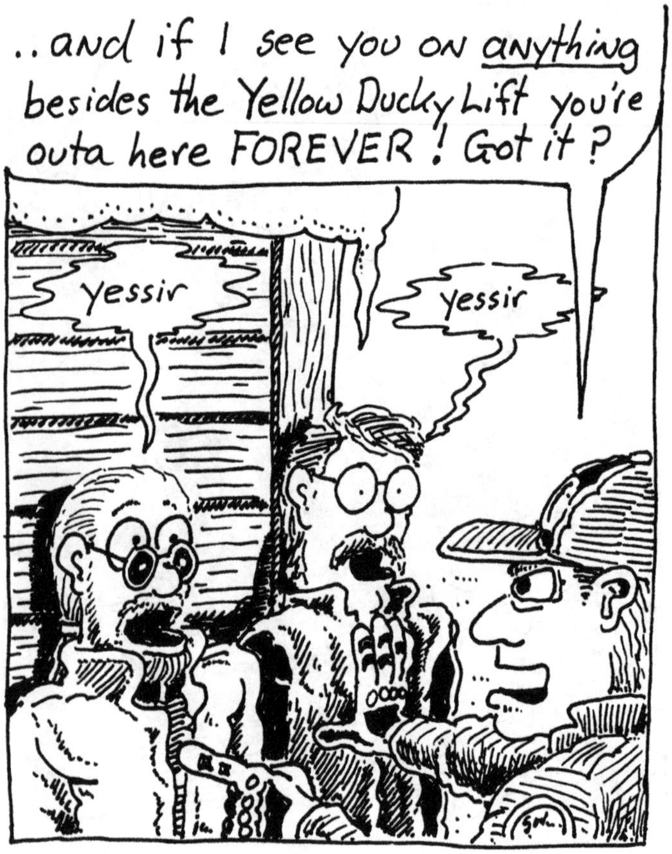
..and if I see you on anything besides the Yellow Ducky Lift you're outa here FOREVER! Got it?
yessir
yessir

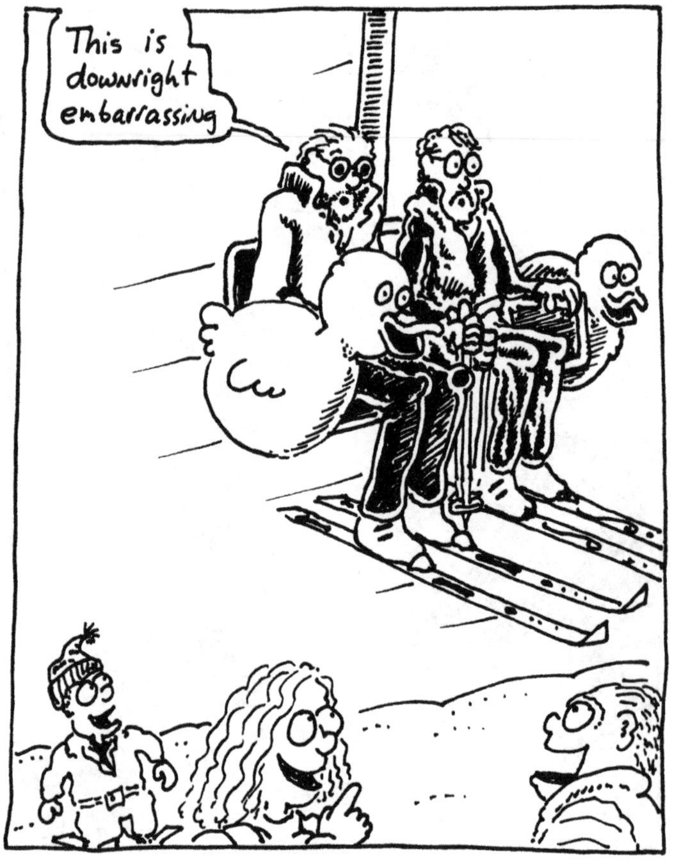
This is downright embarrassing

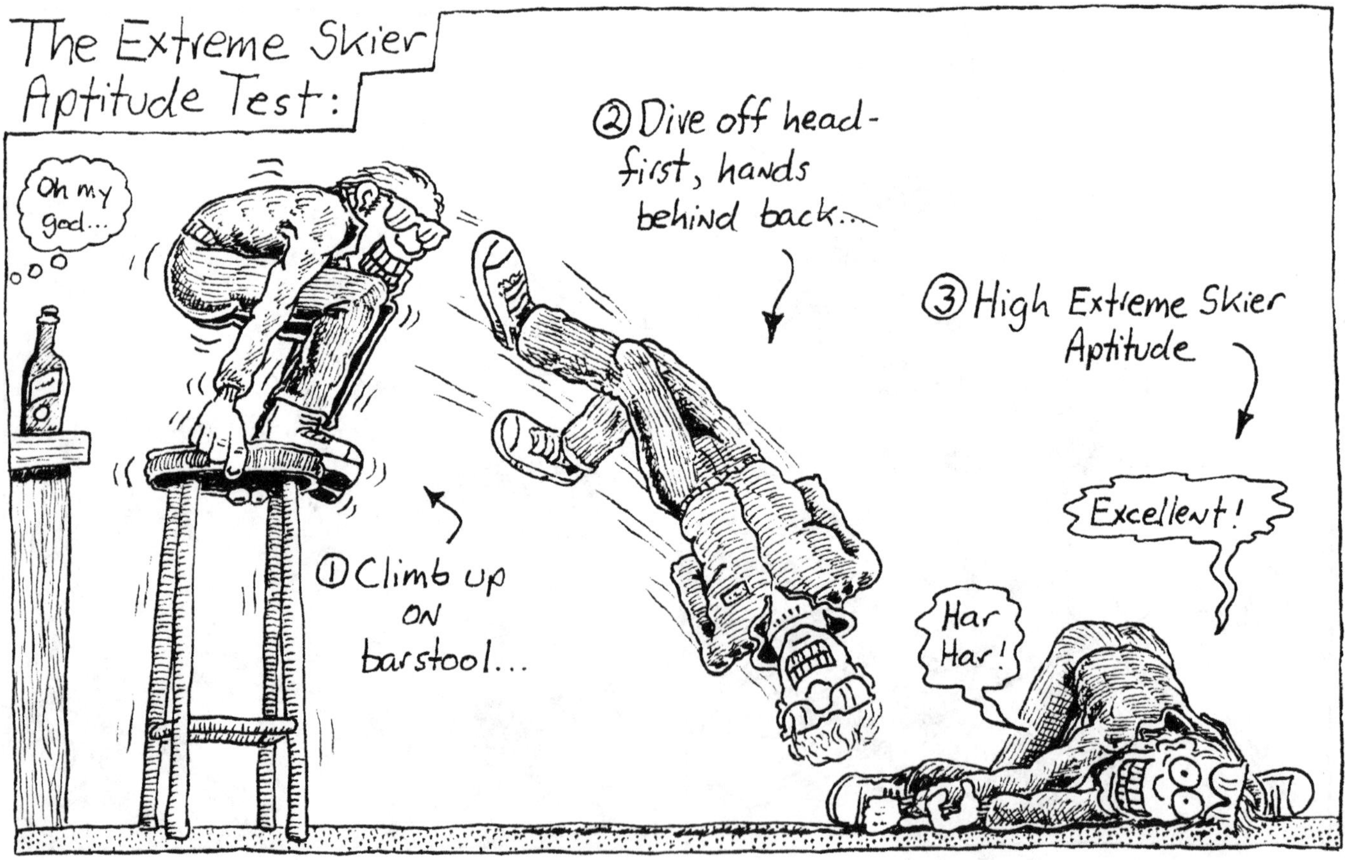
The Extreme Skier Aptitude Test:
Oh my god...
① Climb up on barstool...
② Dive off head-first, hands behind back...
③ High Extreme Skier Aptitude
Excellent!
Har Har!

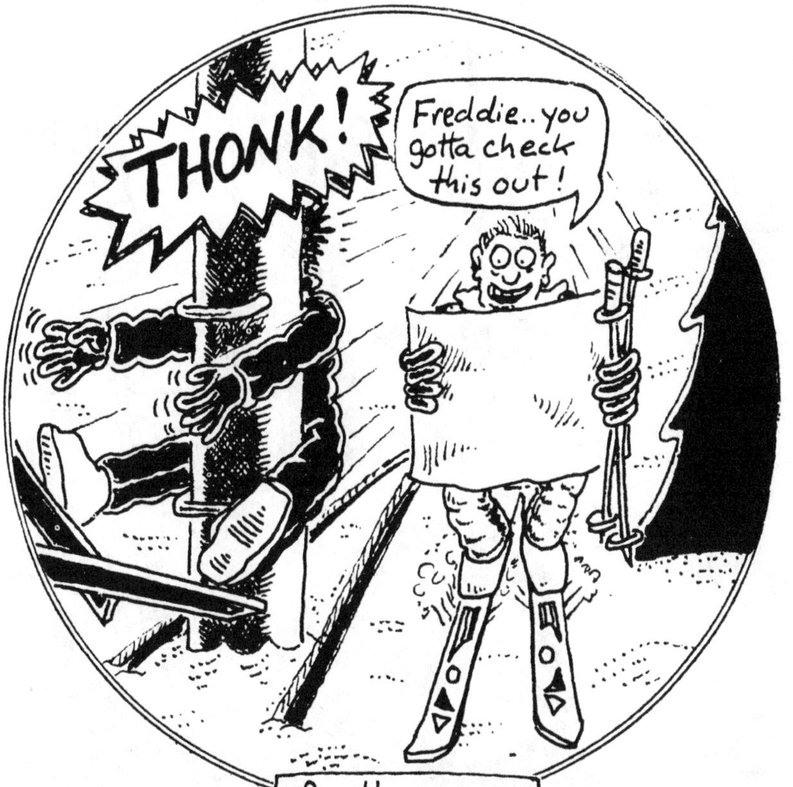
THONK!
Freddie.. you gotta check this out!

Another map related injury..

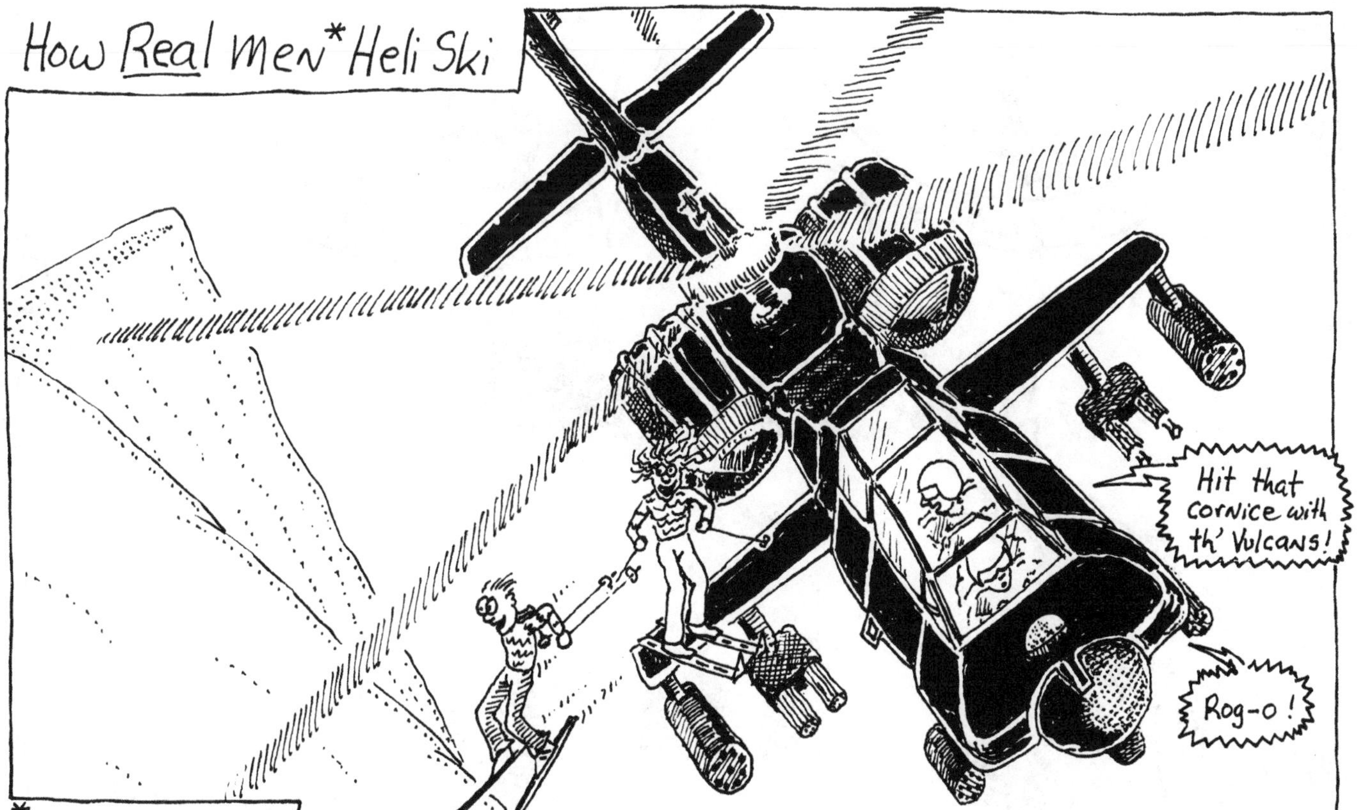
How Real men* Heli Ski
Hit that cornice with th' Vulcans!
Rog-o!
*and wimmen!

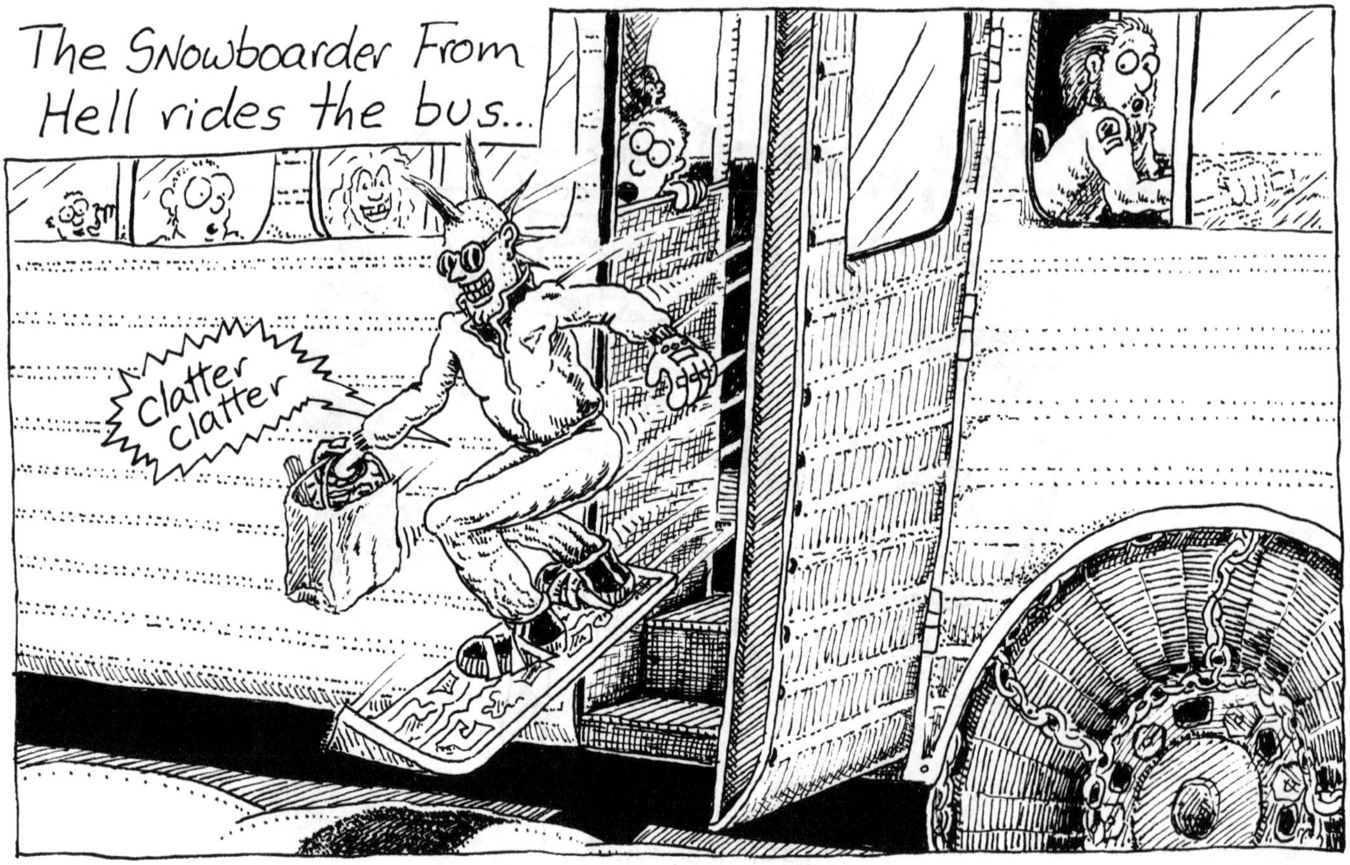
The Snowboarder From Hell rides the bus...
Clatter clatter

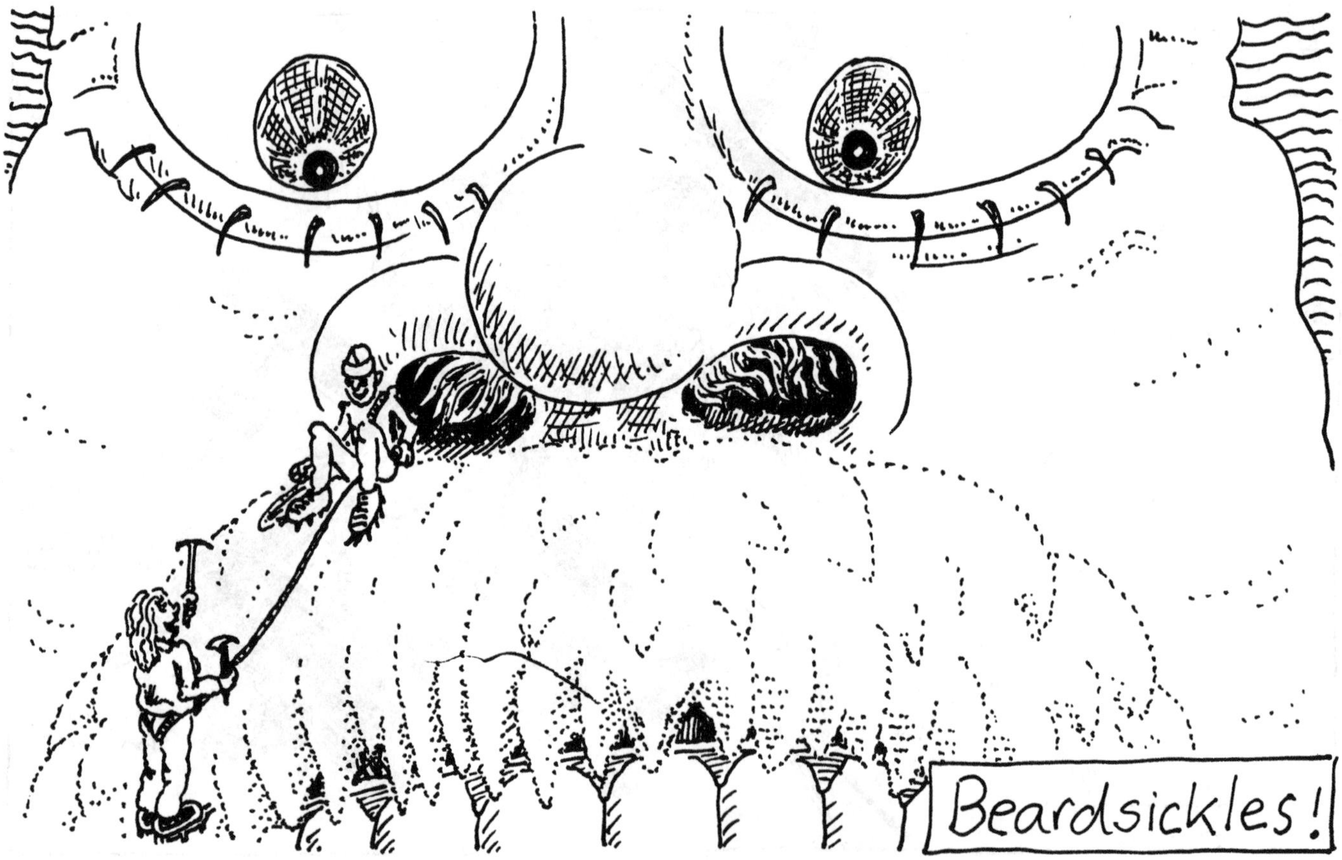
Beardsickles!

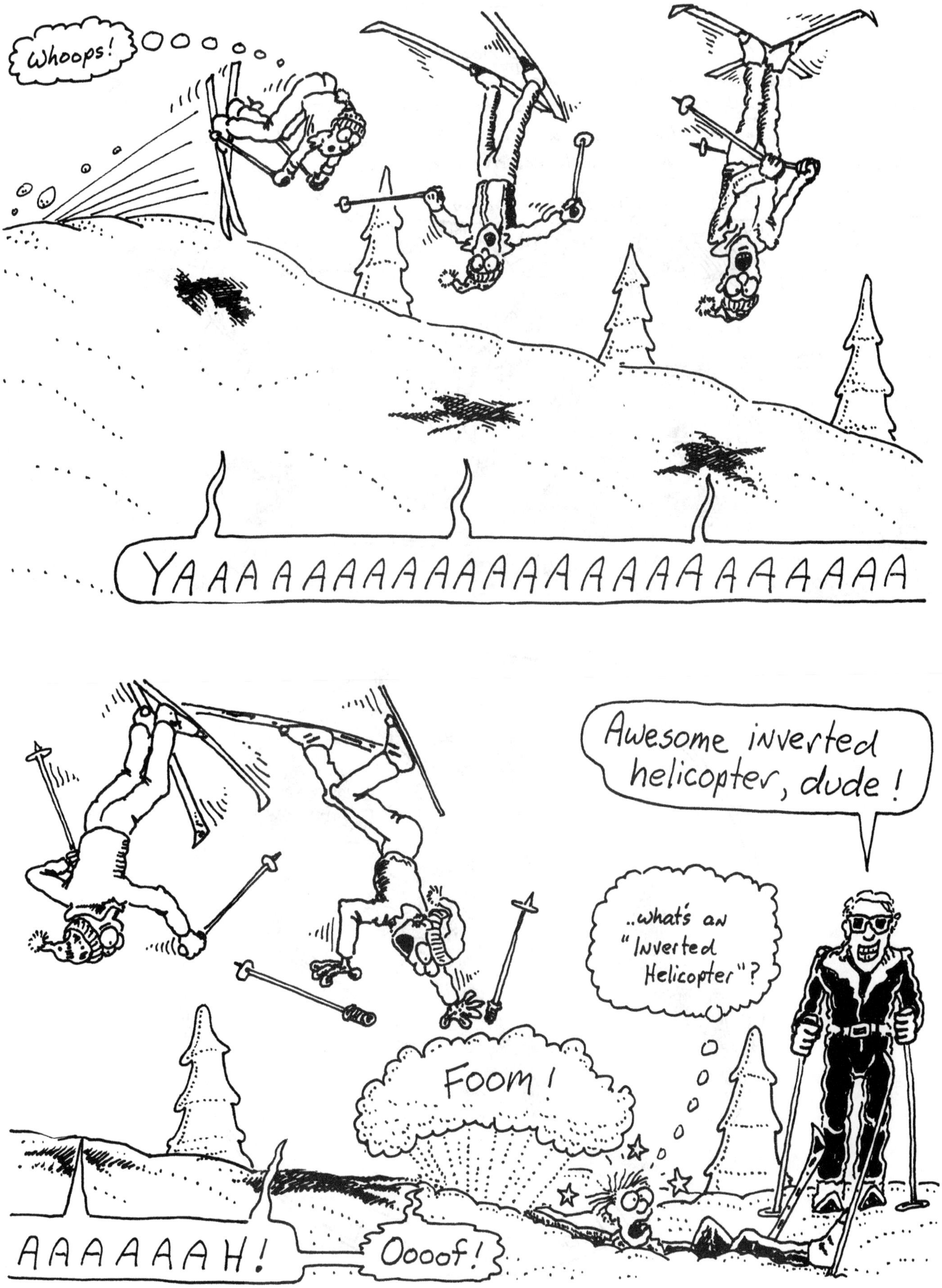
Whoops!
YAAAAAAAAAAAAAAAAAAAAAAA
Awesome inverted helicopter, dude!
..what's an "Inverted Helicopter"?
Foom!
AAAAAAH!
Oooof!

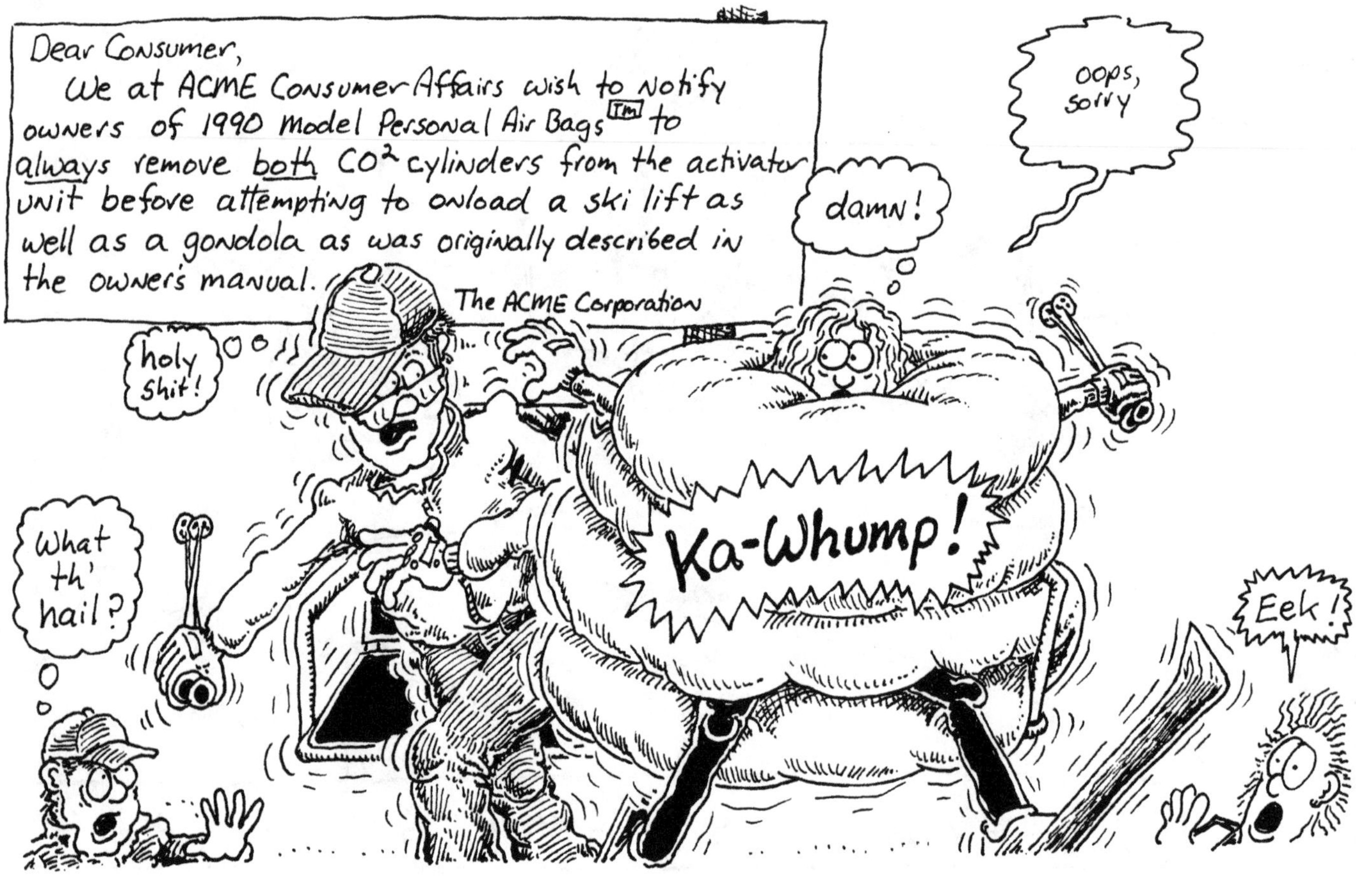
Dear Consumer,
We at ACME Consumer Affairs wish to notify owners of 1990 Model Personal Air Bags(TM) to always remove both CO2 cylinders from the activator unit before attempting to onload a ski lift as well as a gondola as was originally described in the owner's manual.
The ACME Corporation
oops, sorry
damn!
holy shit!
Ka-Whump!
What th' hail?
Eek!

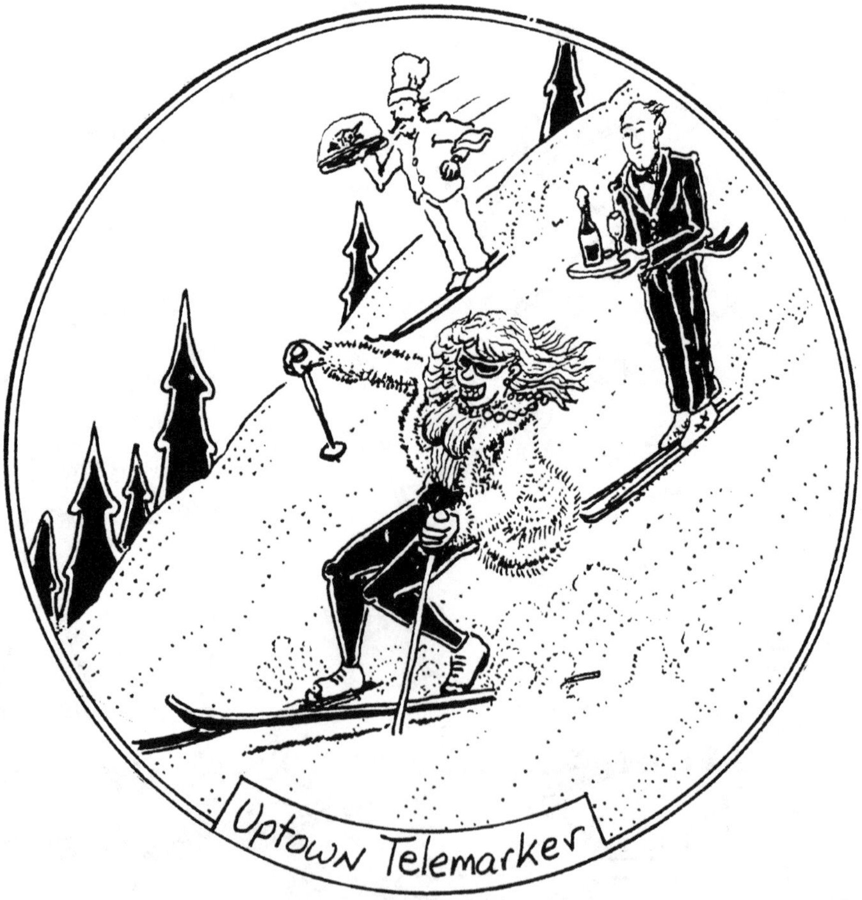
Uptown Telemarker

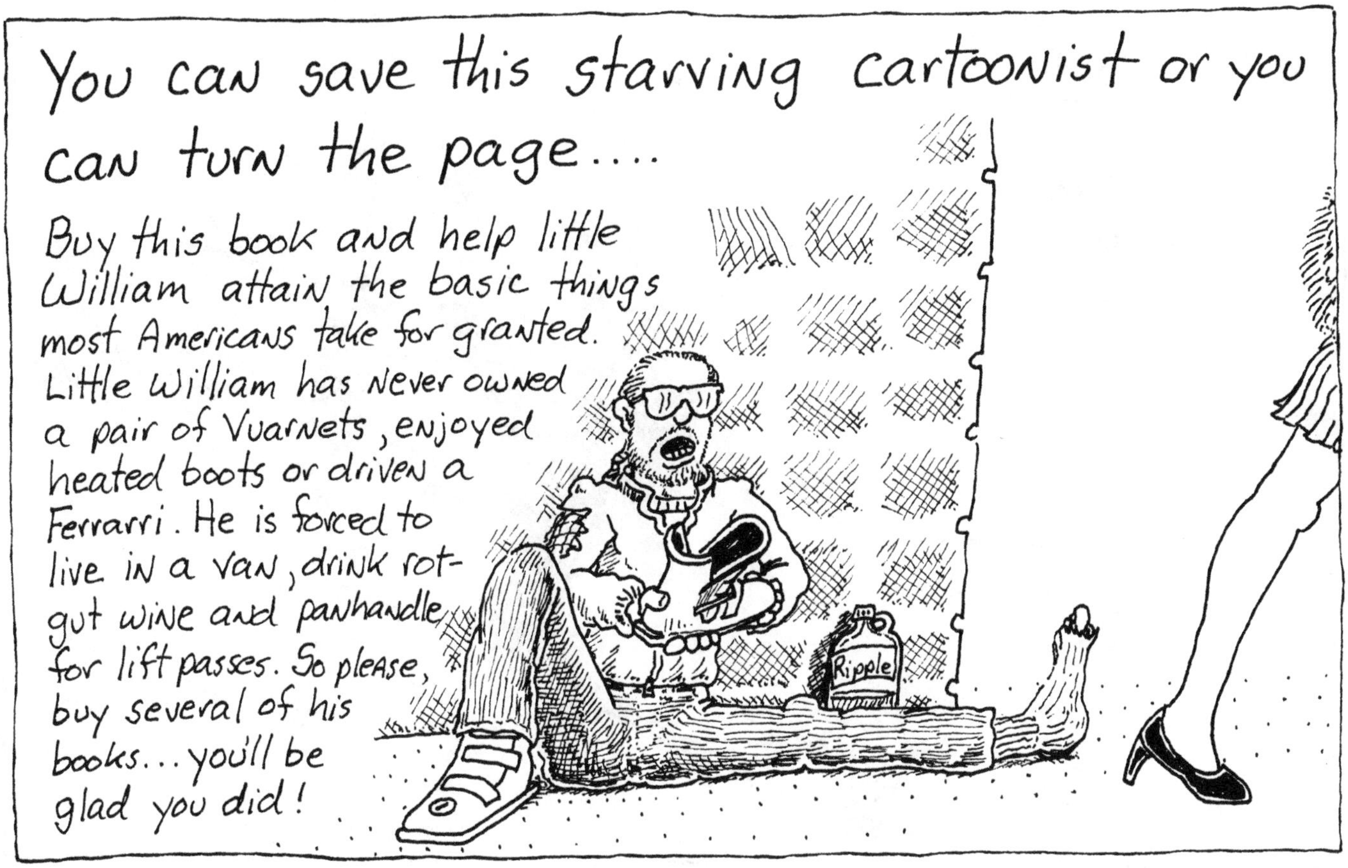
You can save this starving cartoonist or you can turn the page....
Buy this book and help little William attain the basic things most Americans take for granted. Little William has never owned a pair of Vuarnets, enjoyed heated boots or driven a Ferrarri. He is forced to live in a van, drink rot-gut wine and panhandle for lift passes. So please, buy several of his books... you'll be glad you did!
Ripple

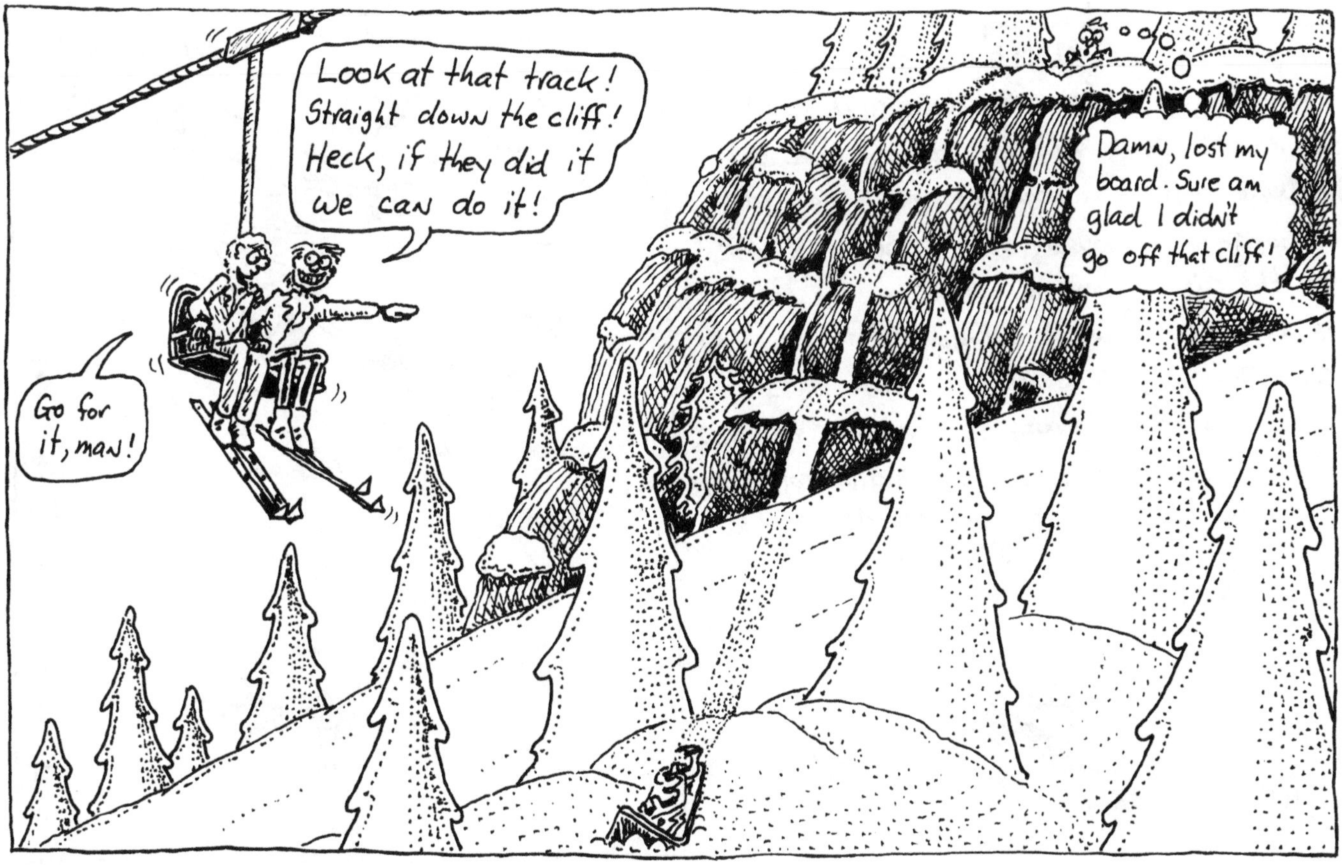
Look at that track! Straight down the cliff! Heck, if they did it we can do it!
Go for it, man!
Damn, lost my board. Sure am glad I didn't go off that cliff!

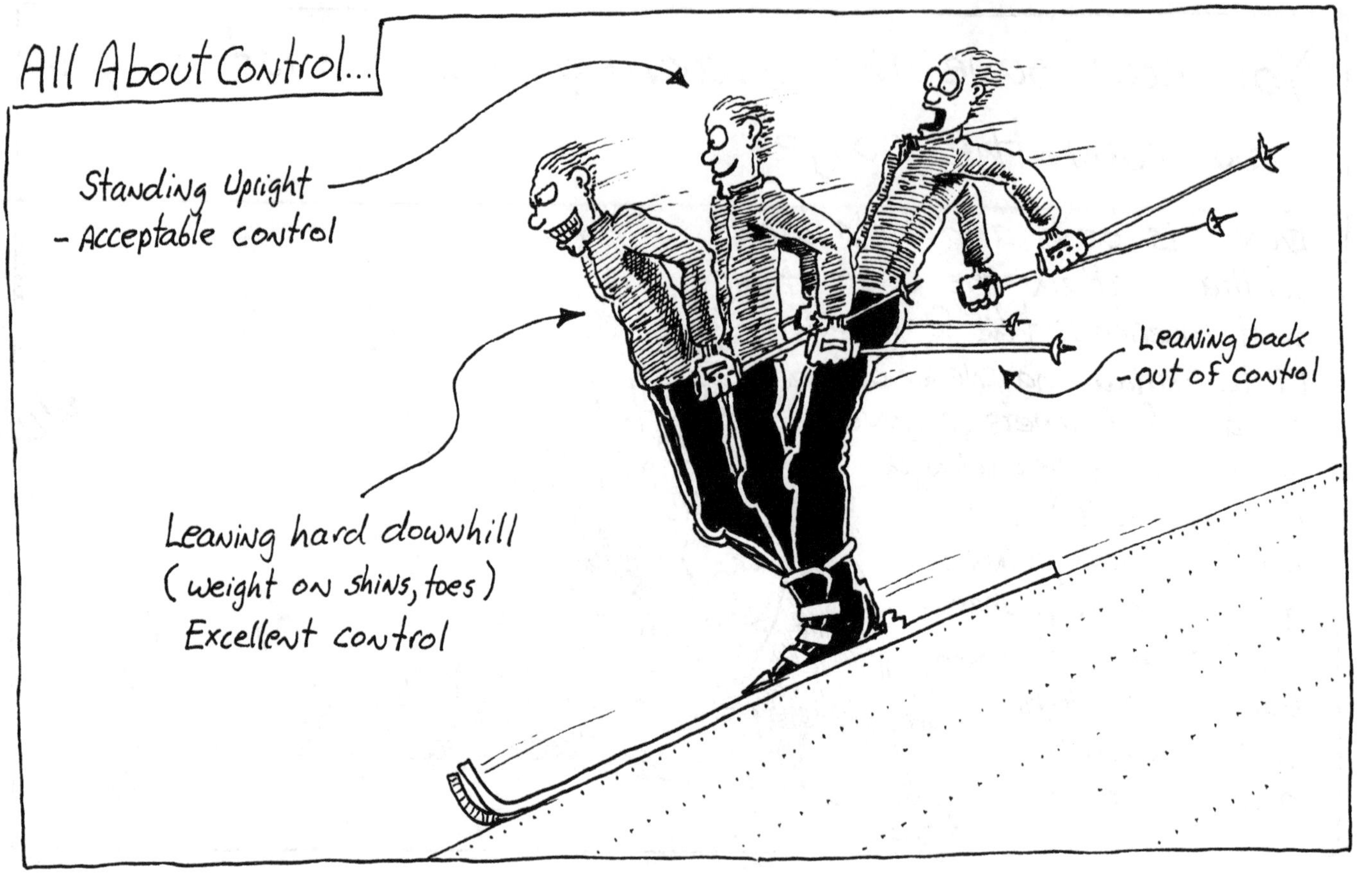
All About Control...
Standing Upright
- Acceptable control
Leaning back
- out of control
Leaning hard downhill
(weight on shins, toes)
Excellent control

Fear

Yes Virginia, fear is alive and well on ski slopes, especially for beginners. Even teenage ninja snowboarders experience fear although it is usually fear of being carded at the disco. Anyhow, fear on the mountain is typically fear of falling off the mountain and landing somewhere in town. After a few hundred wipe-outs the beginner will learn that he or she generally remains attached to the mountain in all but the most catastrophic of falls.

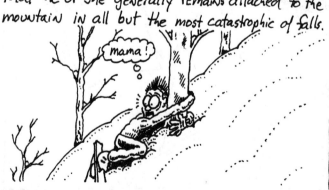

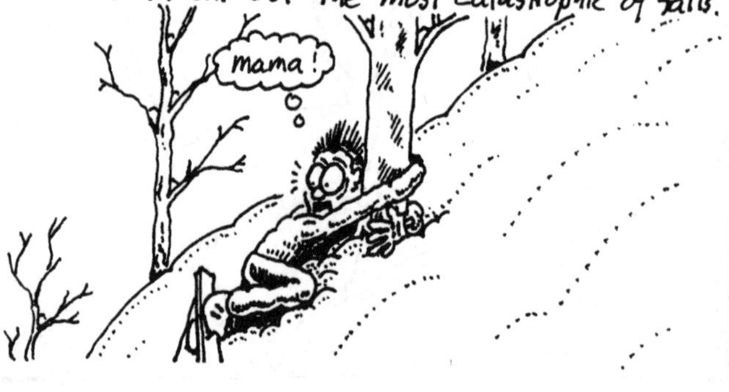
mama!

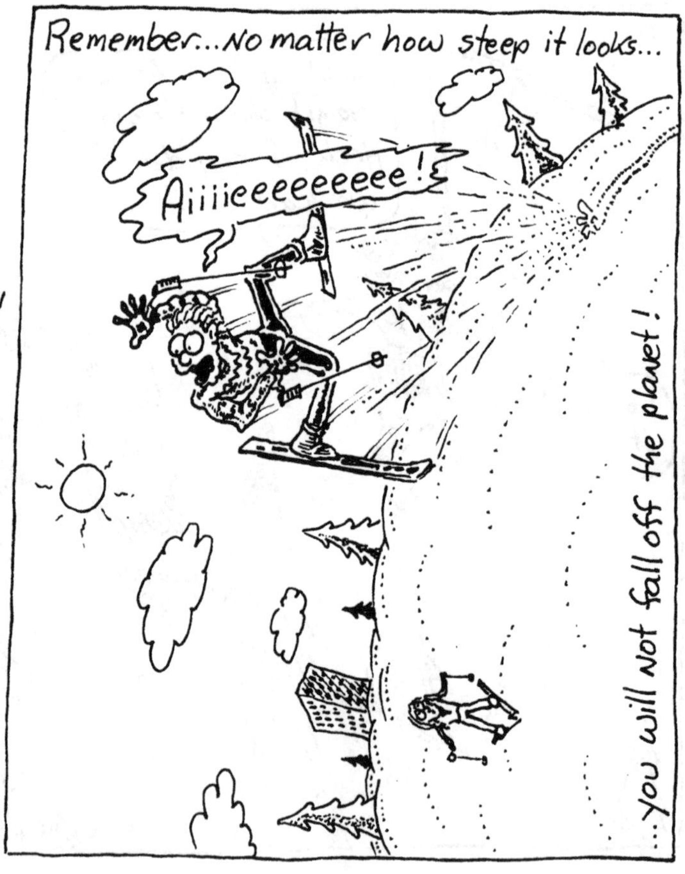
Remember...No matter how steep it looks...
Aiiiieeeeeeeee!
...you will not fall off the planet!

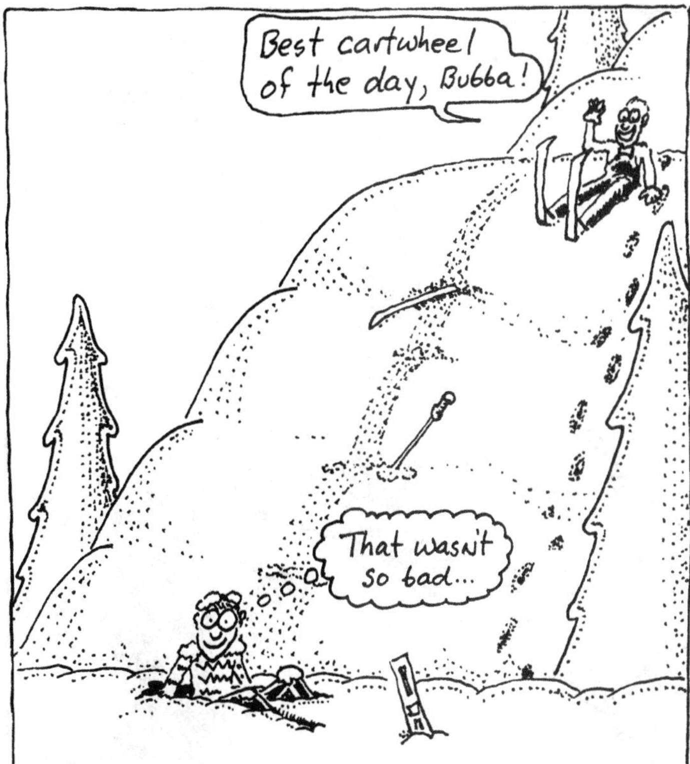
Best cartwheel of the day, Bubba!
That wasn't so bad...

Devise game strategies to habituate yourself to conditions that cause the experience of fear.

The object of the game in skiing is to overcome fear with fun while maintaining a very healthy respect for the dynamic tendencies of gravity. You can overcome fear by habituating yourself to the causes of fear (exposure, steepness, etc) in an amusing and safe context. For instance you might choose to butt glissade a steep pitch until you get acclimatized to the steepness, then ski it. You may want to climb up a steep pitch and ski it ten feet at a time going a little bit higher on each successive attempt. Eventually you'll be skiing the whole slope without fear. Avoid pushing yourself too hard and overdosing on fear... do it a little bit at a time and quit when you stop having fun. Remember: Positive experiences build "Mojo", Negative experiences kill "Mojo". See "Mojo"

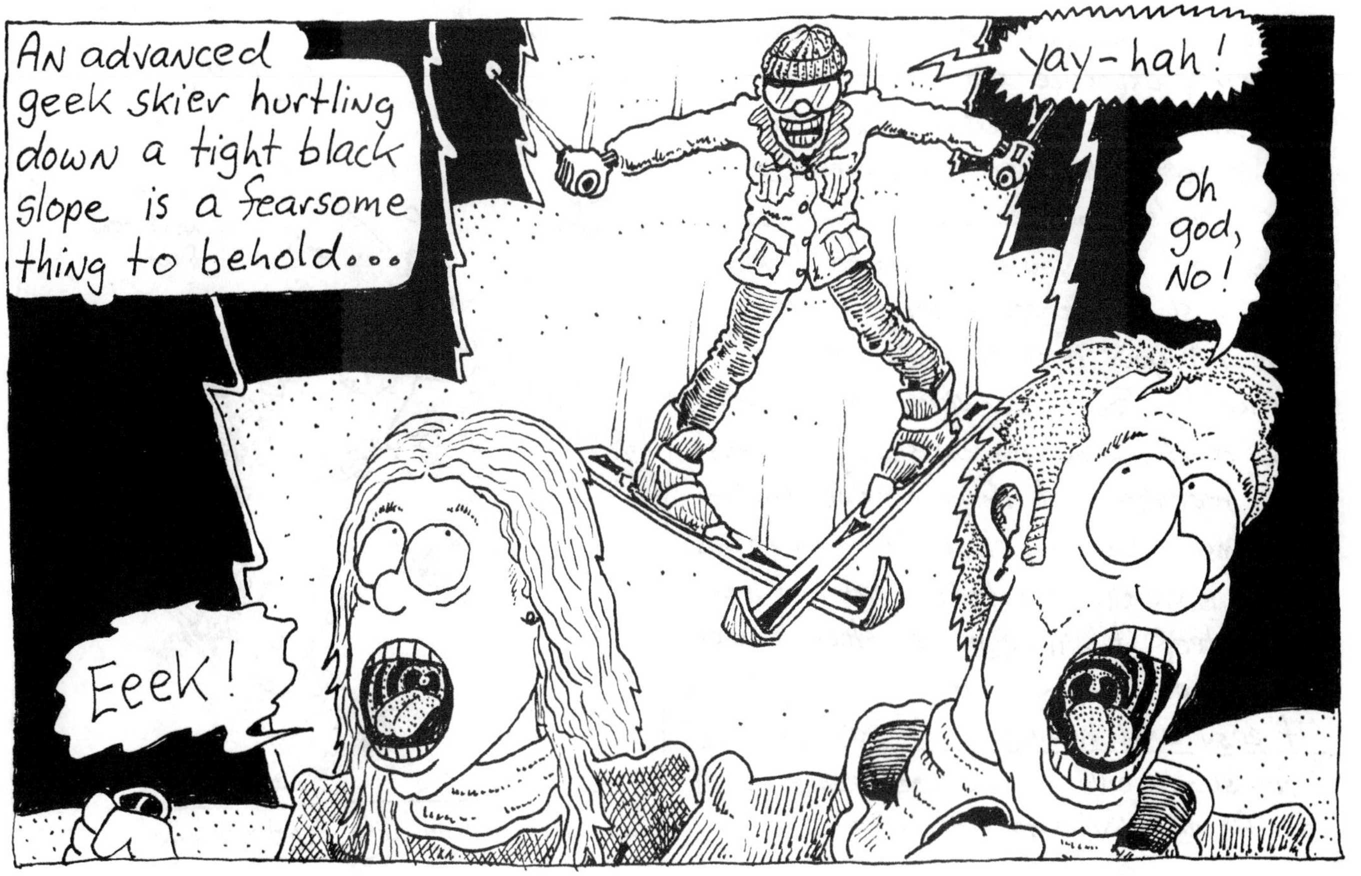
An advanced geek skier hurtling down a tight black slope is a fearsome thing to behold...
Yay-hah!
Oh god, No!
Eeek!

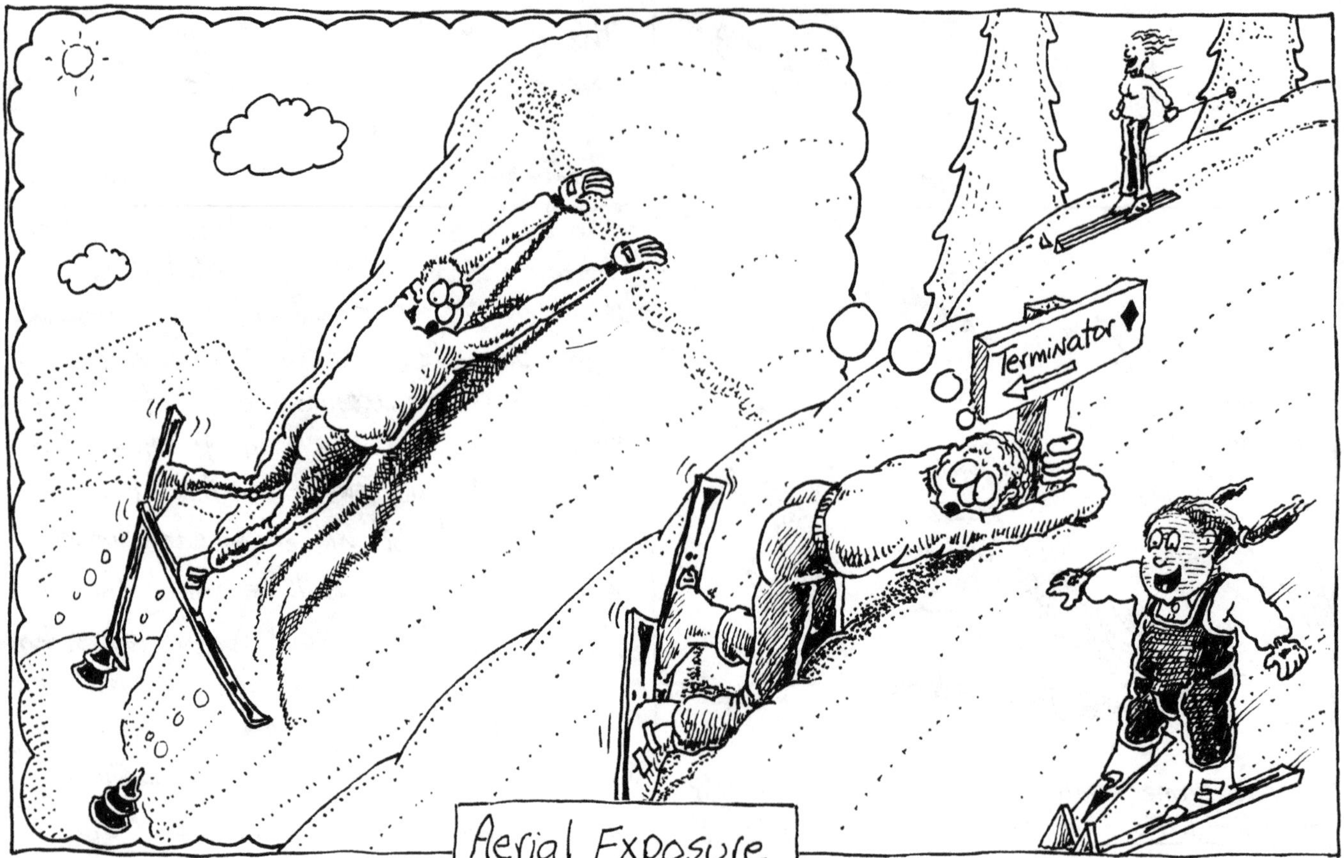
Terminator
Aerial Exposure

There are two types of serious fear-producing exposure: aerial exposure and transitional exposure (next page). Aerial exposure refers to the disconcerting experience of lots of air under your feet on open steep slopes. If you feel like you are fixing to fly screaming off the slope into space, sit down,* relax and let your eyeballs adjust to the verticality. Focus your vision ten feet below you and concentrate on skiing only that ten feet, then rest. If you're mainly having problems on big open slopes, try skiing trails. A trail is visually restricted and even if it is equally steep it will <u>seem</u> less steep than an open slope. Keep your mojo intact by taking it easy and having fun. This ain't the Army!

* You should only stop on steep slopes out of traffic and visible to those above.

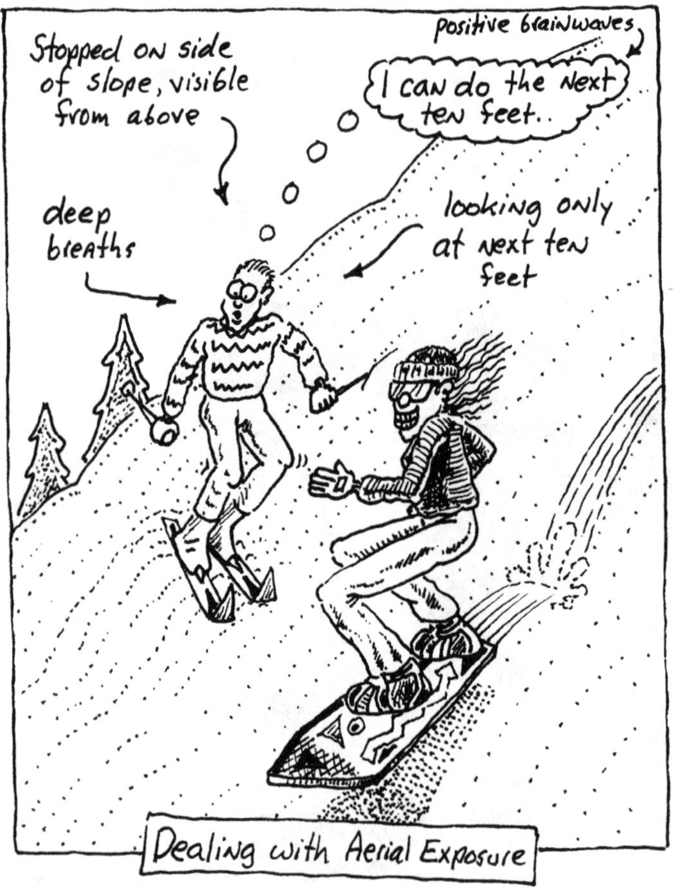
positive brainwaves
I can do the next ten feet.
Stopped on side of slope, visible from above
deep breaths
looking only at next ten feet
Dealing with Aerial Exposure

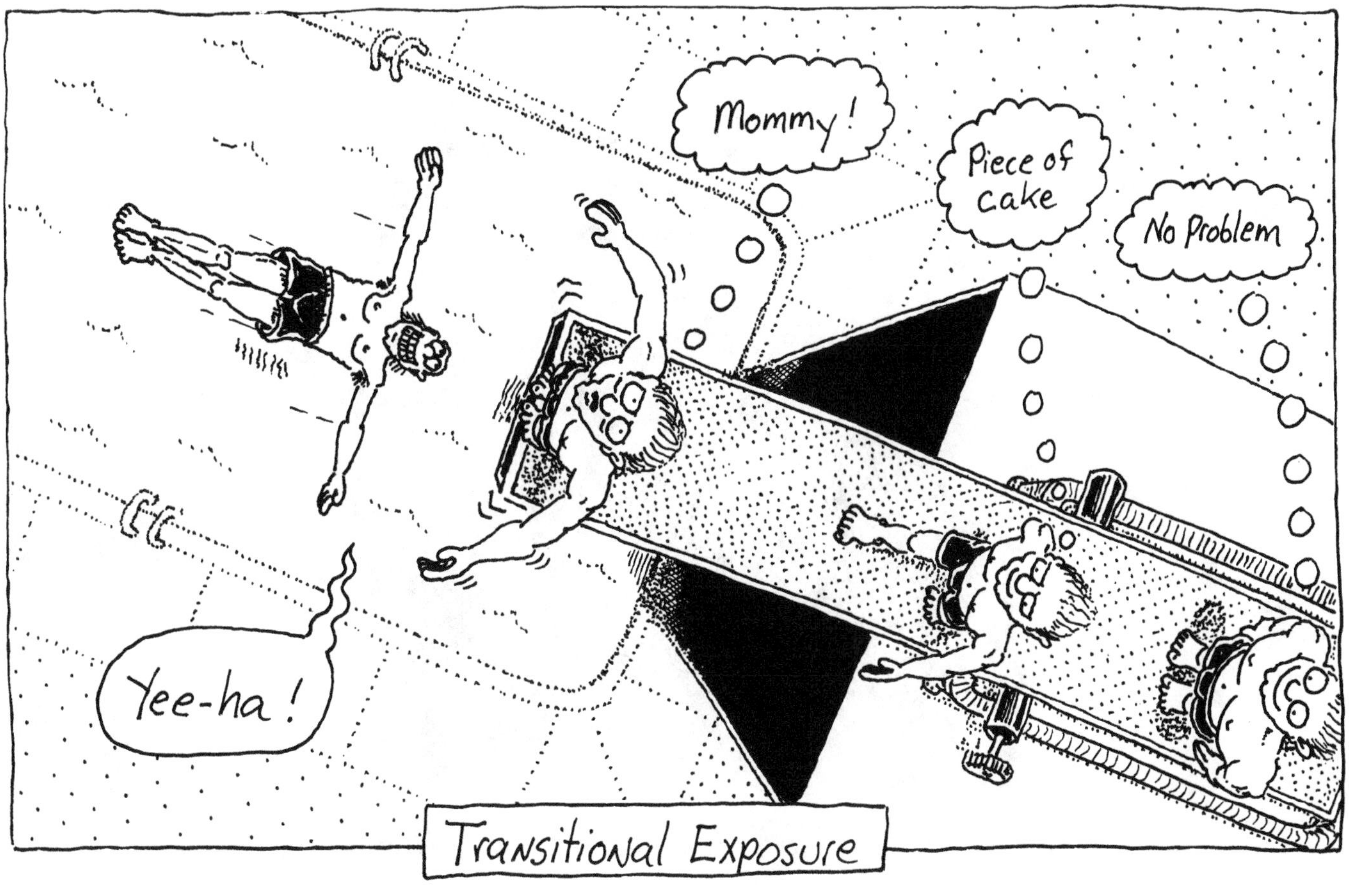
Mommy!
Piece of cake
No Problem
Yee-ha!

Transitional Exposure

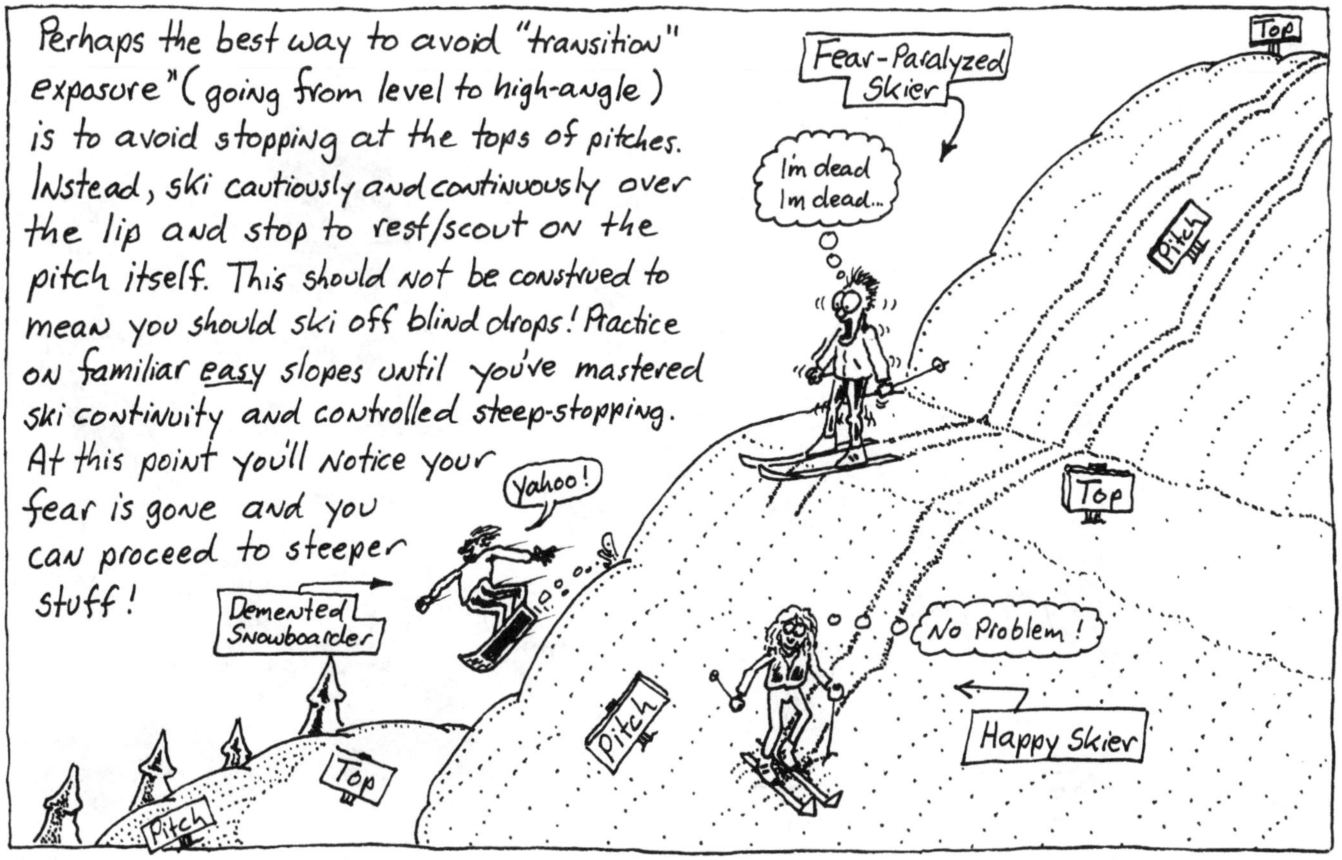
Perhaps the best way to avoid "transition" exposure" (going from level to high-angle) is to avoid stopping at the tops of pitches. Instead, ski cautiously and continuously over the lip and stop to rest/scout on the pitch itself. This should not be construed to mean you should ski off blind drops! Practice on familiar easy slopes until you've mastered ski continuity and controlled steep-stopping. At this point you'll notice your fear is gone and you can proceed to steeper stuff!
Fear-Paralyzed Skier
I'm dead I'm dead...
Top
Pitch
Yahoo!
Demented Snowboarder
Top
No Problem!
Happy Skier
Pitch
Top
Pitch

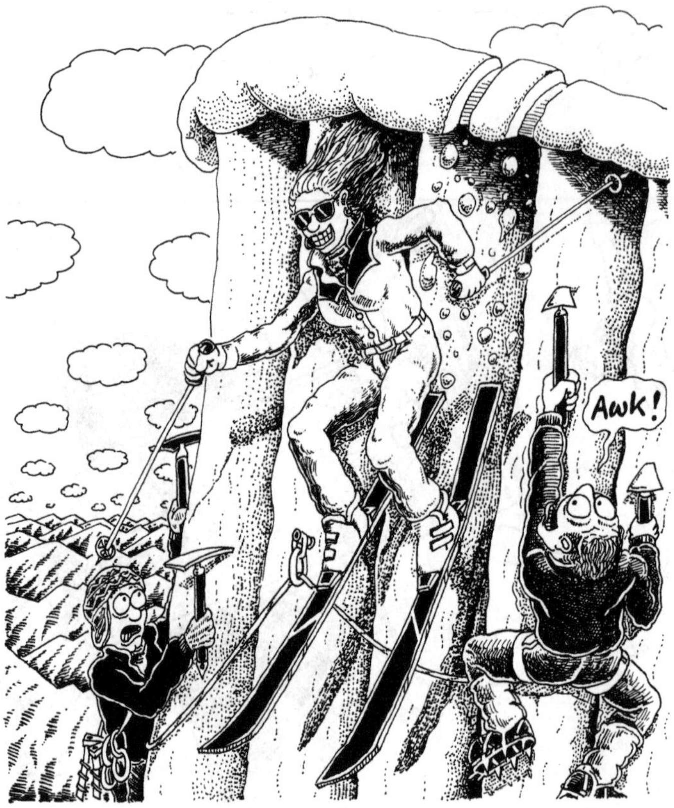
Awk!

Why Ice Climbers Hate Extreme Skiers...

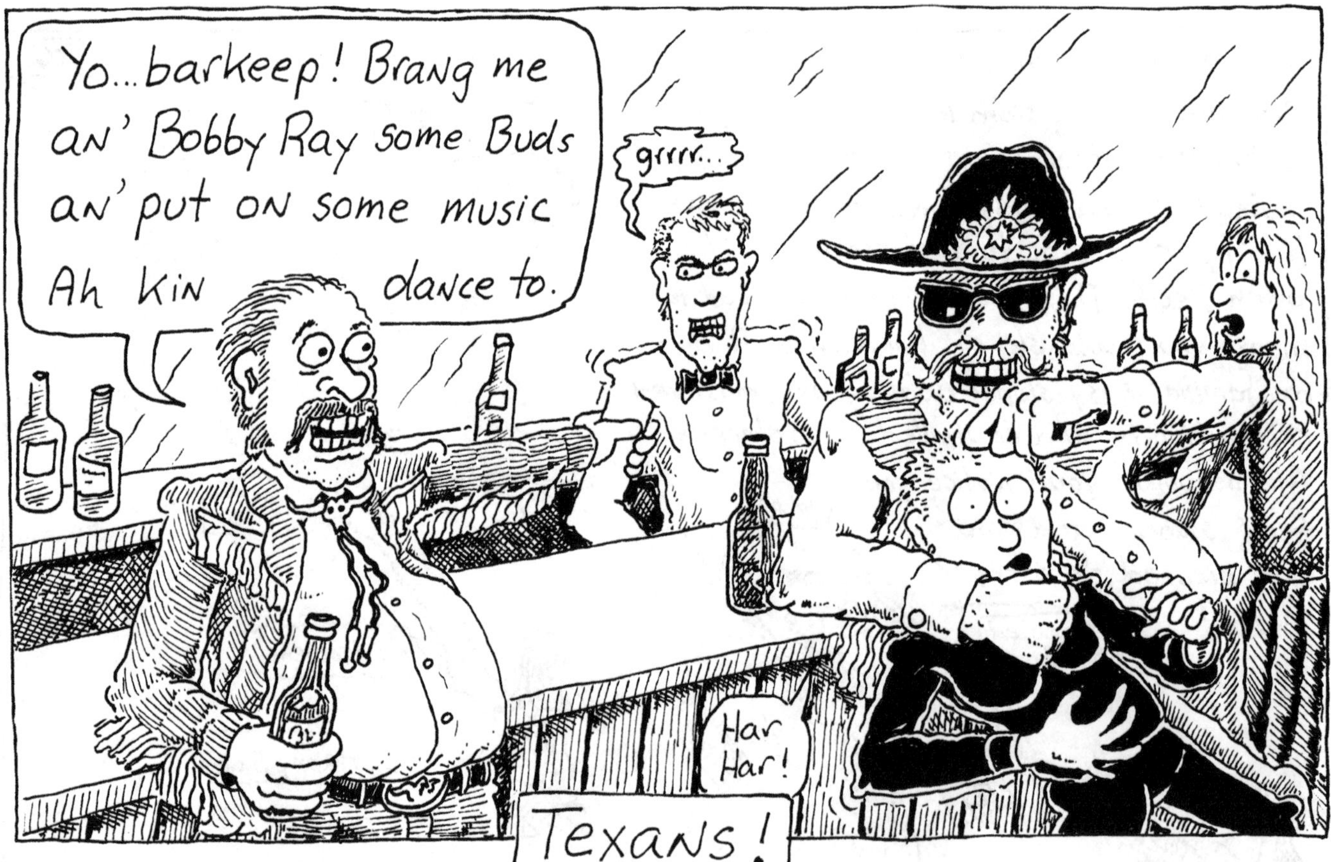
Yo...barkeep! Brang me an' Bobby Ray some Buds an' put on some music Ah kin dance to.
grrrr...
Har Har!
Texans!

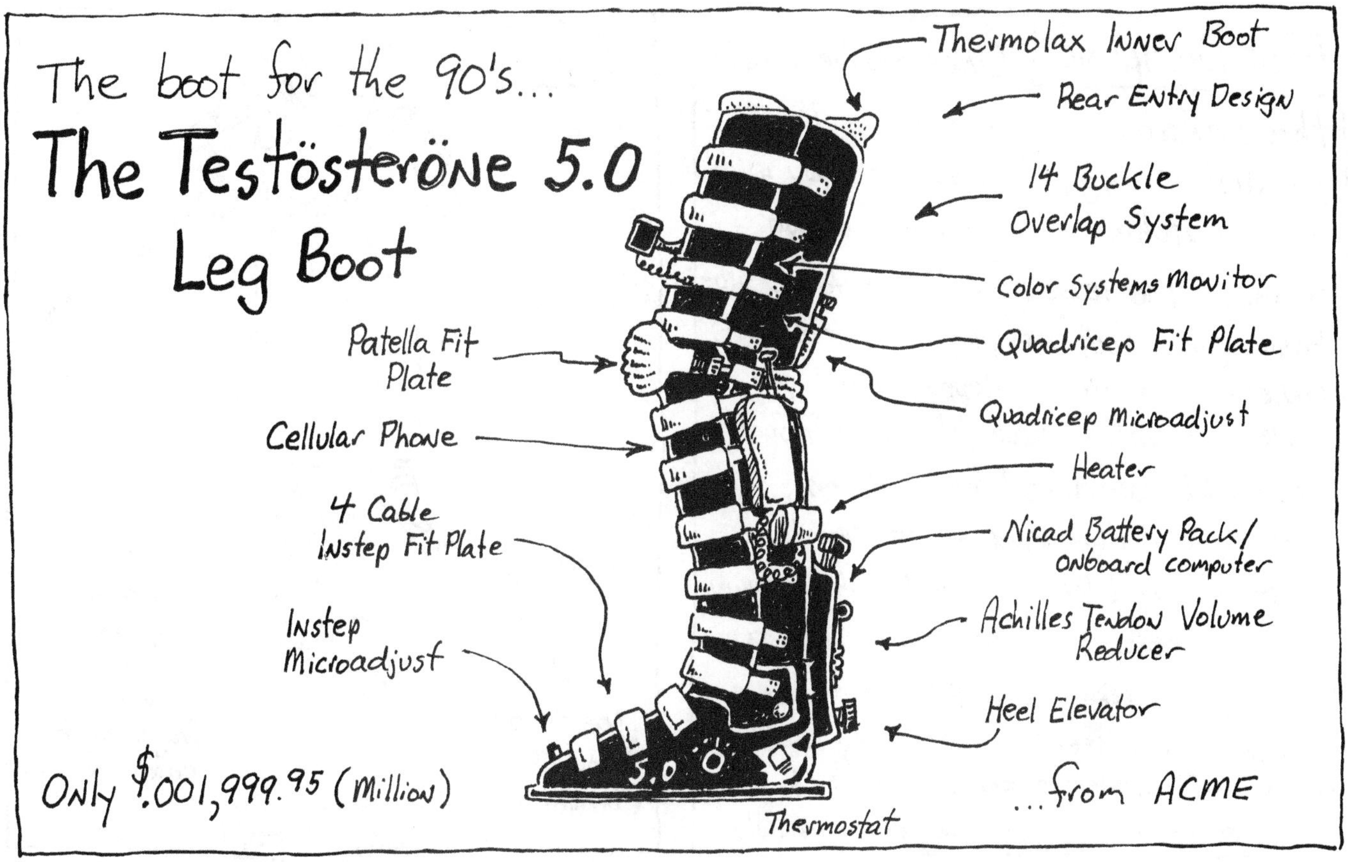

The boot for the 90's...
The Testösteröne 5.0
Leg Boot
Thermolax Inner Boot
Rear Entry Design
14 Buckle
Overlap System
Color Systems Monitor
Quadricep Fit Plate
Quadricep Microadjust
Heater
Nicad Battery Pack/
onboard computer
Achilles Tendon Volume
Reducer
Heel Elevator
Patella Fit
Plate
Cellular Phone
4 Cable
Instep Fit Plate
Instep
Microadjust
5.0
Only $.001,999.95 (Million)
Thermostat
...from ACME

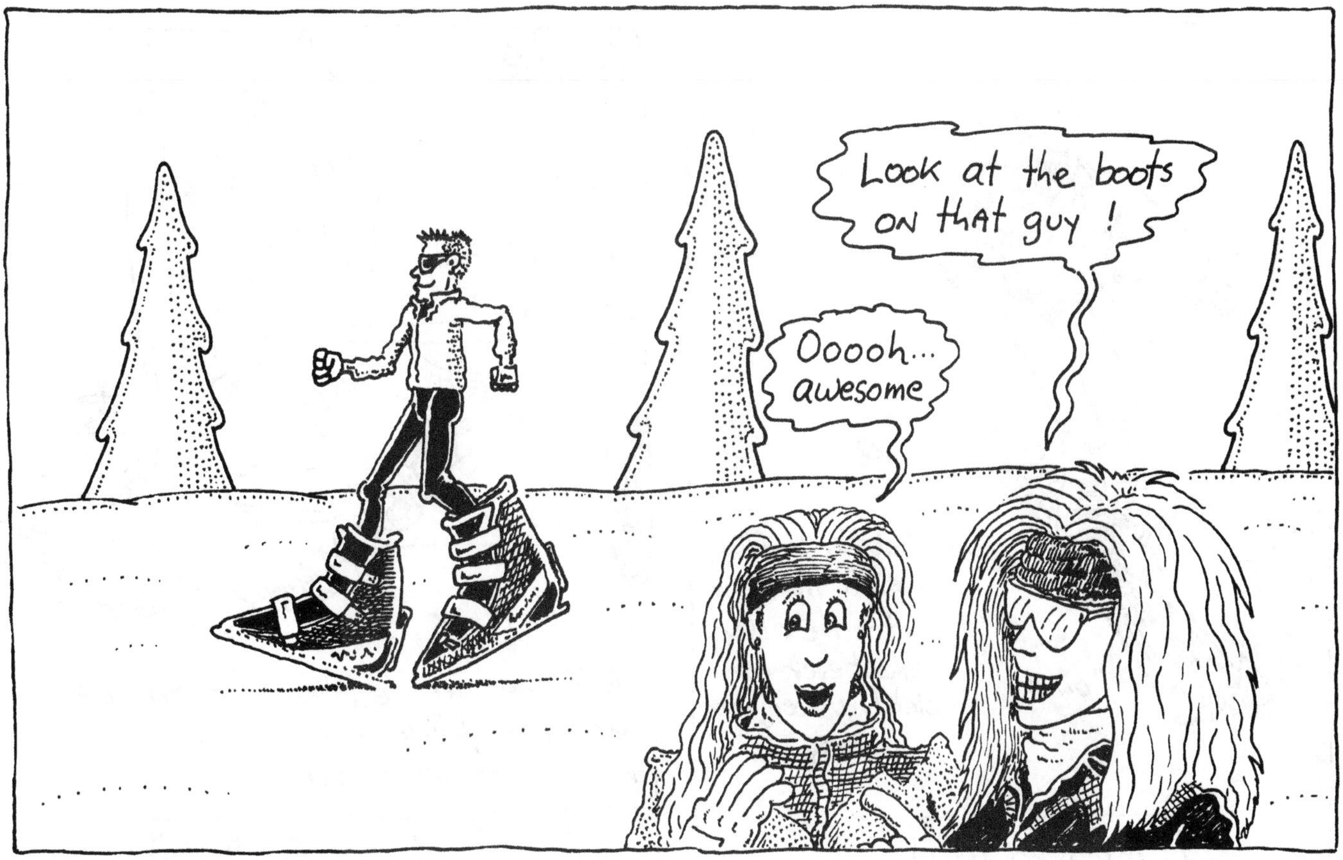

Look at the boots on that guy !
Ooooh... awesome

Foot Discipline

Once you've made the transition from snowplow to semi-parallel skiing, chances are you will begin catching edges and getting trashed. The reason for this is you've probably got a foot "unemployed" (your "off foot"). Unless you're doing "stepped turns" you never completely unweight your "off foot"! To avoid unemployed foot problems, establish a rhythm kind of like pedalling a teeny-tiny bike: one foot pushing down and the other foot rotating around a micro-axis preparing to press down. Concentrate on keeping your body quiet and shifting weight on the balls of your feet so you're using your inside edges only...

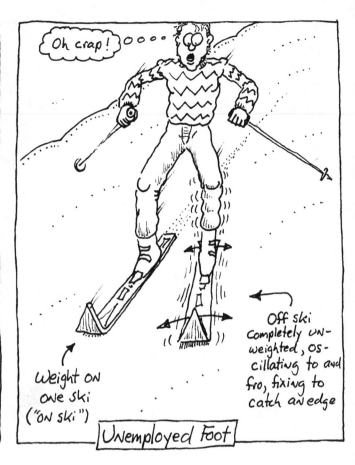

Oh crap!

Weight on one ski ("on ski")

Off ski completely unweighted, oscillating to and fro, fixing to catch an edge

Unemployed Foot

"off ski"

"on ski"

Subtly shifting weight from one foot to the other without ever completely unweighting the "off ski"

Employed Foot

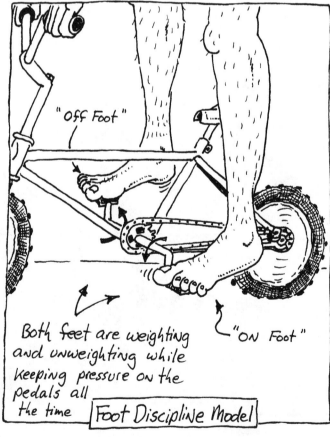

"Off Foot"

"On Foot"

Both feet are weighting and unweighting while keeping pressure on the pedals all the time

Foot Discipline Model

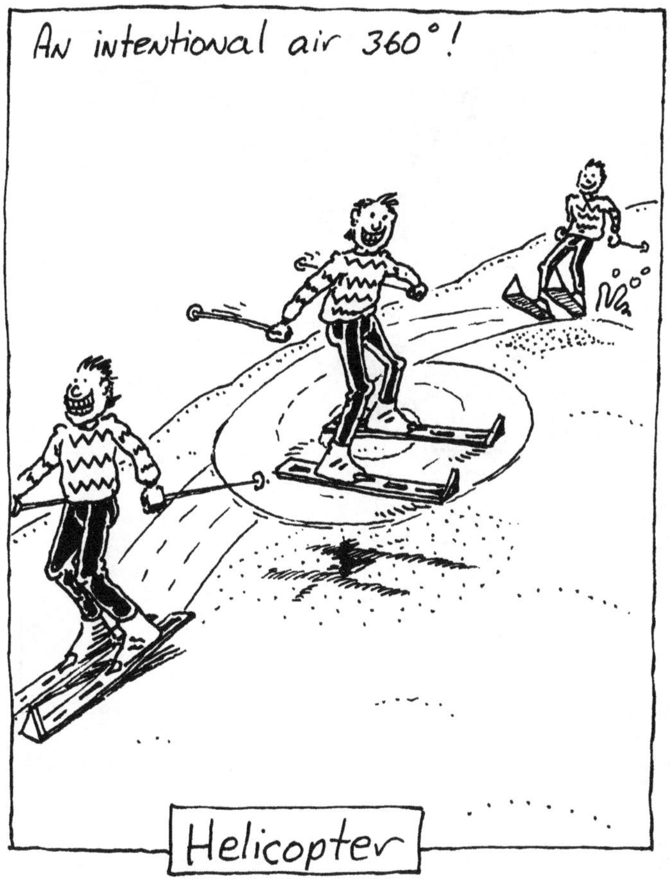
An intentional air 360°!
Helicopter

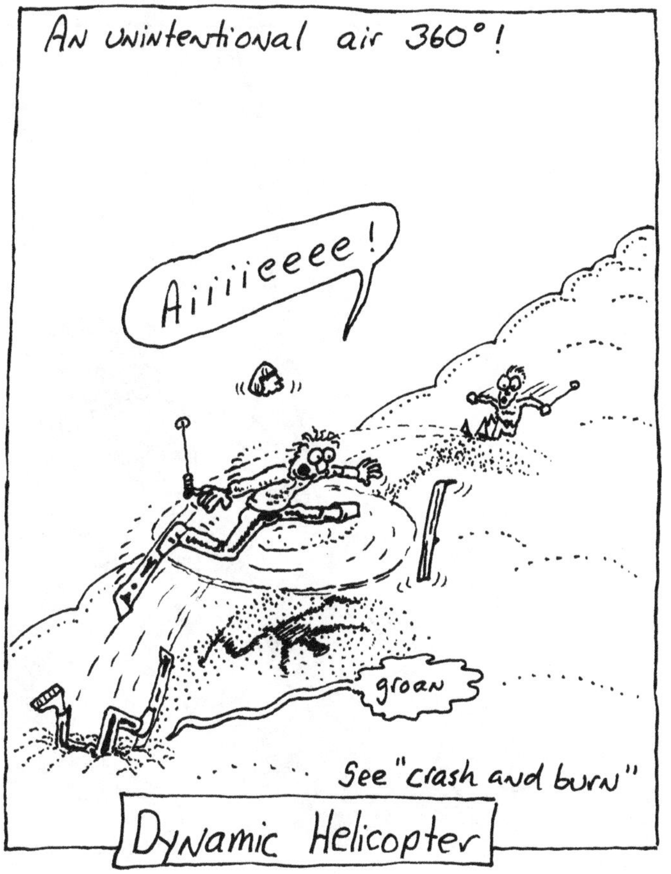
An unintentional air 360°!
Aiiiieeee!
groan
See "crash and burn"
Dynamic Helicopter

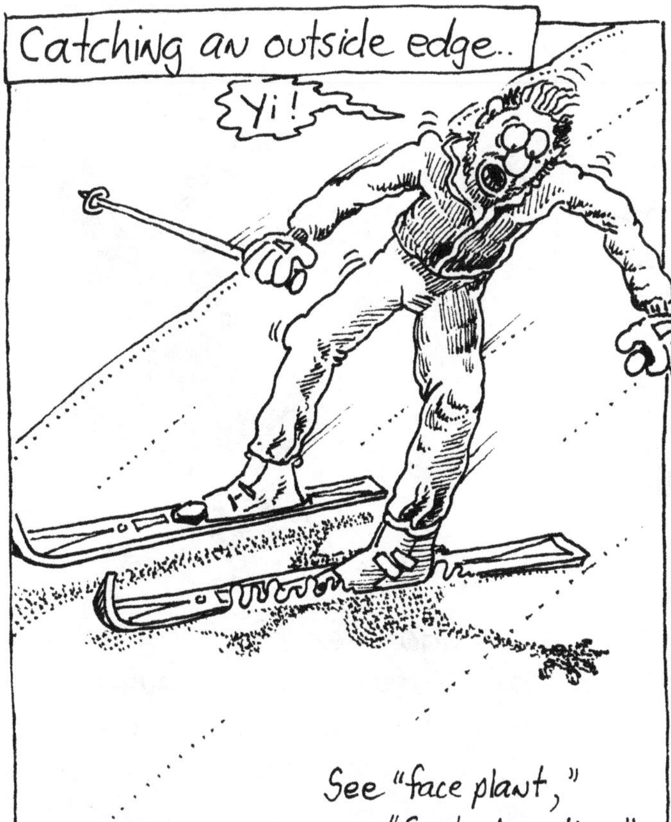
Catching an outside edge..
Yi!
See "face plant,"
"foot discipline"

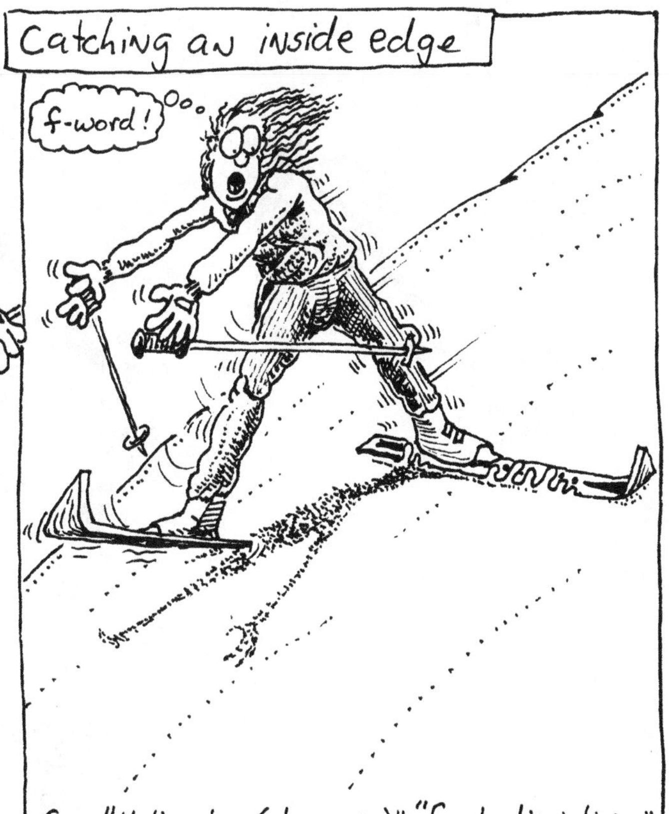
Catching an inside edge
f-word!
See "Helicopter (dynamic)", "foot discipline"

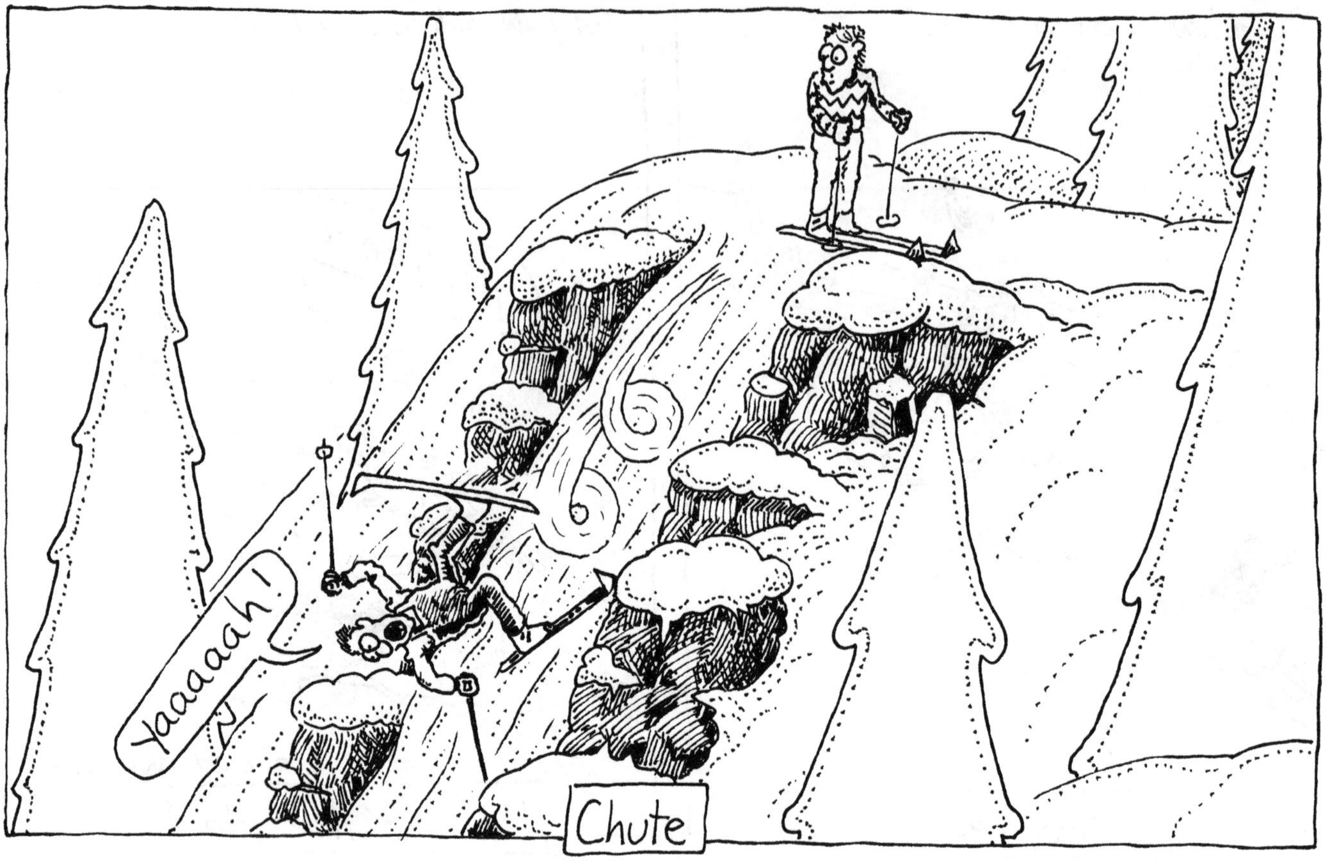
Yaaaaah!
Chute

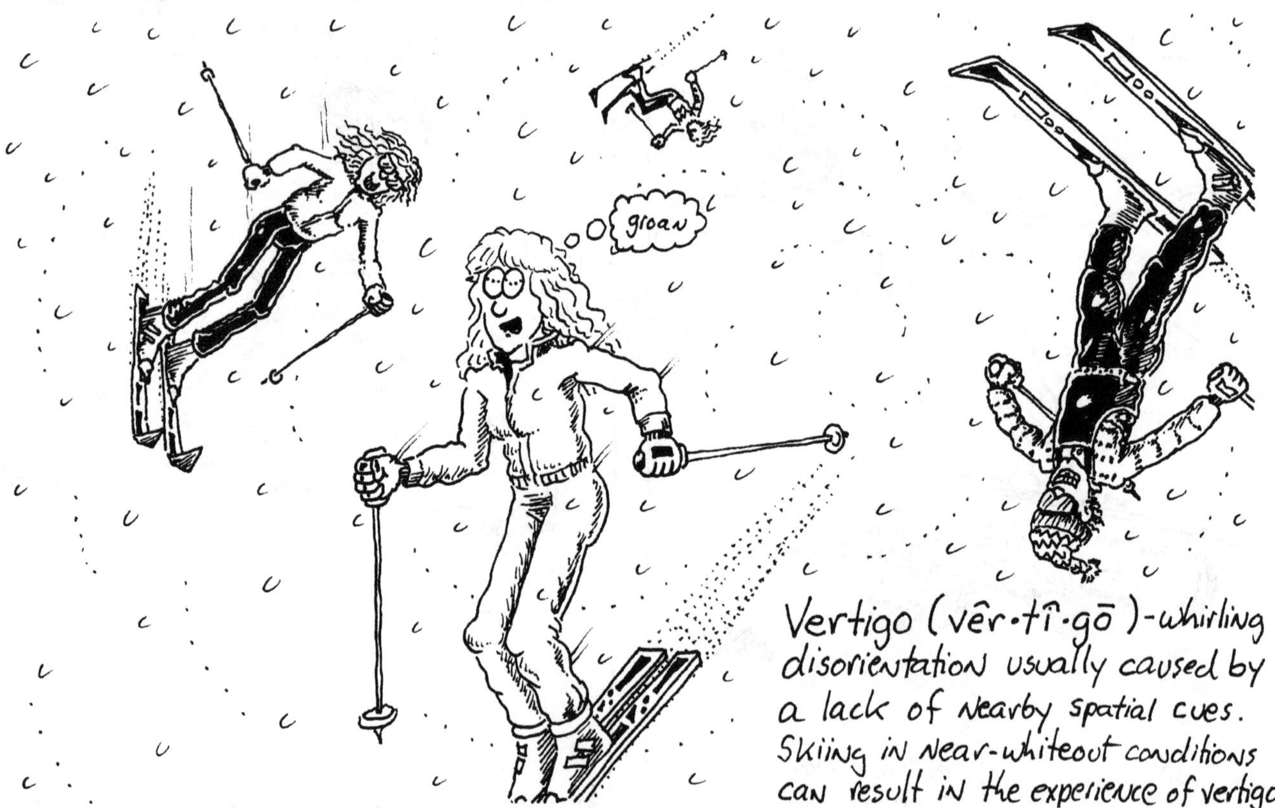
groan

Vertigo (vêr·tĭ·gō)-whirling disorientation usually caused by a lack of nearby spatial cues. Skiing in near-whiteout conditions can result in the experience of vertigo.

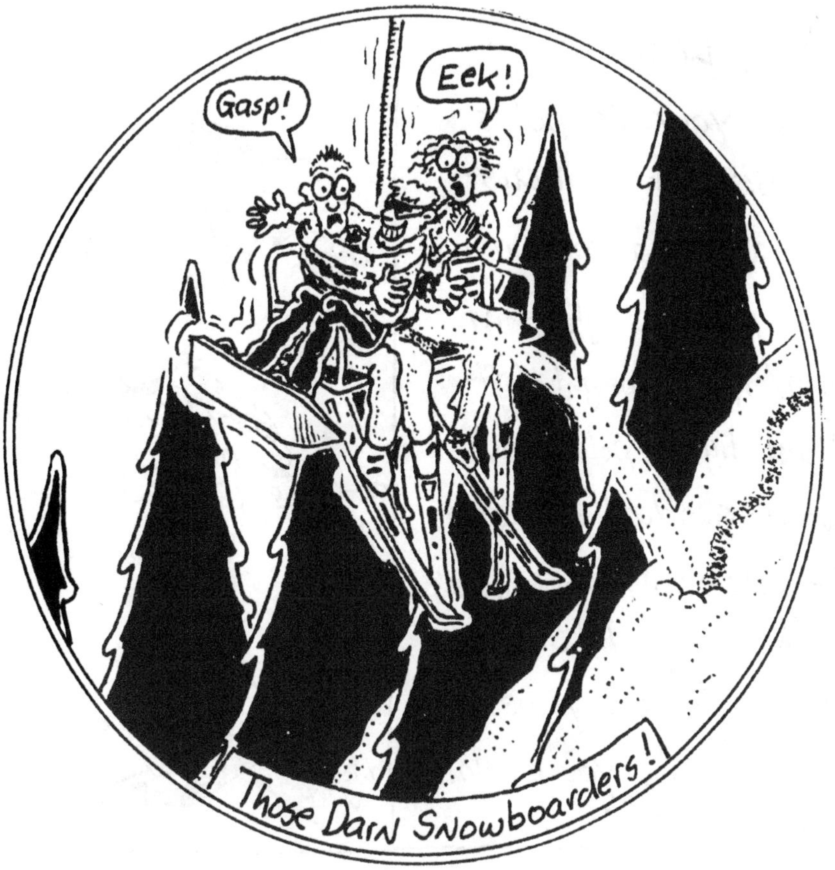
Gasp!
Eek!
Those Darn Snowboarders!

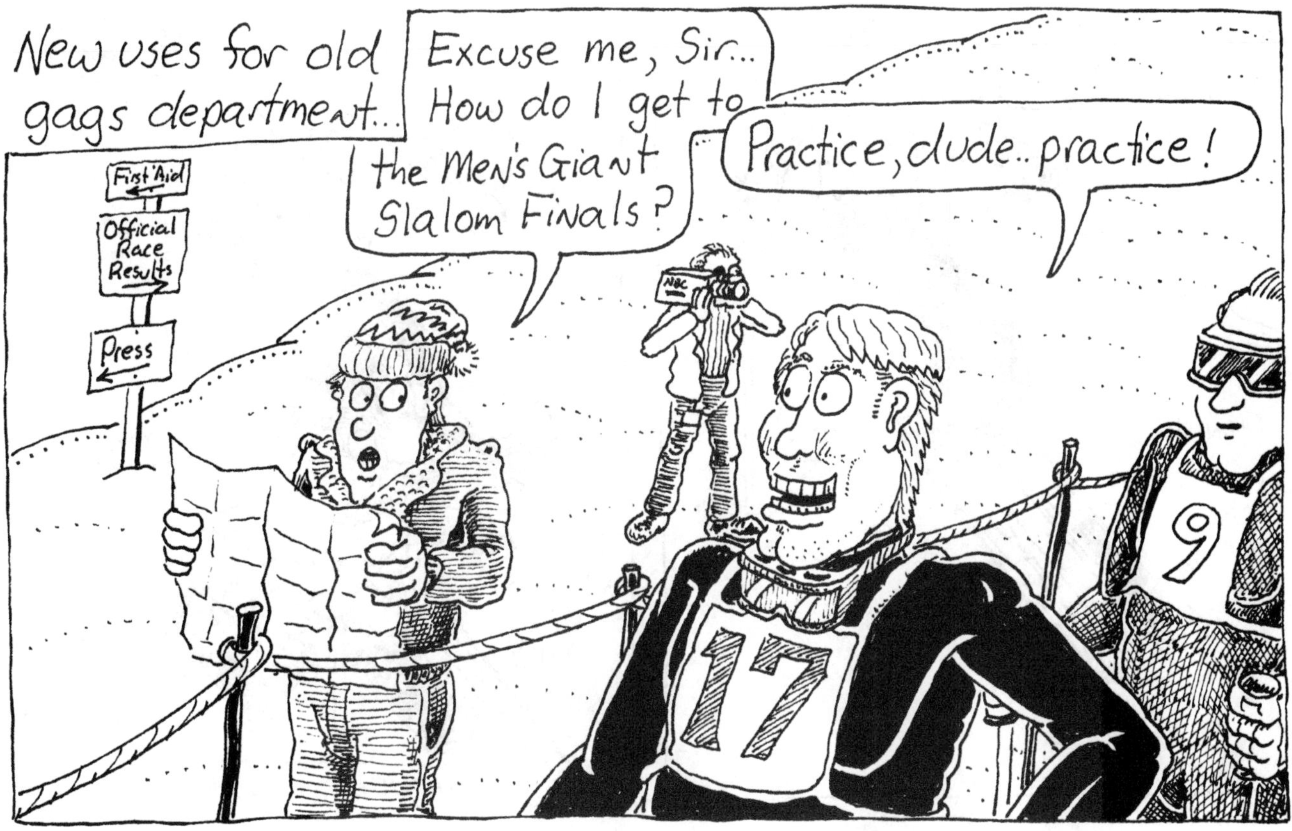
New uses for old gags department...
Excuse me, Sir... How do I get to the Men's Giant Slalom Finals?
Practice, dude.. practice!
First Aid
Official Race Results
Press
17
9

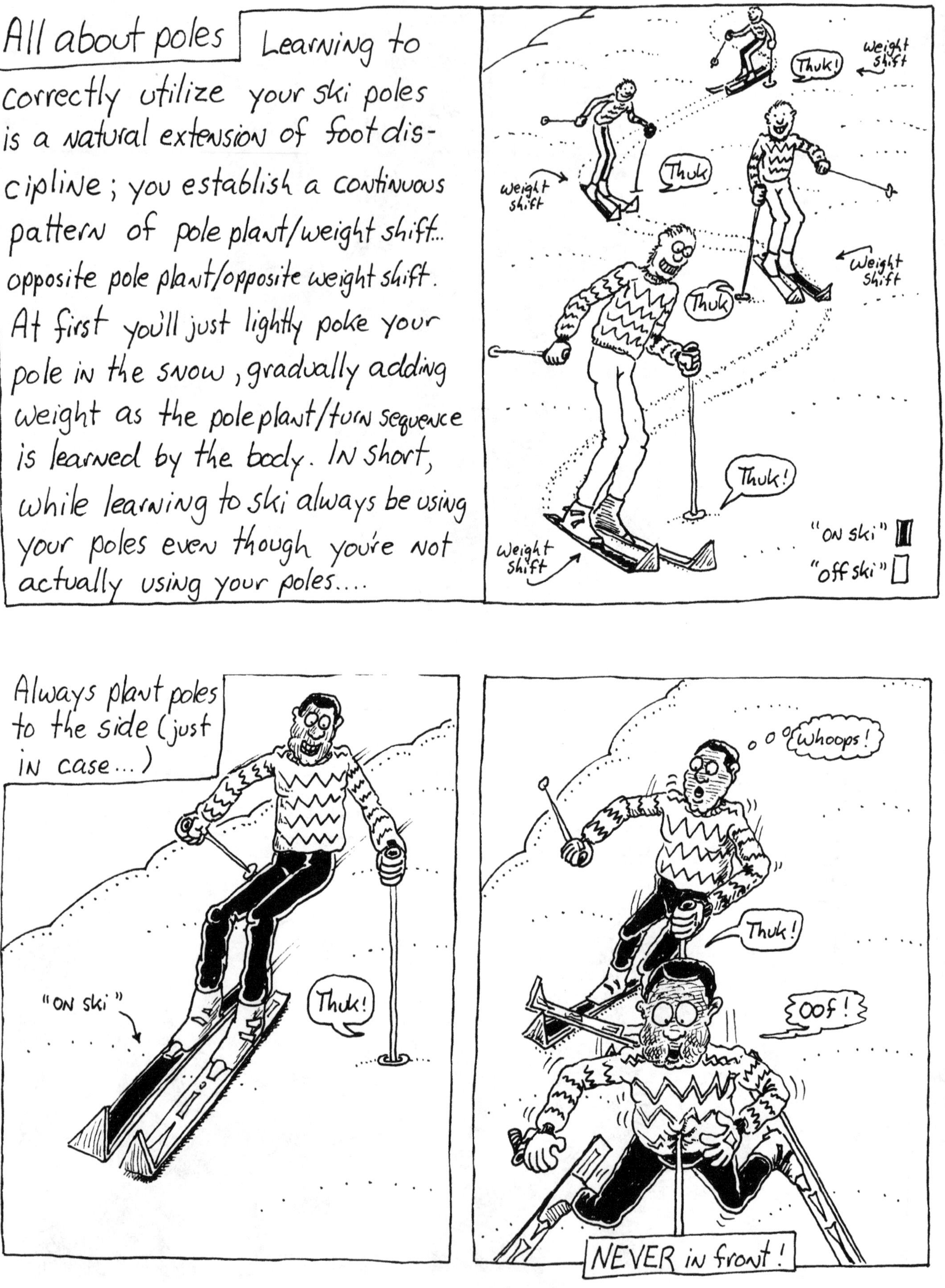
All about poles
Learning to correctly utilize your ski poles is a natural extension of foot discipline; you establish a continuous pattern of pole plant/weight shift... opposite pole plant/opposite weight shift. At first you'll just lightly poke your pole in the snow, gradually adding weight as the pole plant/turn sequence is learned by the body. In short, while learning to ski always be using your poles even though you're not actually using your poles....
Thuk!
weight shift
Thuk
weight shift
Weight shift
Thuk
Thuk!
Weight shift
"ON ski"
"off ski"
Always plant poles to the side (just in case...)
Thuk!
"ON ski"
Whoops!
Thuk!
Oof!
NEVER in front!

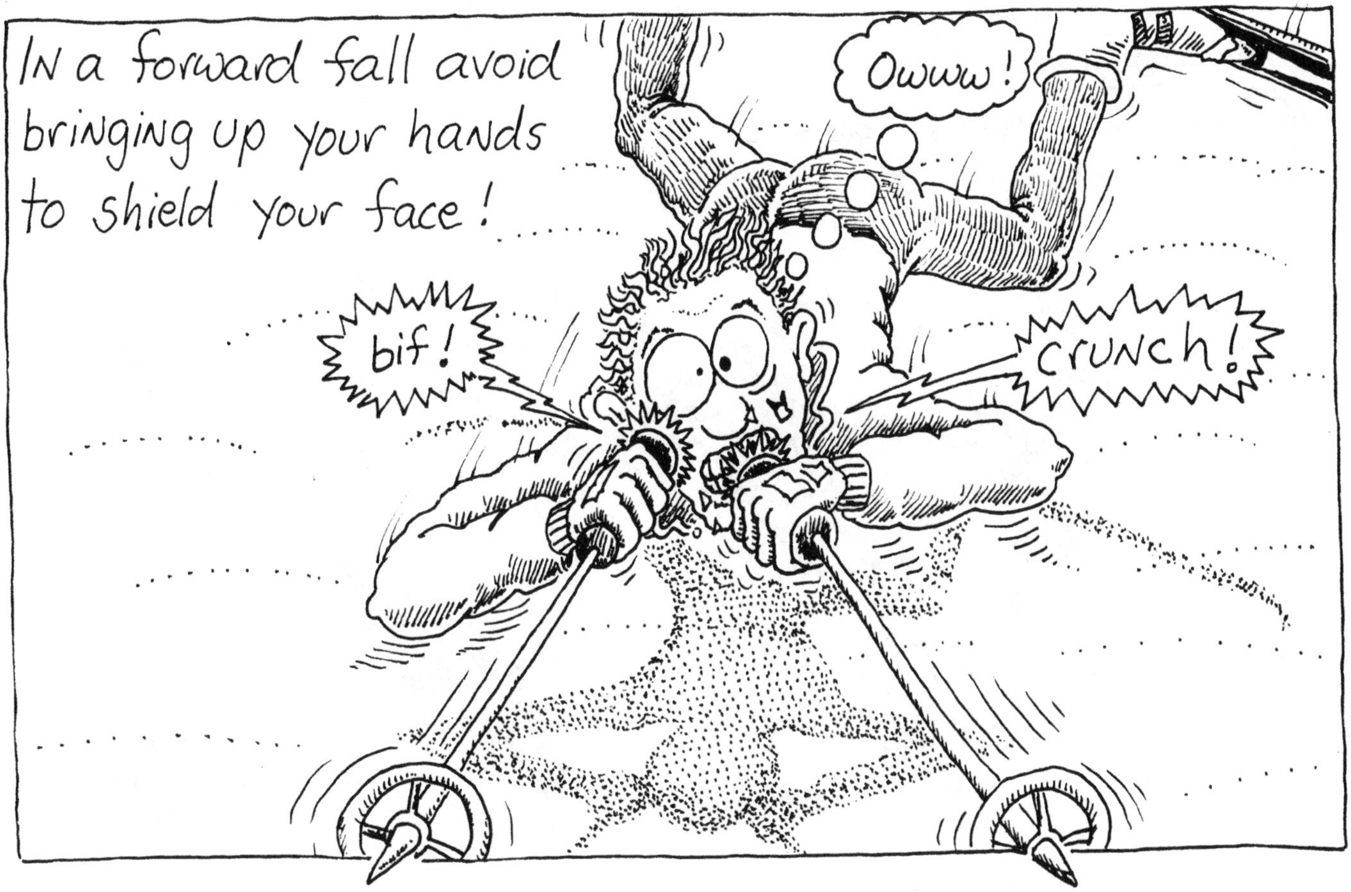
In a forward fall avoid bringing up your hands to shield your face!
Owww!
bif!
crunch!

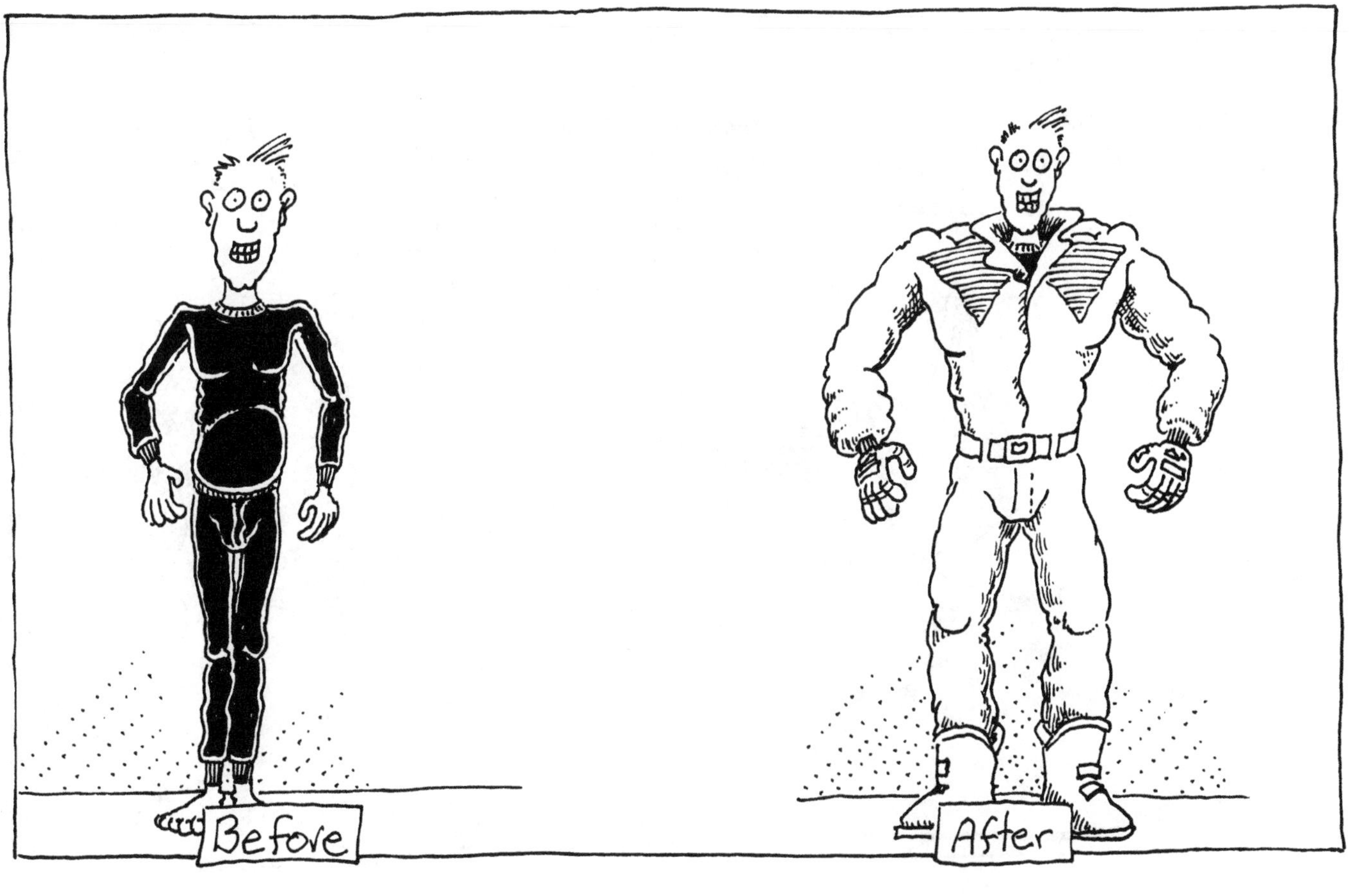
Before
After

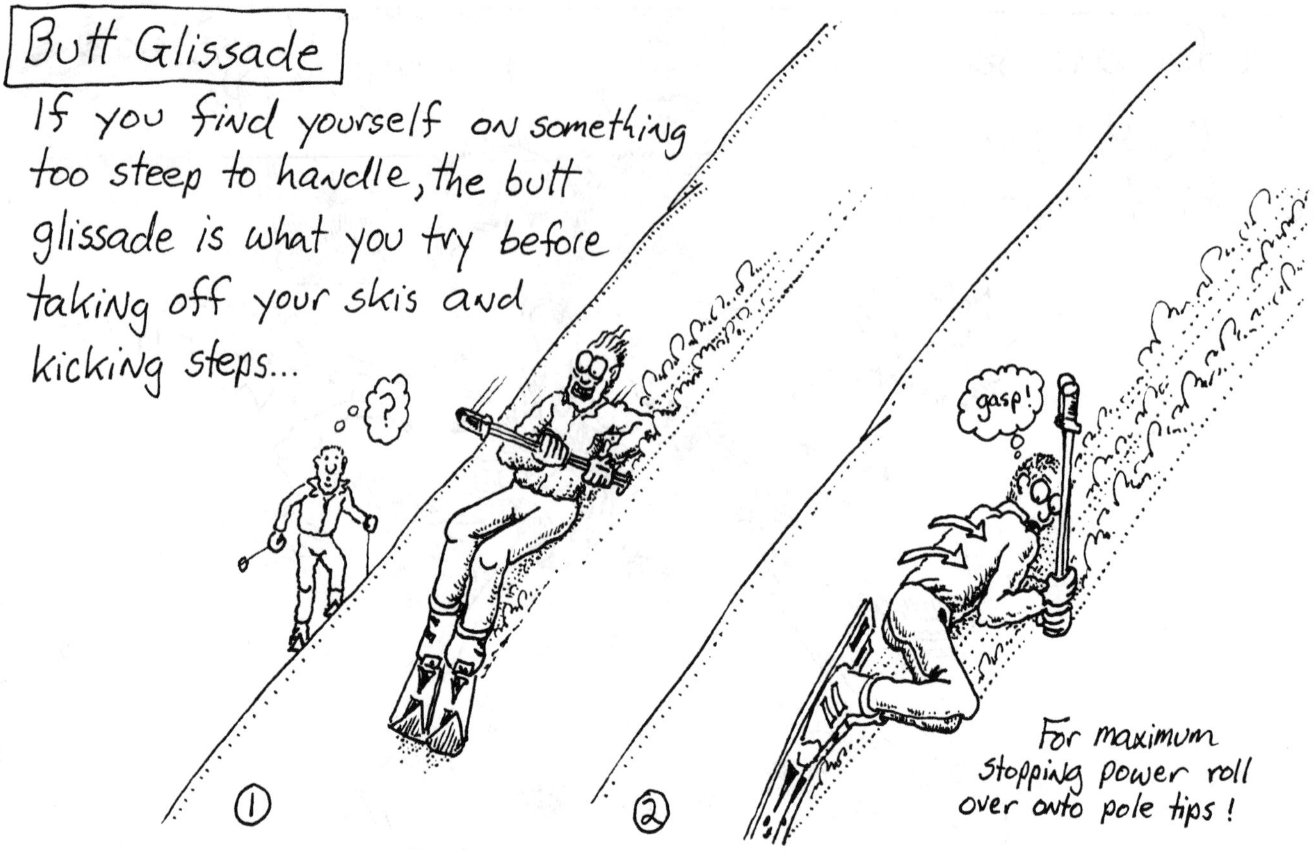
Butt Glissade
If you find yourself on something too steep to handle, the butt glissade is what you try before taking off your skis and kicking steps...
?
gasp!
1
2
For maximum stopping power roll over onto pole tips!

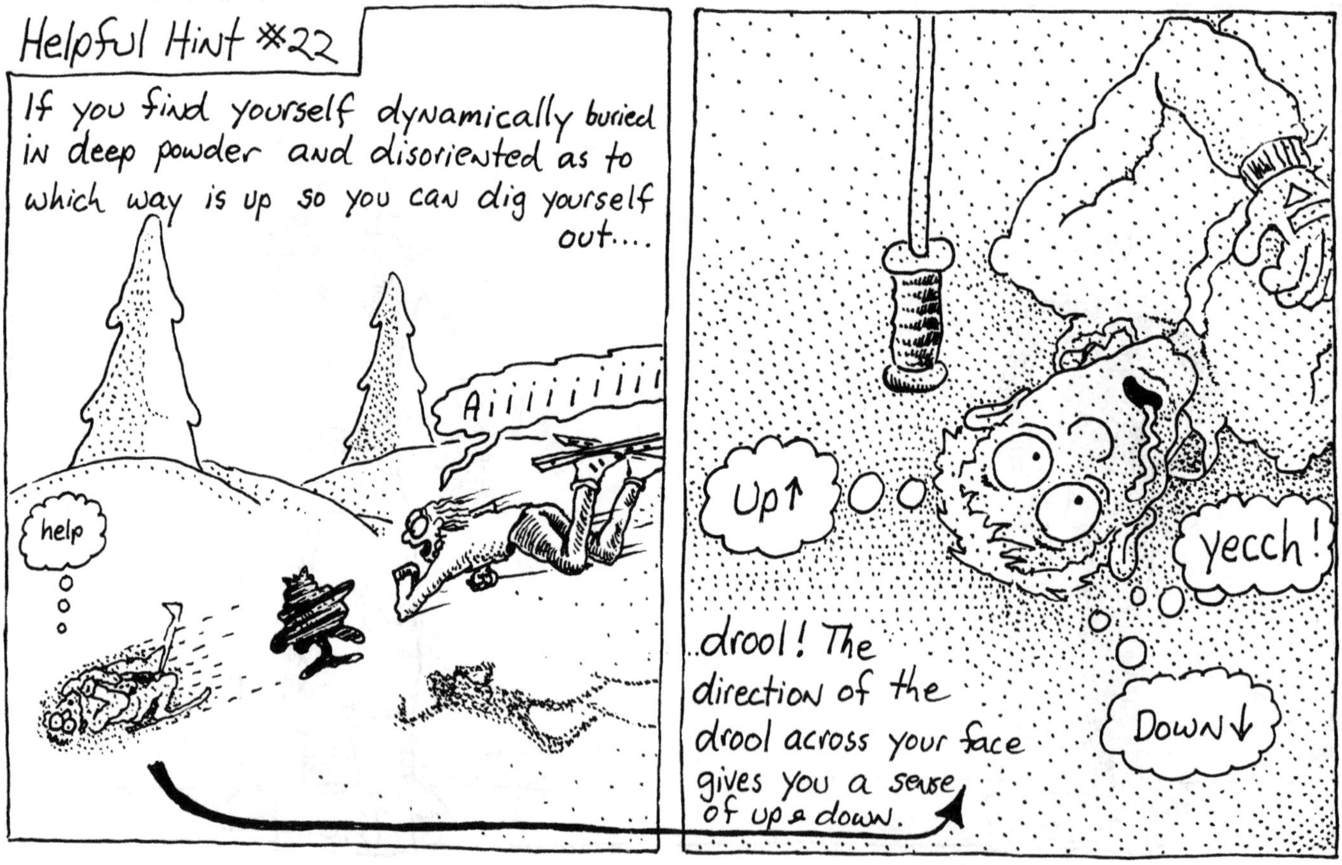
Helpful Hint #22
If you find yourself dynamically buried in deep powder and disoriented as to which way is up so you can dig yourself out....
Aiiiiiiii
help
Up↑
yecch!
Down↓
drool! The direction of the drool across your face gives you a sense of up & down.

Fall Line Orientation Imagine a line connecting your shoulders (like a T-shirt shoulder seam). Ideally you want to keep this imaginary line perpendicular to the fall line most of the time. Once you've mastered this technique you'll find yourself doing fewer exhausting traverses. Instead, you'll have more control and your skiing will be smoother and more continuous. Use "short swings"* to bleed off speed and maintain control. If you're doing this correctly your feet will turn and twist independently of your upper torso.

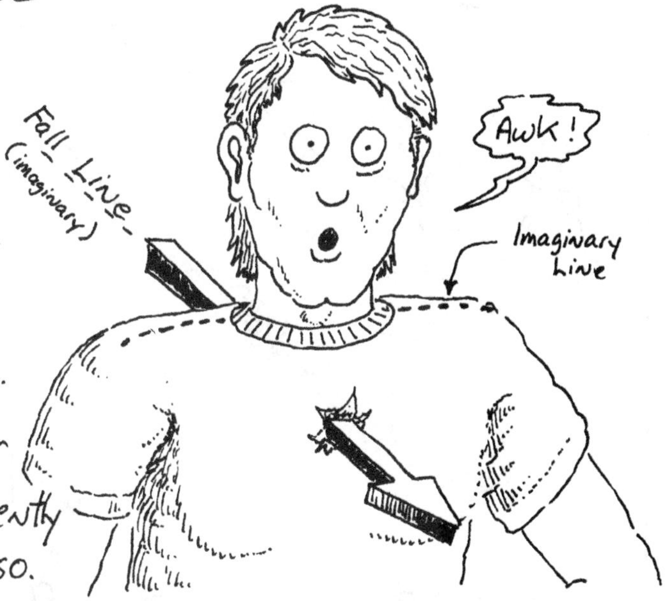
Fall Line (imaginary)
Awk!
Imaginary Line

* See "Short Swings"

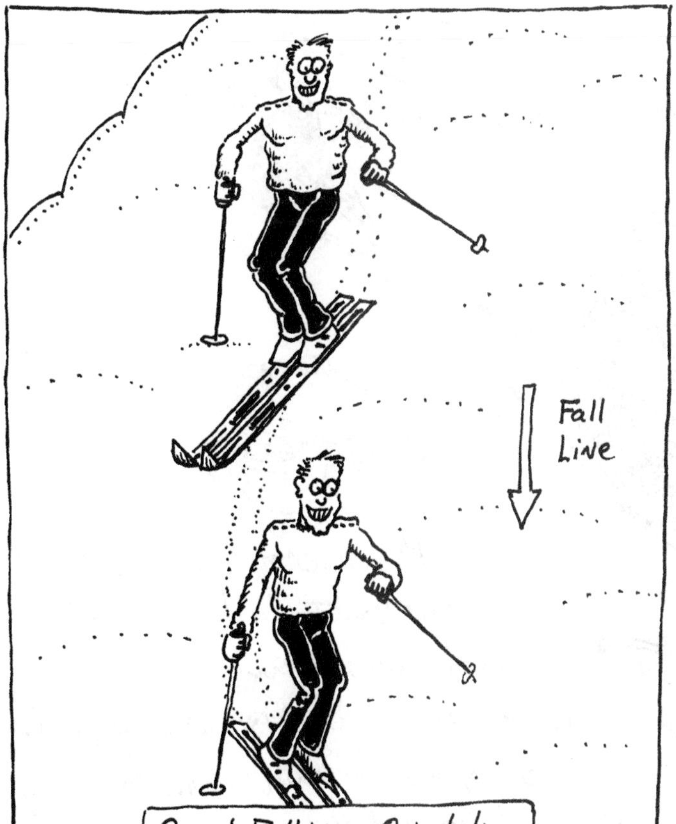
Fall Line

Good Fall Line Orientation

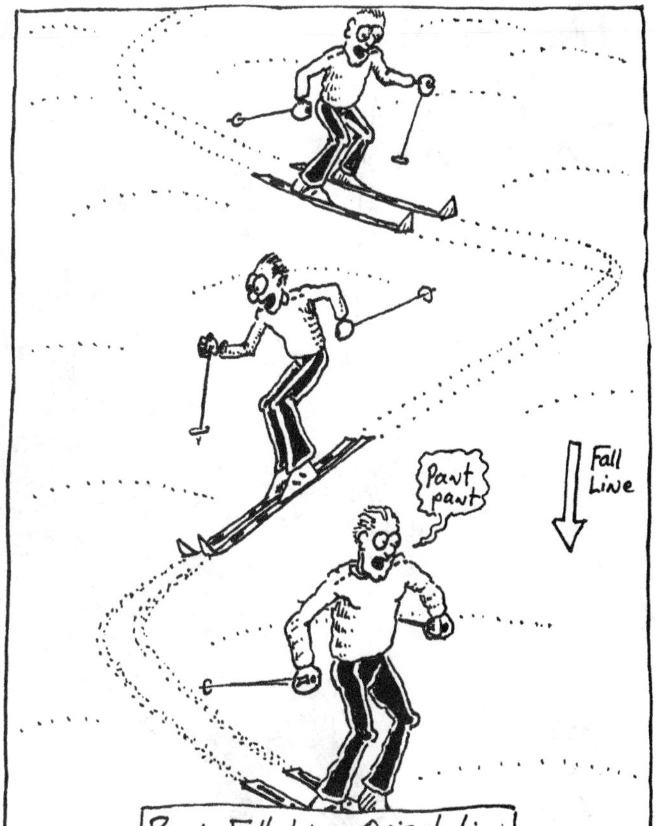
Pant pant
Fall Line

Bad Fall Line Orientation

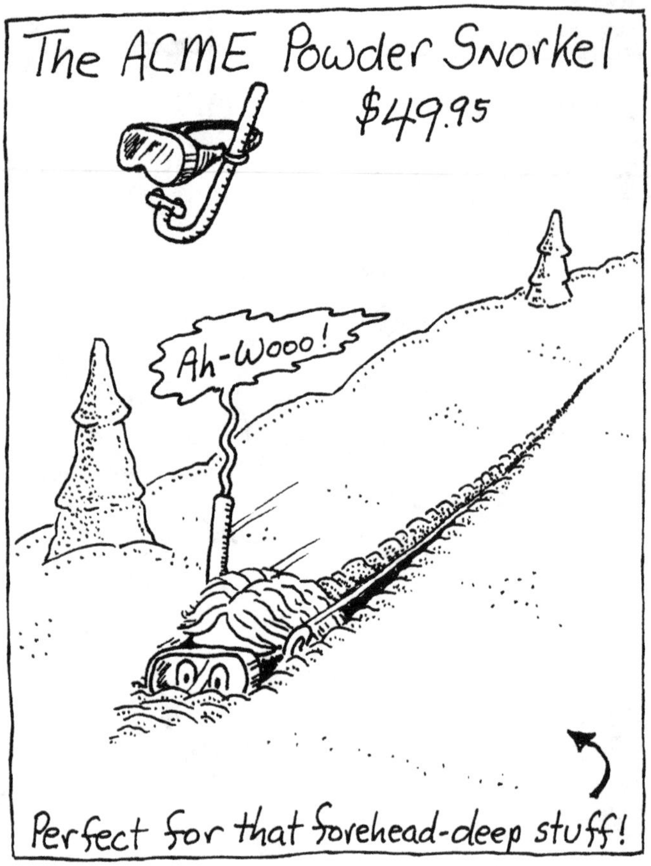
The ACME Powder Snorkel
$49.95
Ah-Wooo!
Perfect for that forehead-deep stuff!

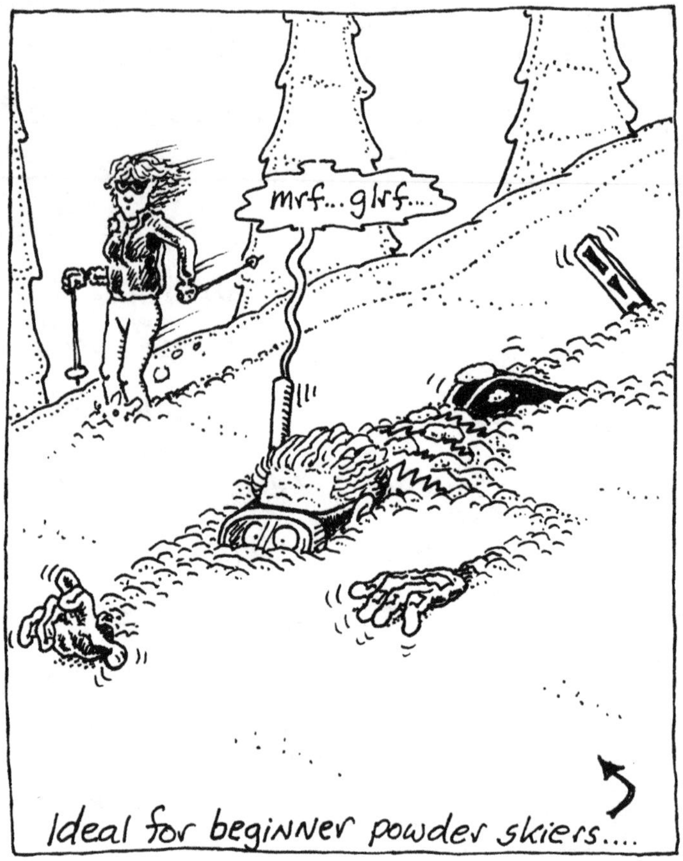
mrf... glrf...
Ideal for beginner powder skiers....

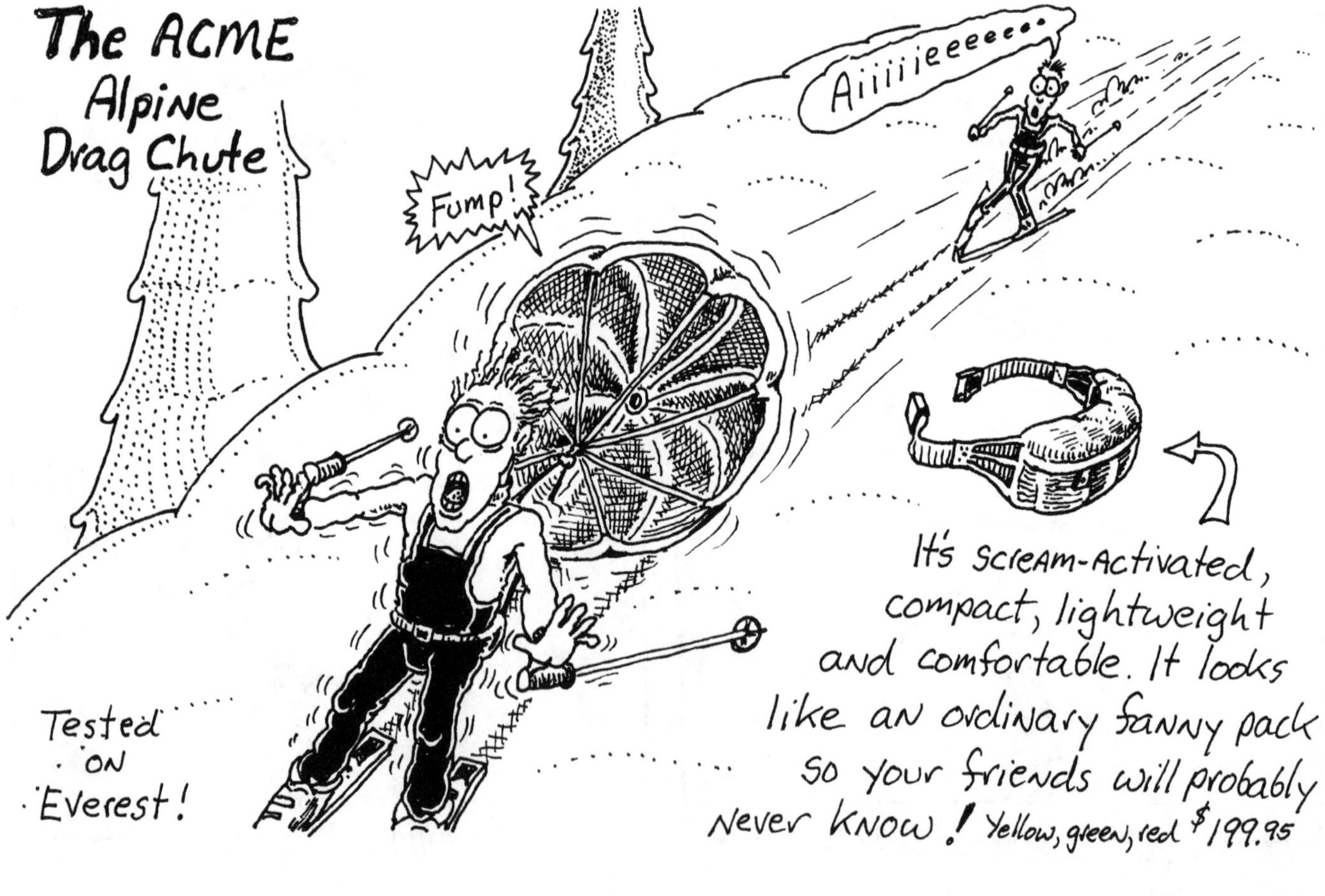
The ACME Alpine Drag Chute
Aiiiiieeeee...
Fump!
It's scream-activated, compact, lightweight and comfortable. It looks like an ordinary fanny pack so your friends will probably never know! Yellow, green, red $199.95
Tested on Everest!

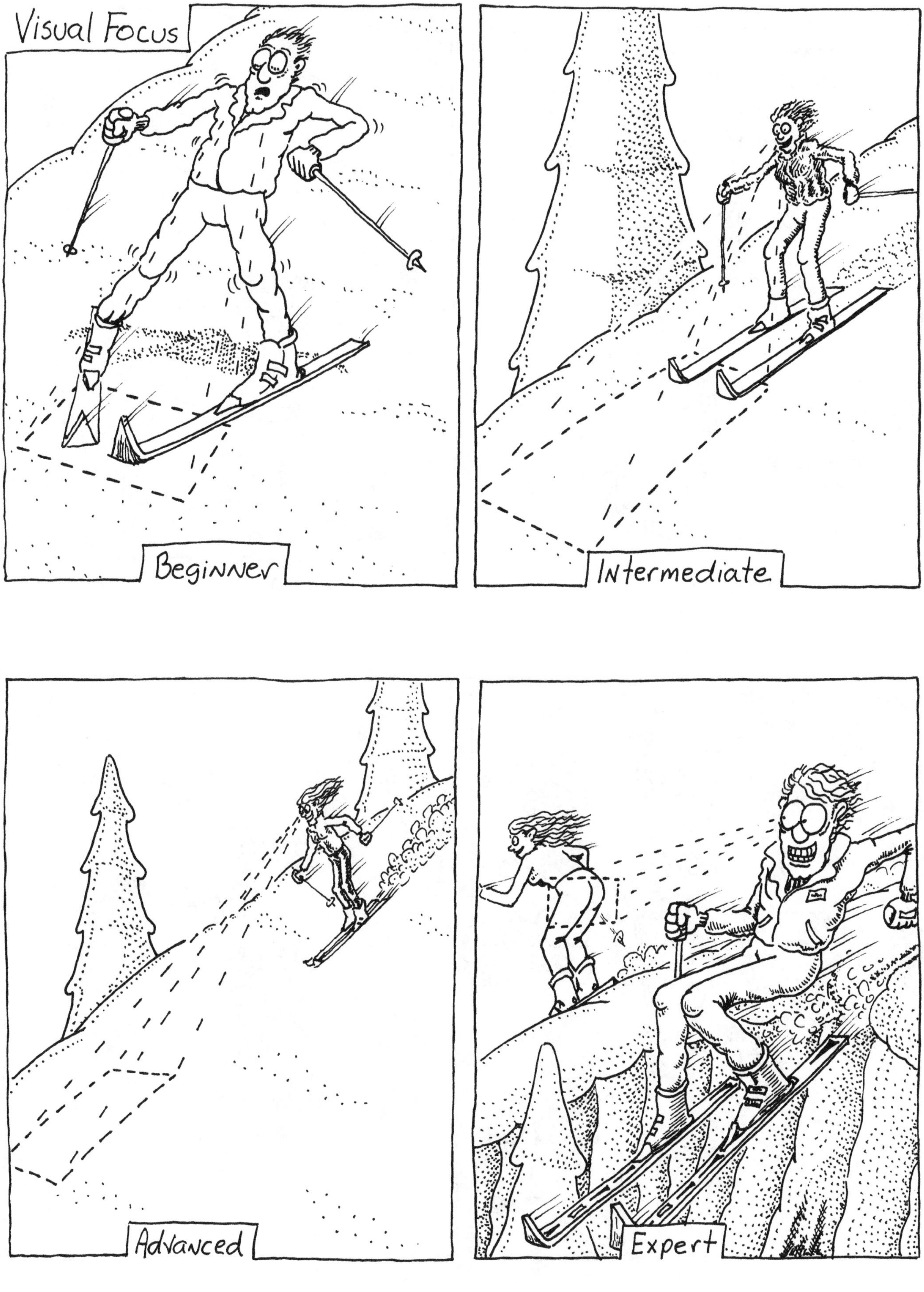
Visual Focus
Beginner
Intermediate
Advanced
Expert

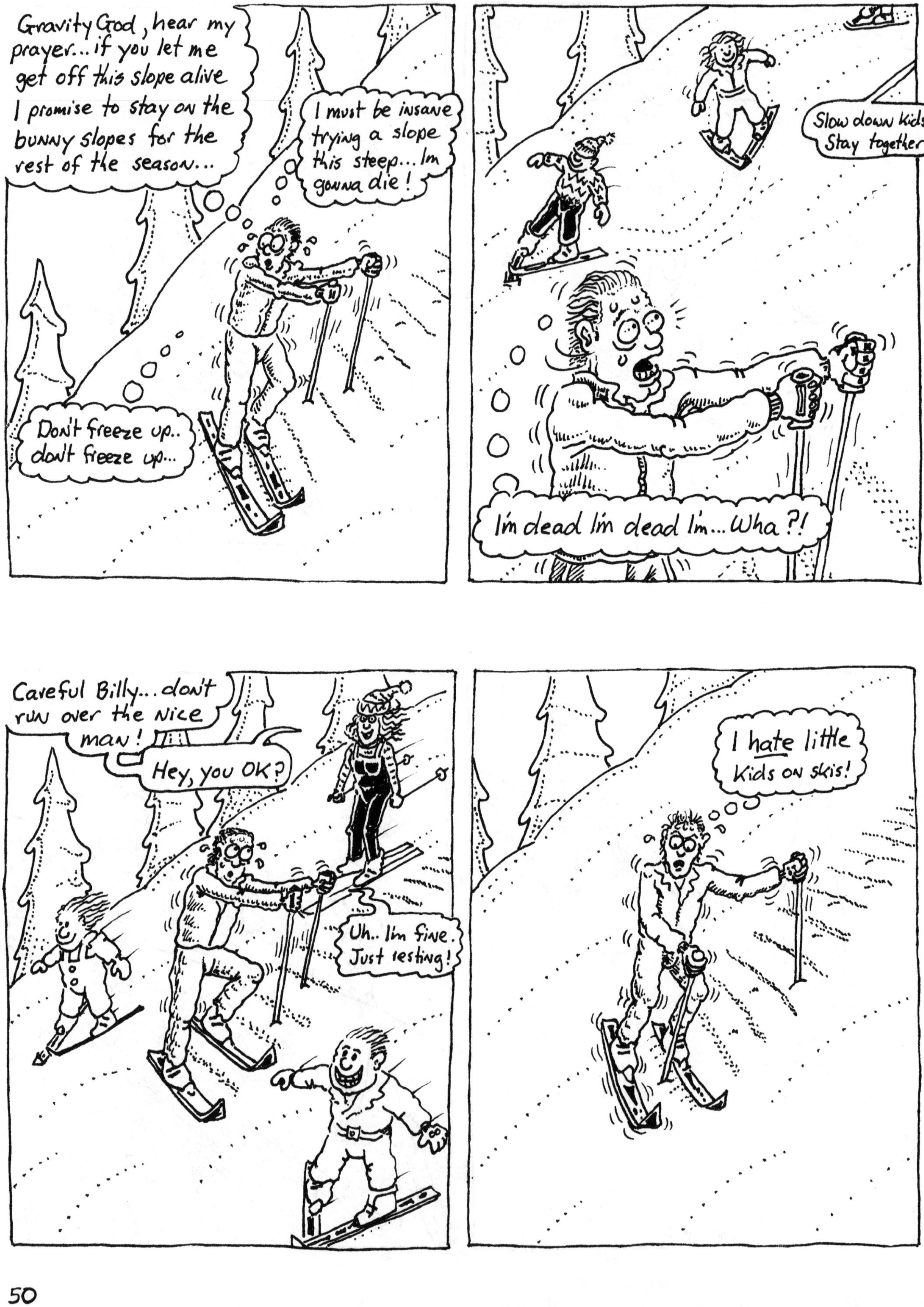

Gravity God, hear my prayer... if you let me get off this slope alive I promise to stay on the bunny slopes for the rest of the season...
I must be insane trying a slope this steep... Im gonna die!
Don't freeze up.. don't freeze up...
Slow down kids! Stay together
I'm dead I'm dead I'm... Wha?!
Careful Billy... don't run over the nice man!
Hey, you OK?
Uh.. I'm fine. Just resting!
I hate little kids on skis!

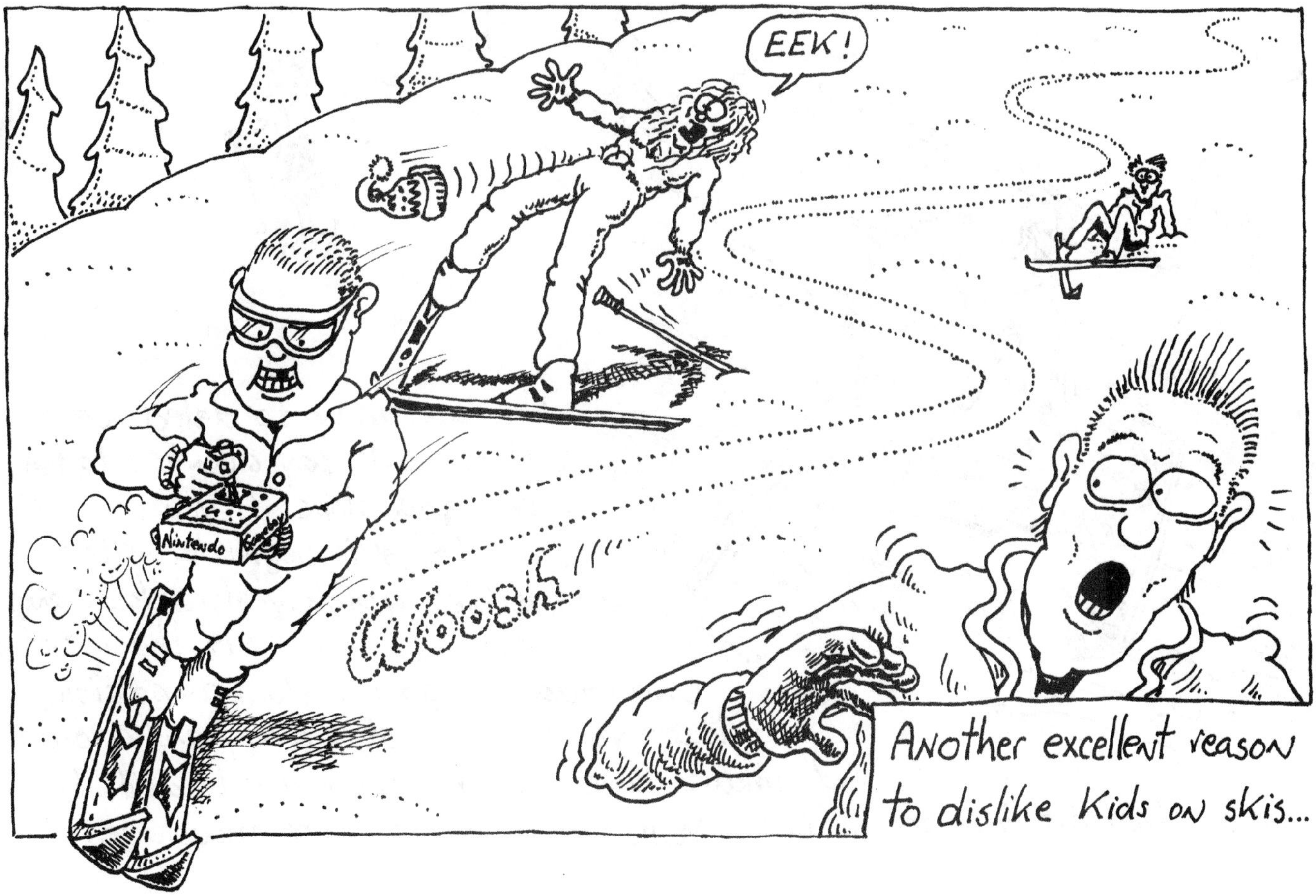
EEK!
Woosh
Nintendo
Another excellent reason to dislike Kids on skis...

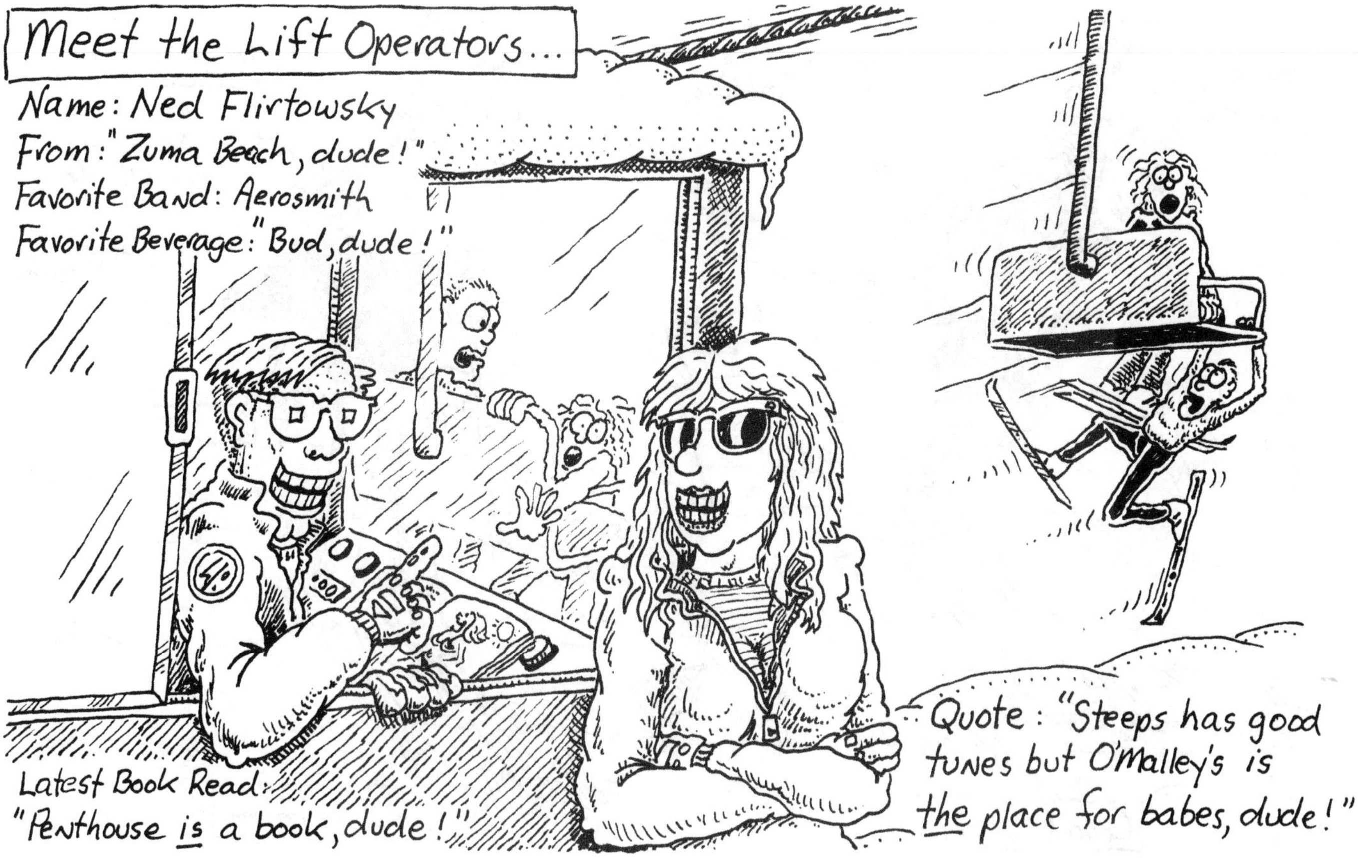
Meet the Lift Operators...
Name: Ned Flirtowsky
From: "Zuma Beach, dude!"
Favorite Band: Aerosmith
Favorite Beverage: "Bud, dude!"
Latest Book Read: "Penthouse is a book, dude!"
Quote: "Steeps has good tunes but O'Malley's is the place for babes, dude!"

Skiing Ice

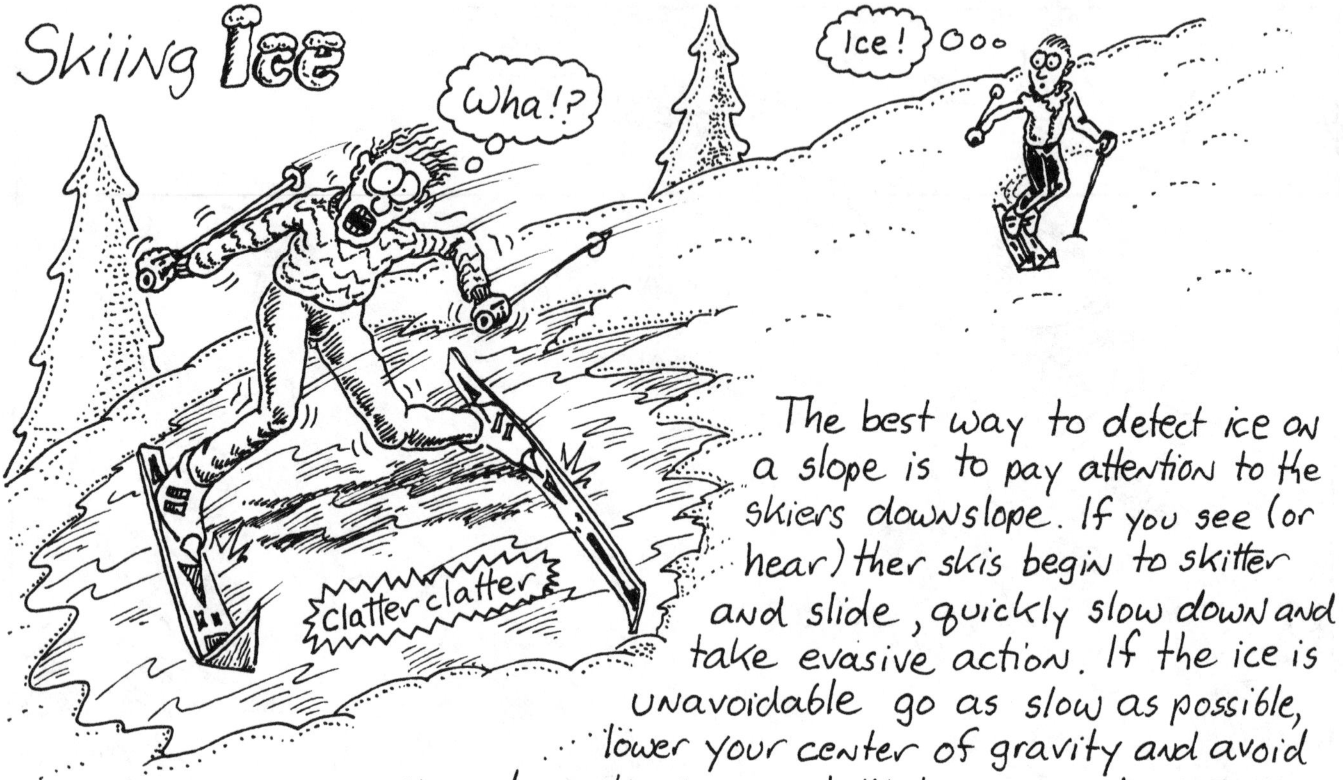

Wha!?
Ice! ooo
clatter clatter

The best way to detect ice on a slope is to pay attention to the skiers downslope. If you see (or hear) ther skis begin to skitter and slide, quickly slow down and take evasive action. If the ice is unavoidable go as slow as possible, lower your center of gravity and avoid dramatic movement. Motion on ice tends to be in a straight line but you can <u>gently</u> use your edges to maneuver.

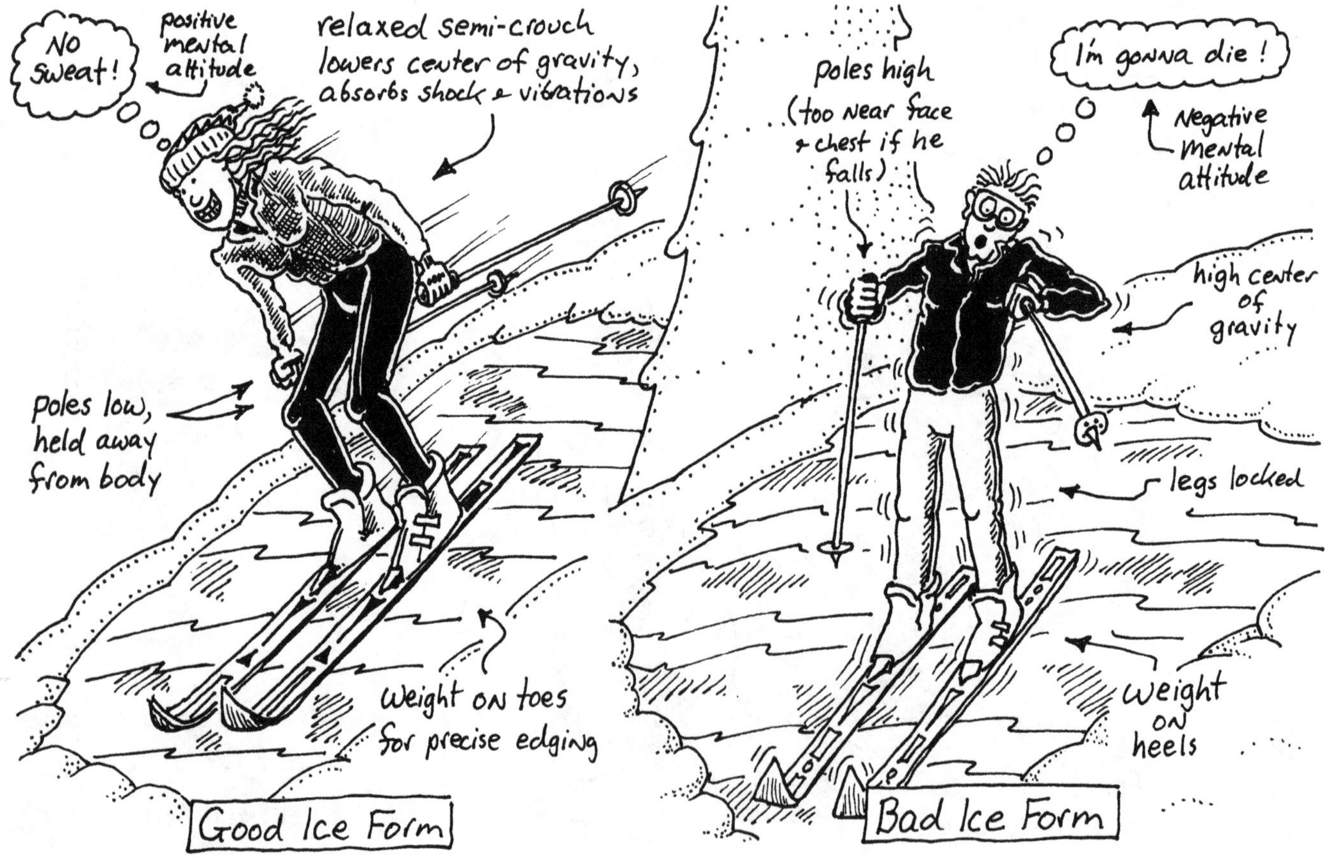

No sweat!
positive mental attitude
relaxed semi-crouch lowers center of gravity, absorbs shock & vibrations
poles low, held away from body
weight on toes for precise edging
poles high (too near face & chest if he falls)
I'm gonna die!
Negative mental attitude
high center of gravity
legs locked
weight on heels

Good Ice Form

Bad Ice Form

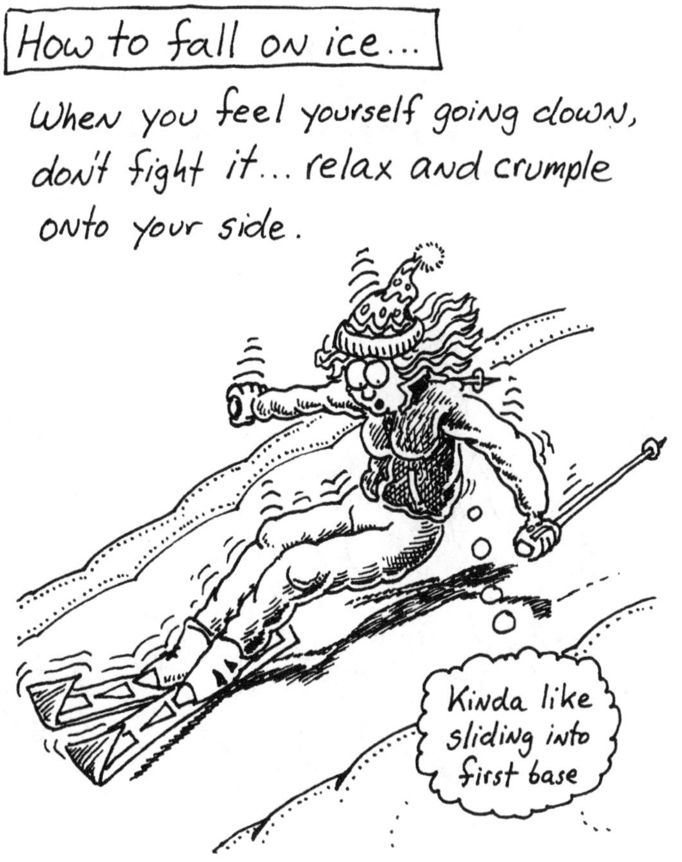
How to fall on ice...
When you feel yourself going down, don't fight it... relax and crumple onto your side.
Kinda like sliding into first base

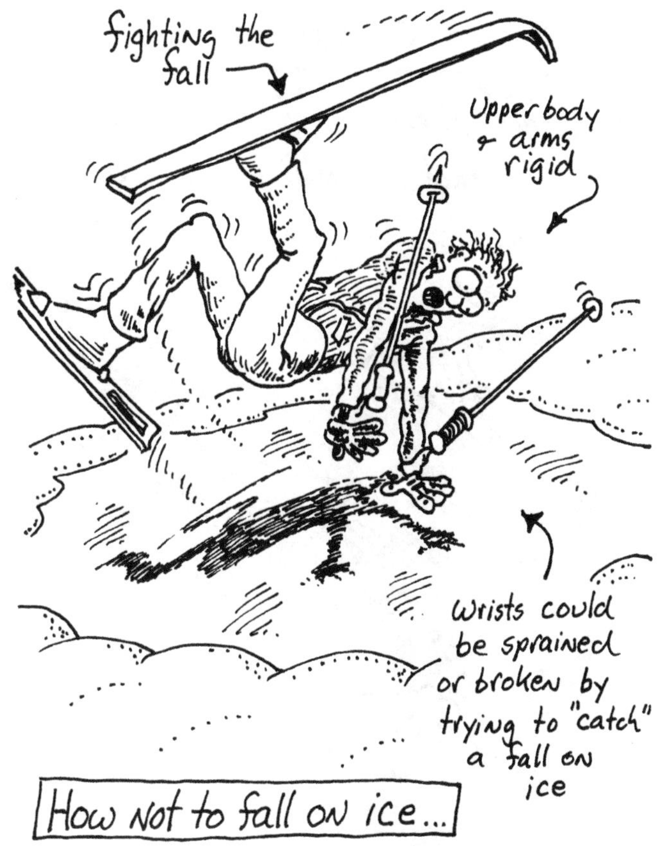
fighting the fall
Upper body & arms rigid
Wrists could be sprained or broken by trying to "catch" a fall on ice
How not to fall on ice...

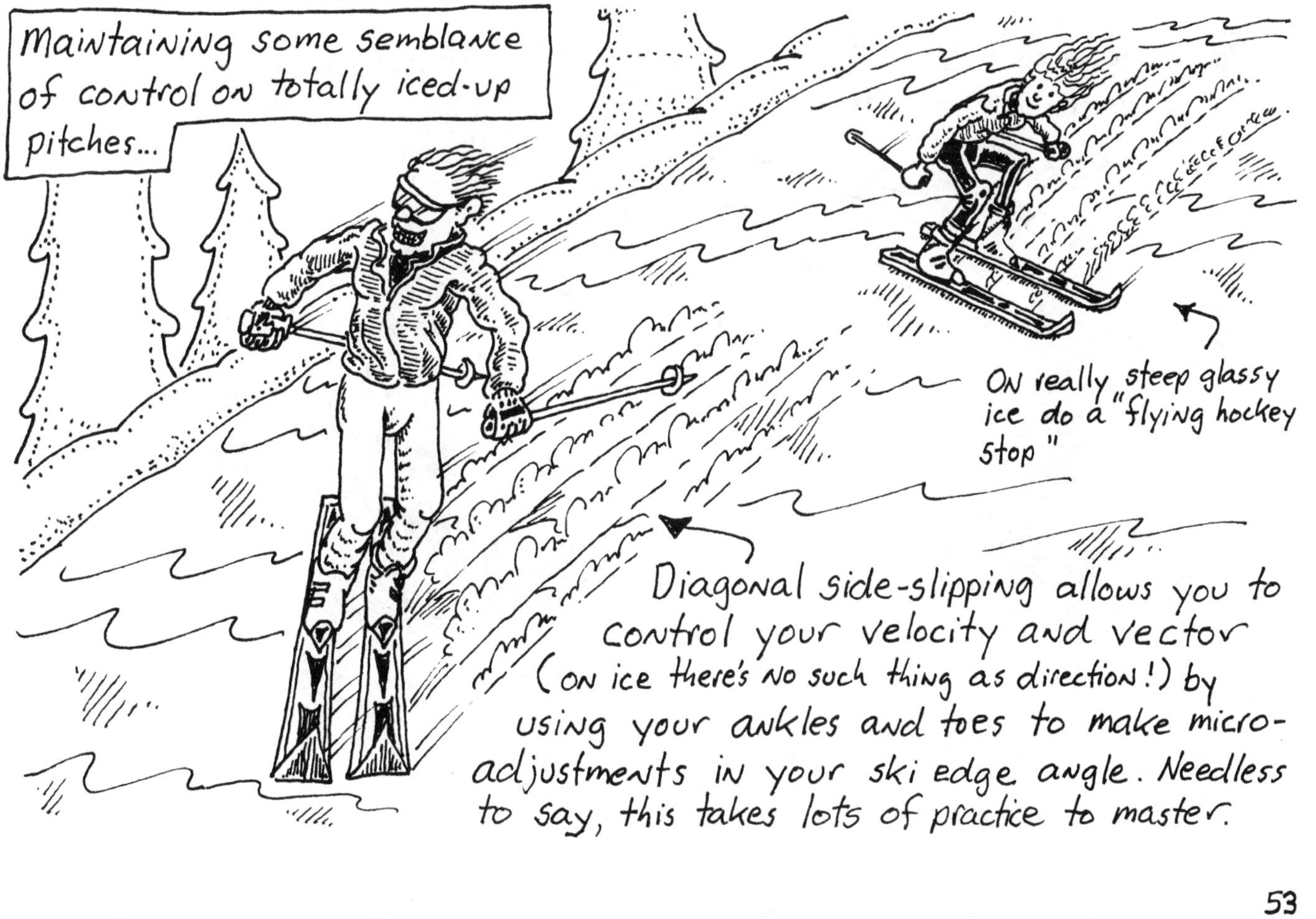
Maintaining some semblance of control on totally iced-up pitches...
On really steep glassy ice do a "flying hockey stop"
Diagonal side-slipping allows you to control your velocity and vector (on ice there's no such thing as direction!) by using your ankles and toes to make micro-adjustments in your ski edge angle. Needless to say, this takes lots of practice to master.

Arresting a screaming slide

① Often when you fall on your back, head downhill, you will find yourself actually picking up speed...

② This is OK if you like being a human bobsled but if the slope runs out in the trees or on a cliff you're gonna get trashed...

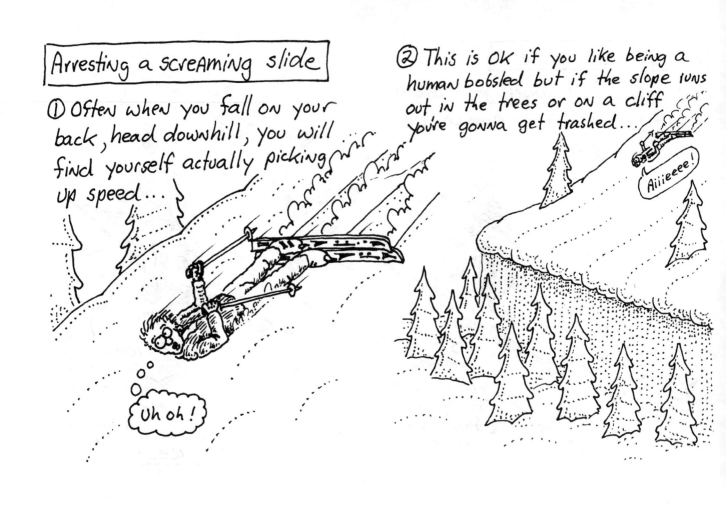

③ To perform a self-arrest, ditch one pole* and grasp the business end of the other one thusly...

④ Twist onto your side and bury the pole tip in the snow with all your weight on it...

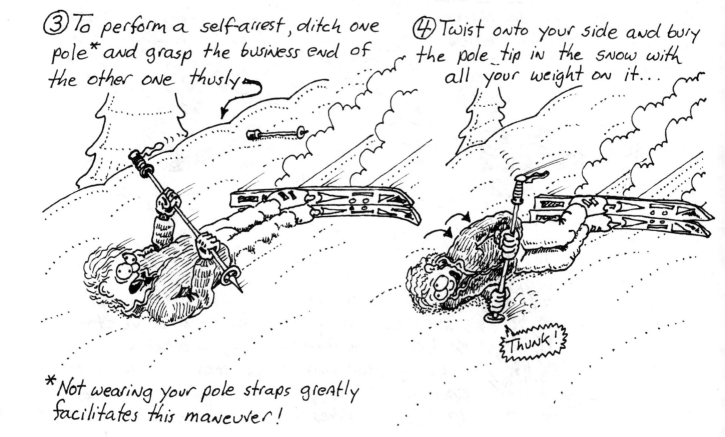

*Not wearing your pole straps greatly facilitates this maneuver!

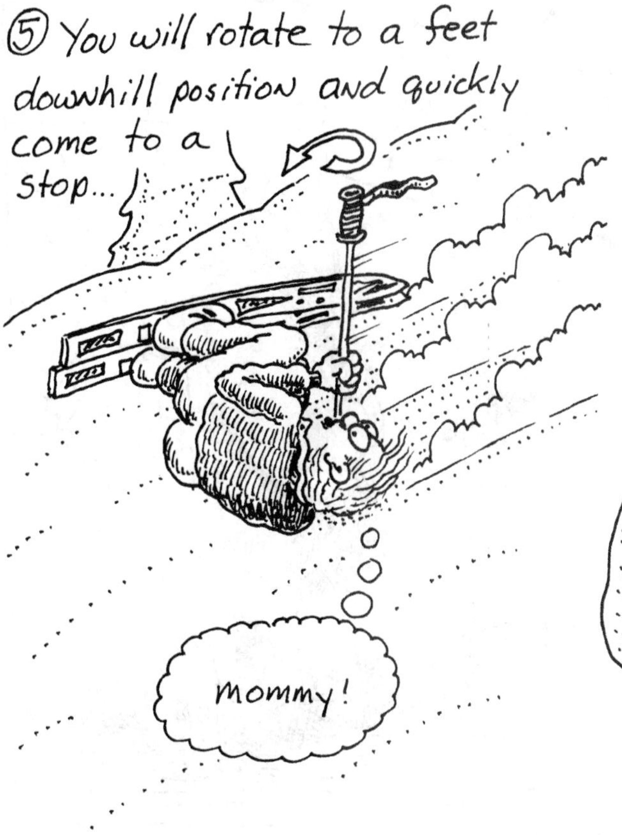
⑤ You will rotate to a feet downhill position and quickly come to a stop...
mommy!

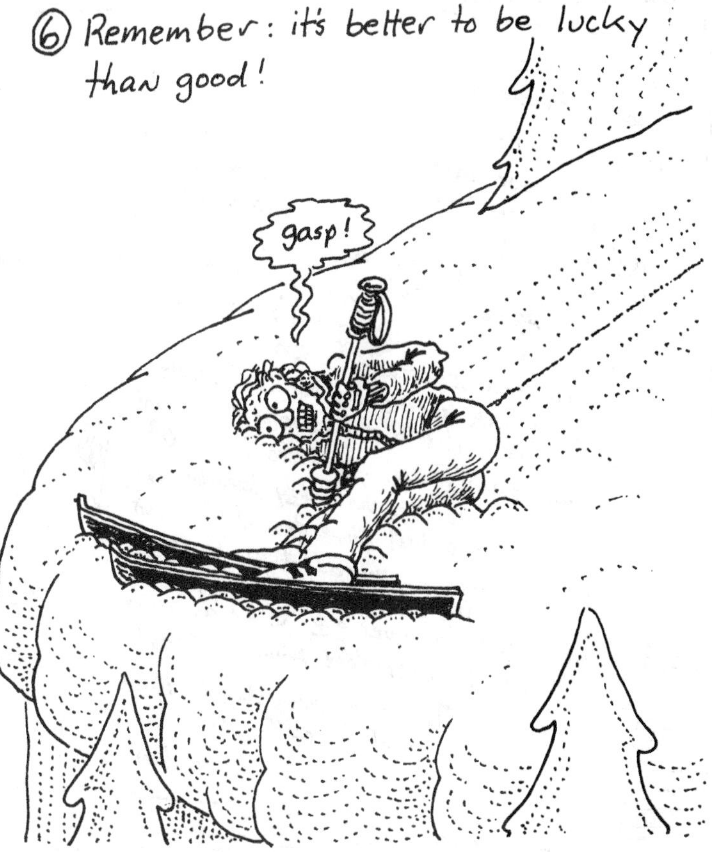
⑥ Remember: it's better to be lucky than good!
gasp!

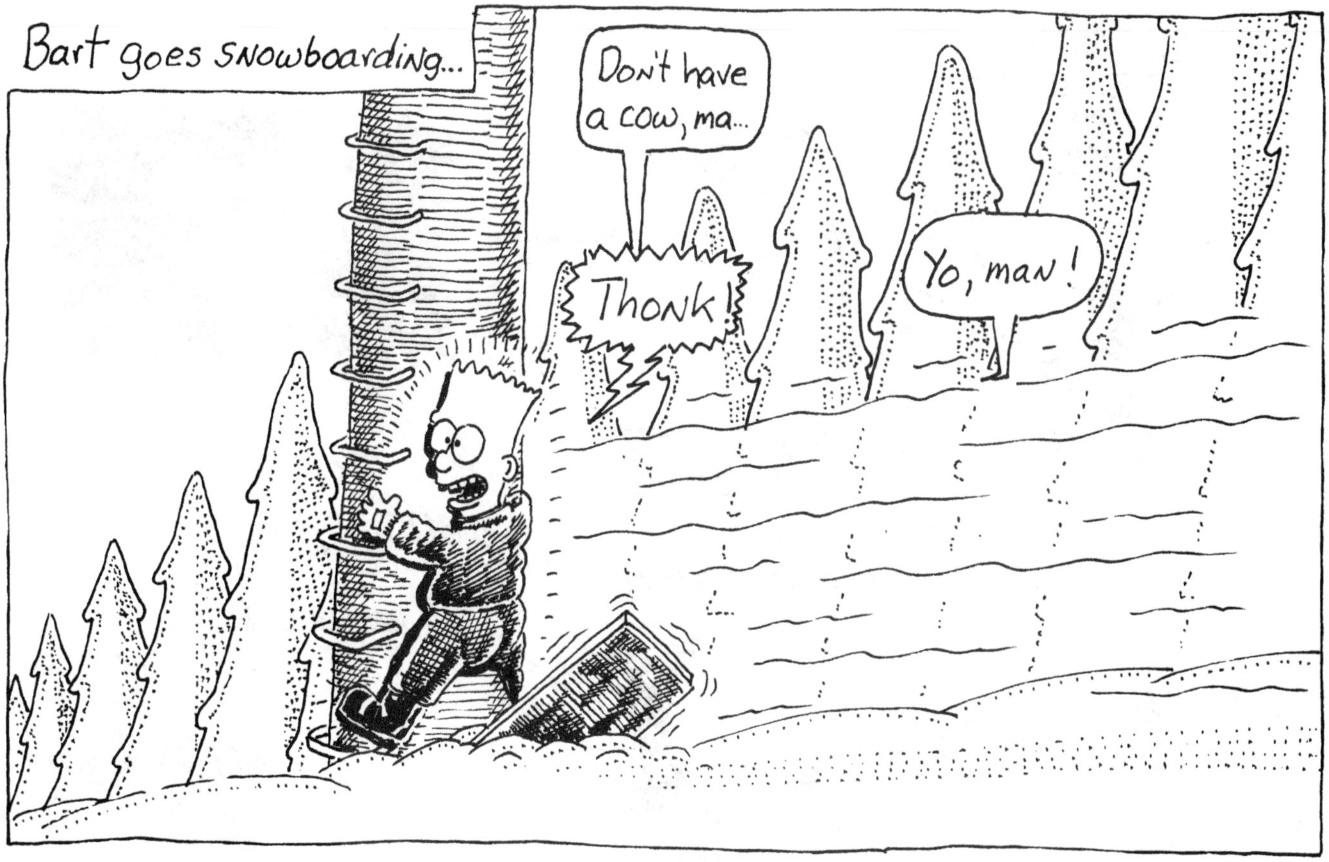
Bart goes SNOWboarding...
Don't have a cow, ma...
Thonk!
Yo, man!

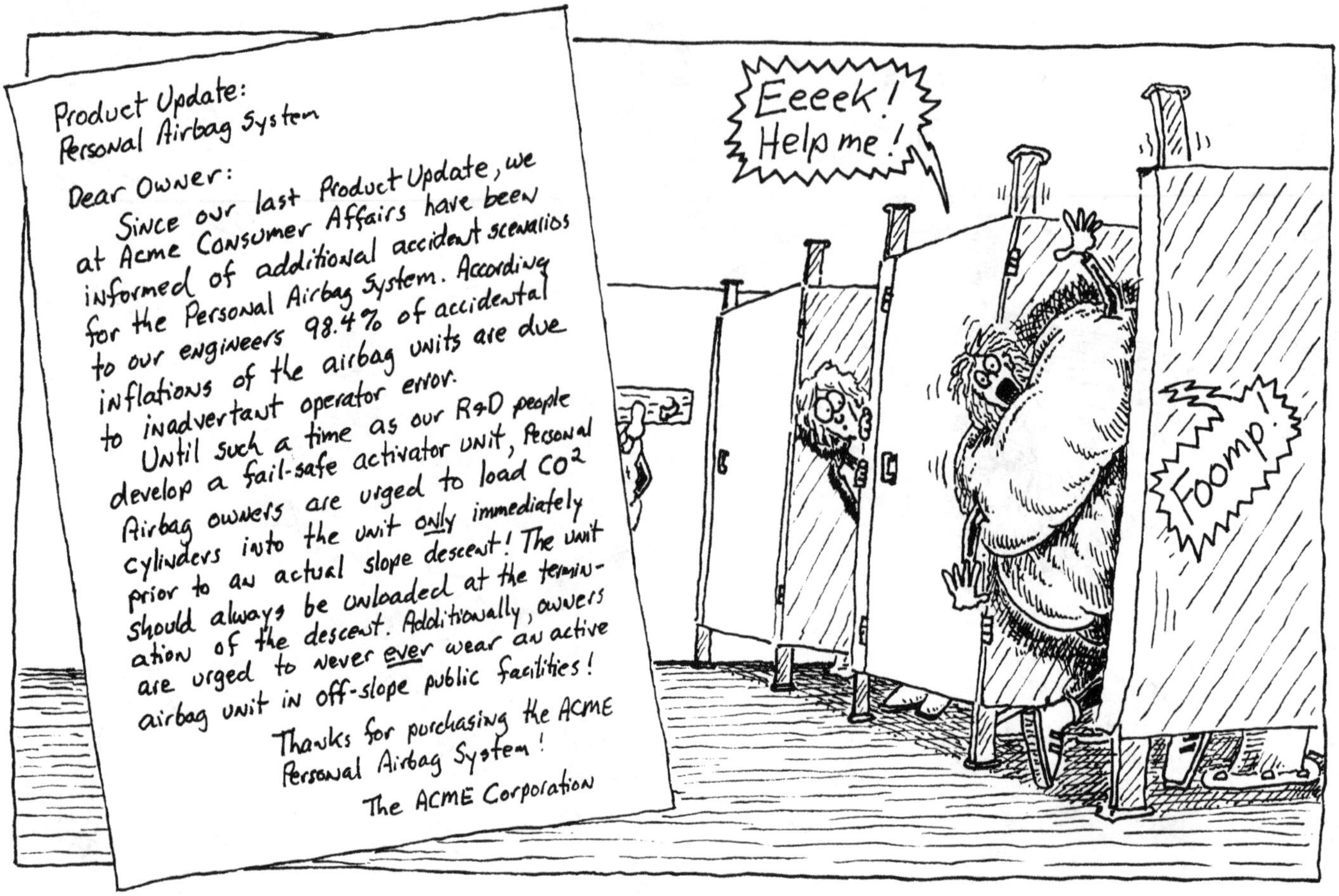
Product Update:
Personal Airbag System
Dear Owner:
Since our last Product Update, we at Acme Consumer Affairs have been informed of additional accident scenarios for the Personal Airbag System. According to our engineers 98.4% of accidental inflations of the airbag units are due to inadvertant operator error.
Until such a time as our R&D people develop a fail-safe activator unit, Personal Airbag owners are urged to load CO2 cylinders into the unit only immediately prior to an actual slope descent! The unit should always be unloaded at the termination of the descent. Additionally, owners are urged to never ever wear an active airbag unit in off-slope public facilities!
Thanks for purchasing the ACME Personal Airbag System!
The ACME Corporation
Eeeek! Help me!
Foomp!

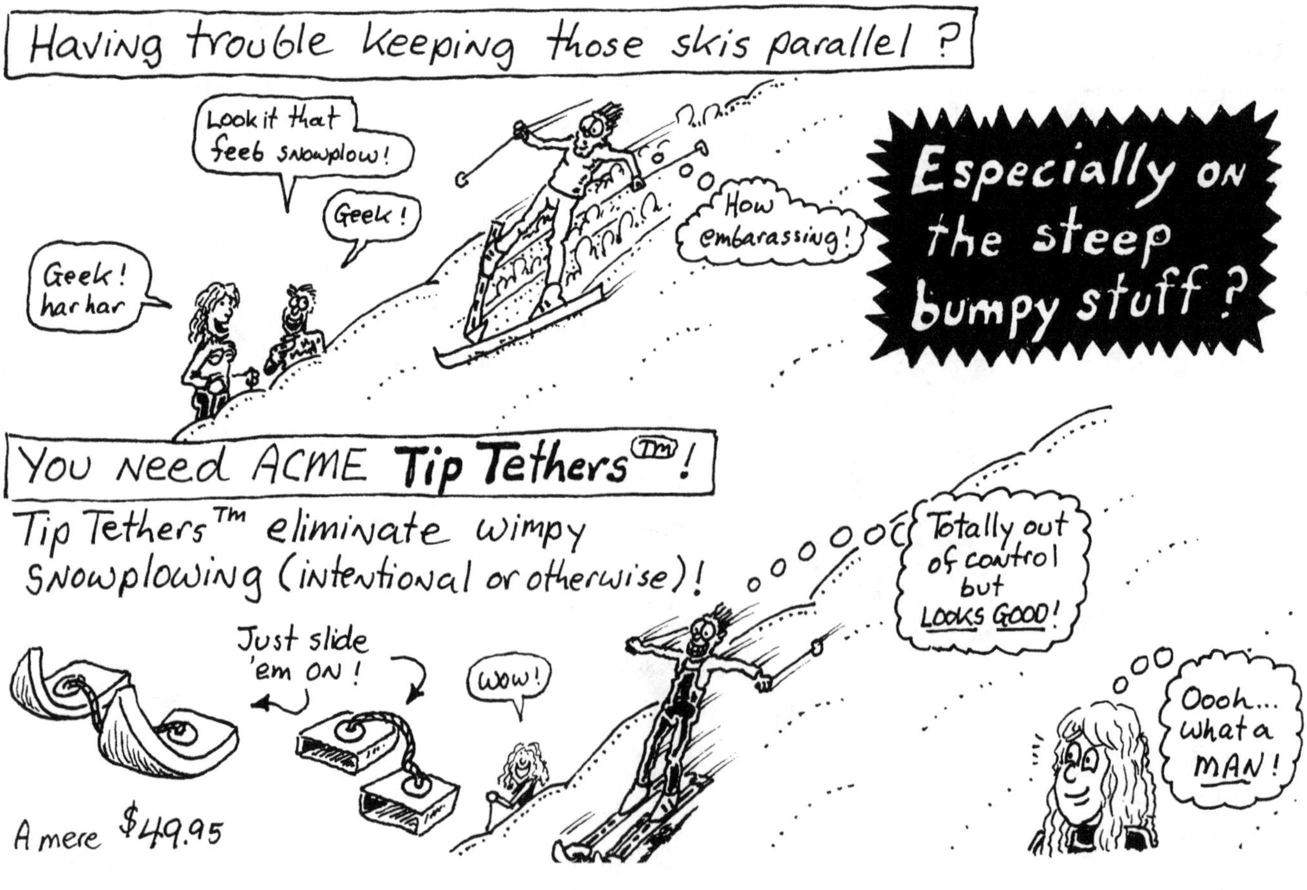
Having trouble keeping those skis parallel?
Look it that feeb snowplow!
Geek!
Geek! har har
How embarassing!
Especially on the steep bumpy stuff?
You need ACME Tip Tethers(TM)!
Tip Tethers™ eliminate wimpy snowplowing (intentional or otherwise)!
Just slide 'em on!
Wow!
Totally out of control but LOOKS GOOD!
Oooh... what a MAN!
A mere $49.95

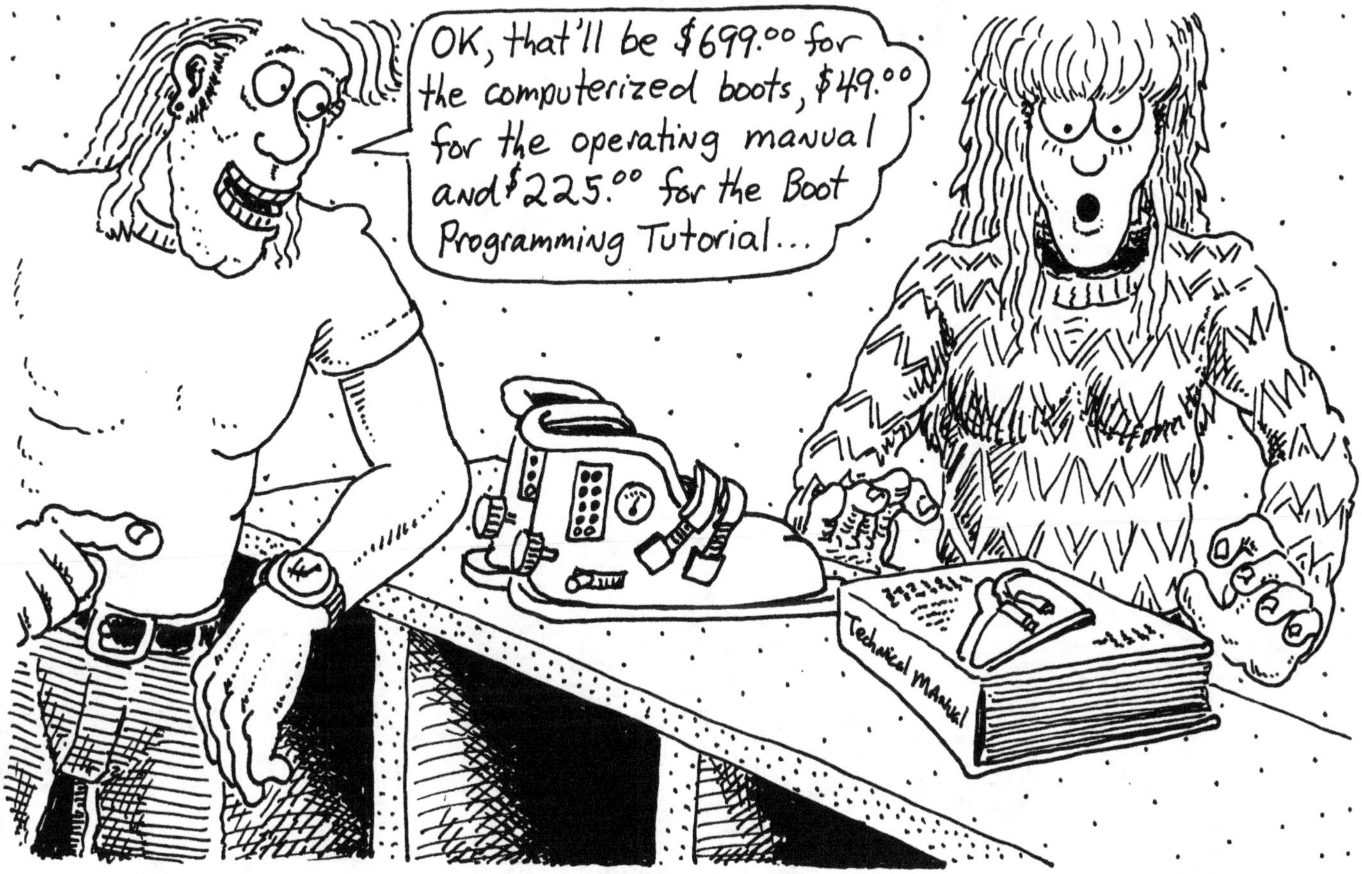
OK, that'll be $699.00 for the computerized boots, $49.00 for the operating manual and $225.00 for the Boot Programming Tutorial...
Technical MANUAL

Apres Ski Cartoons

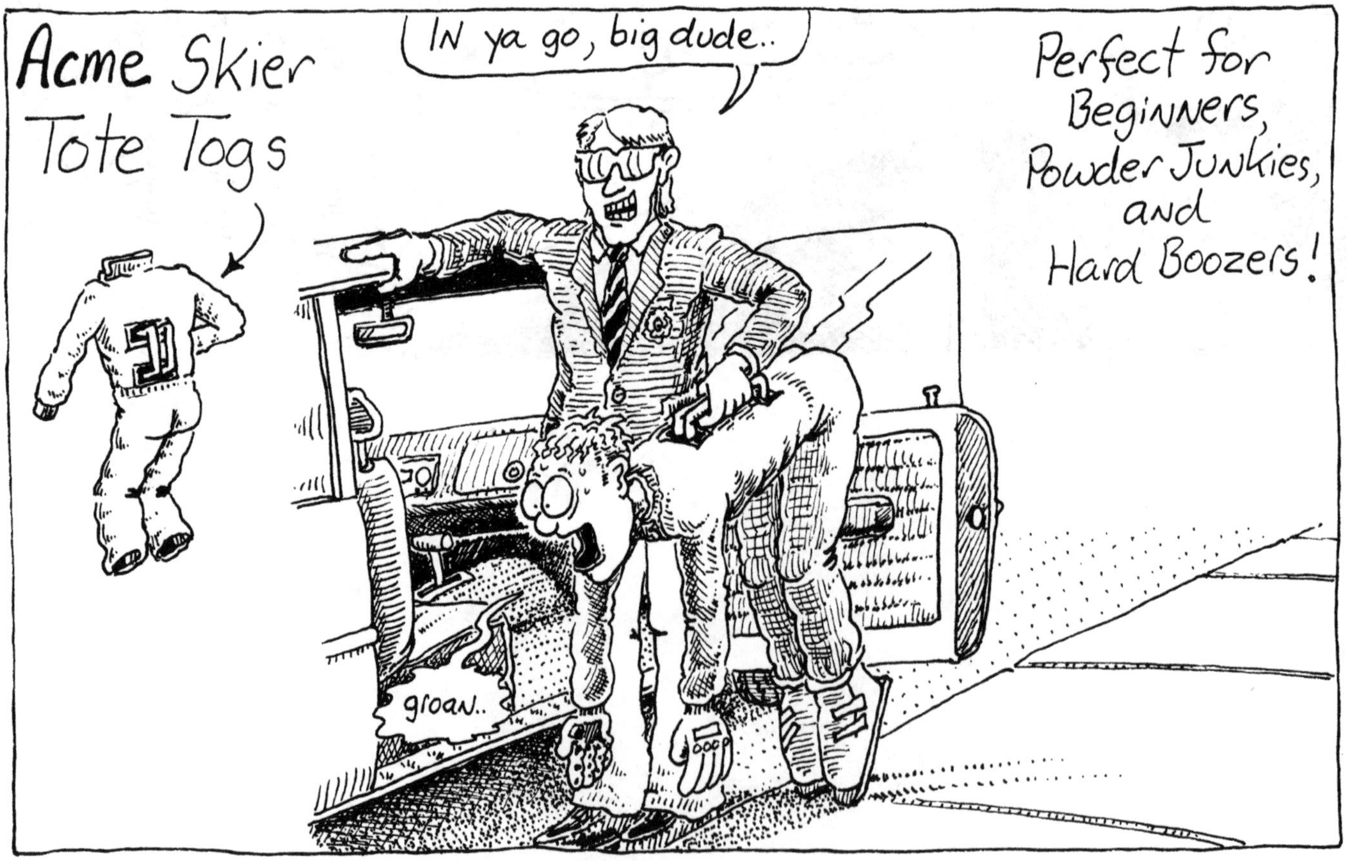
Acme Skier Tote Togs
IN ya go, big dude..
Perfect for Beginners, Powder Junkies, and Hard Boozers!
groan..

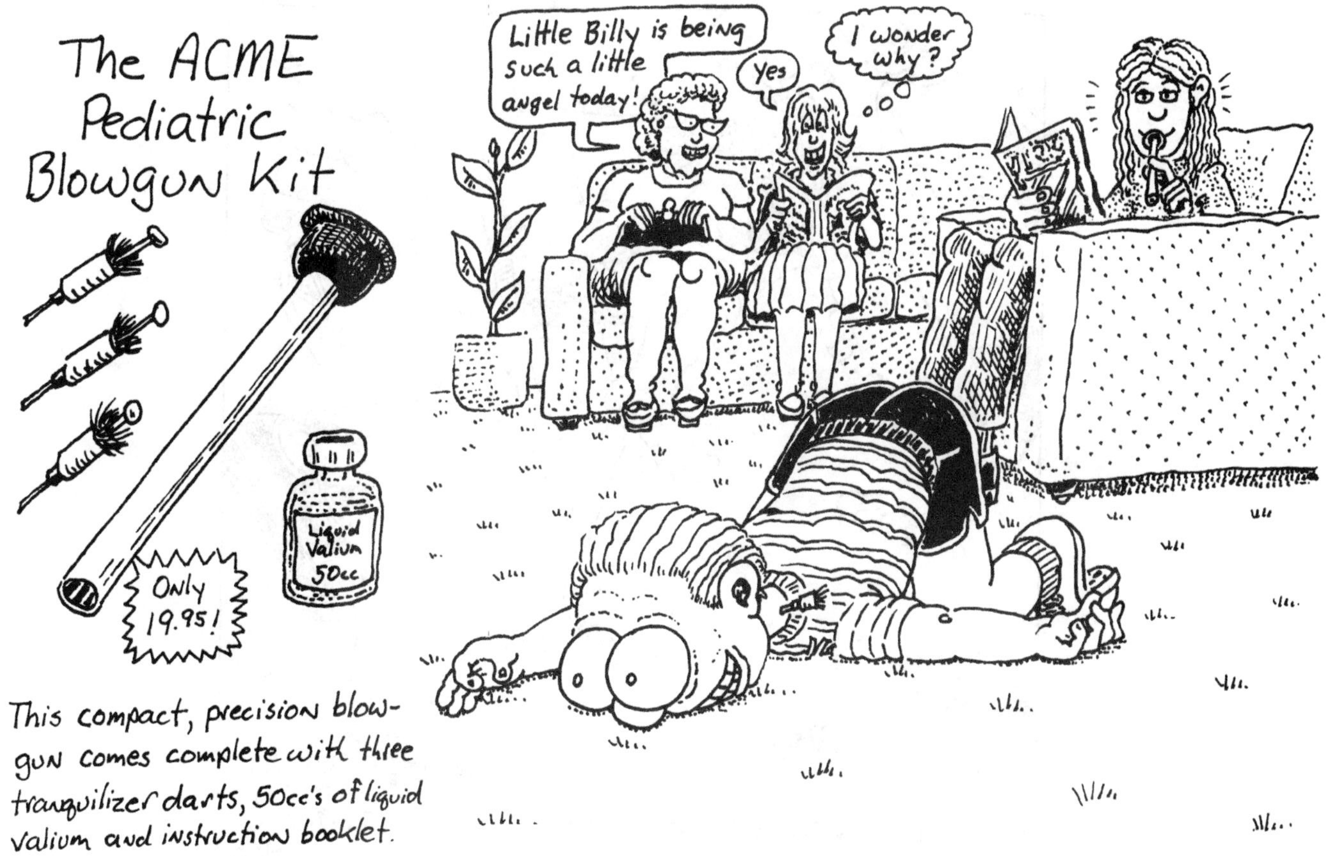
The ACME Pediatric Blowgun Kit
Only 19.95!
Liquid Valium 50cc
This compact, precision blowgun comes complete with three tranquilizer darts, 50cc's of liquid valium and instruction booklet.
Little Billy is being such a little angel today!
Yes
I wonder why?

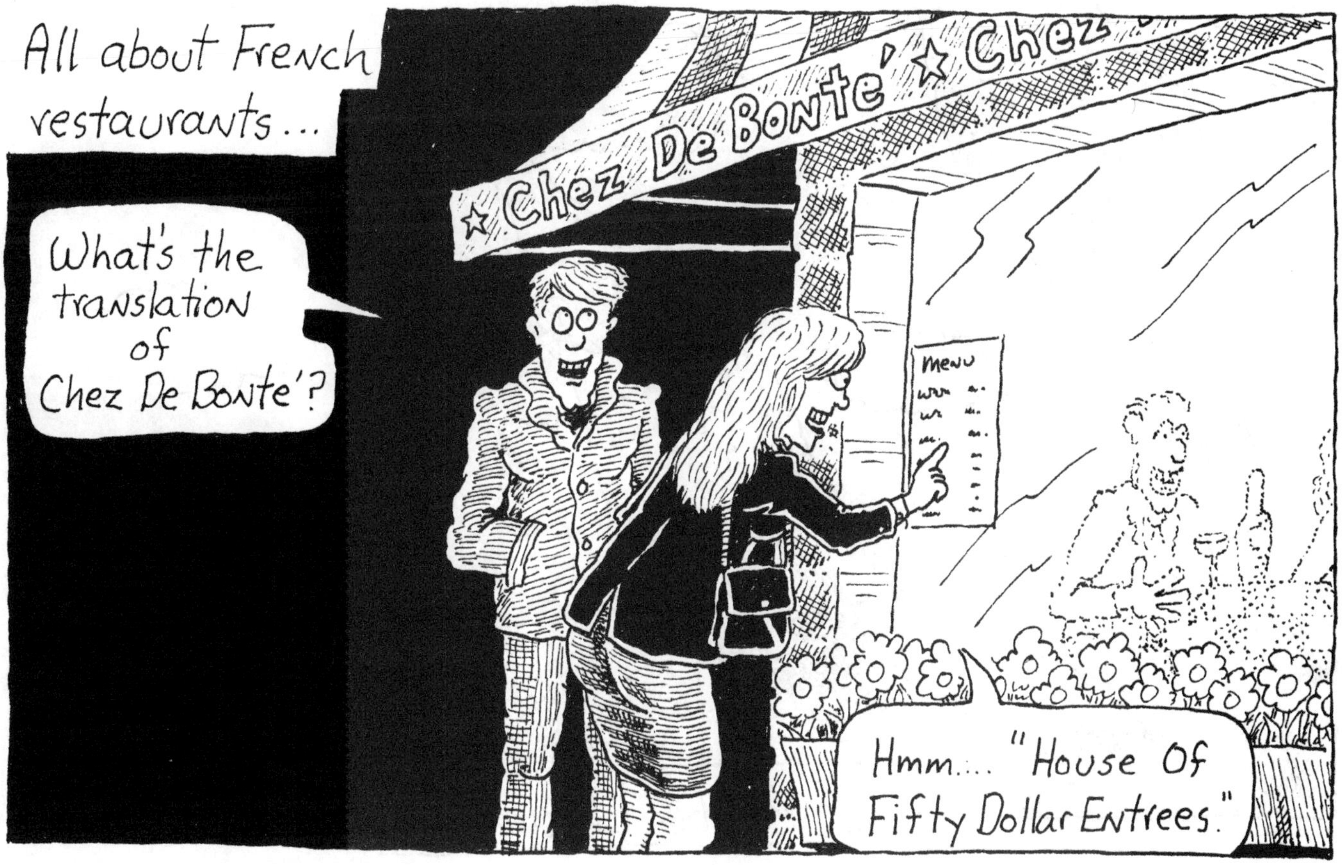
All about French restaurants...
Chez De Bonte' ☆ Chez
What's the translation of Chez De Bonte'?
Menu
Hmm.... "House Of Fifty Dollar Entrees."

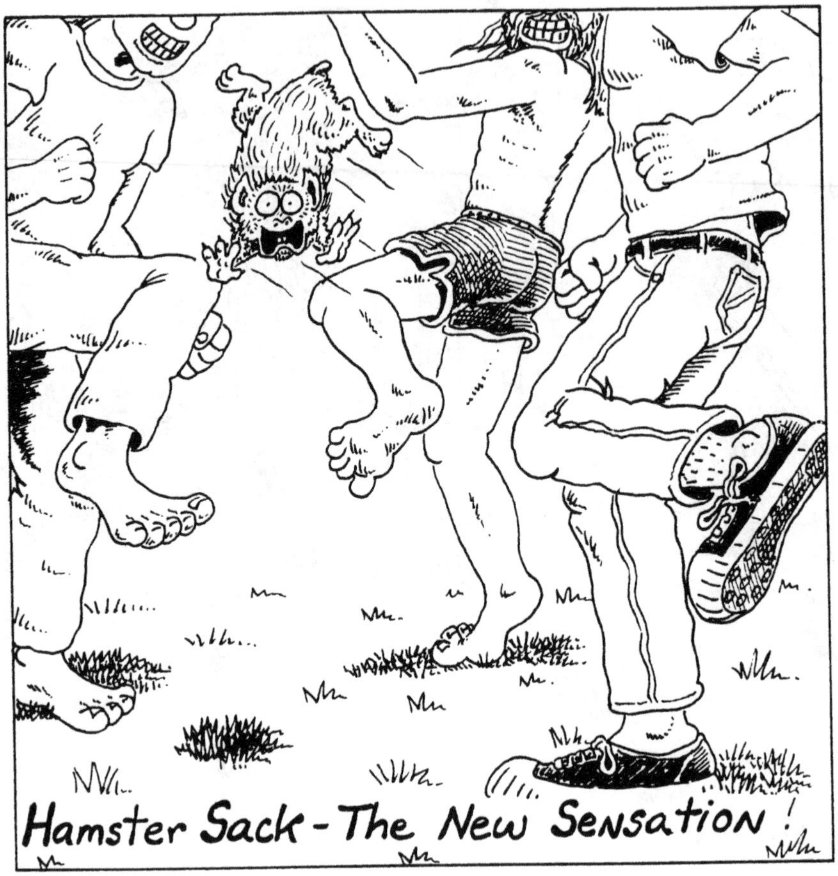
Hamster Sack - The New Sensation!

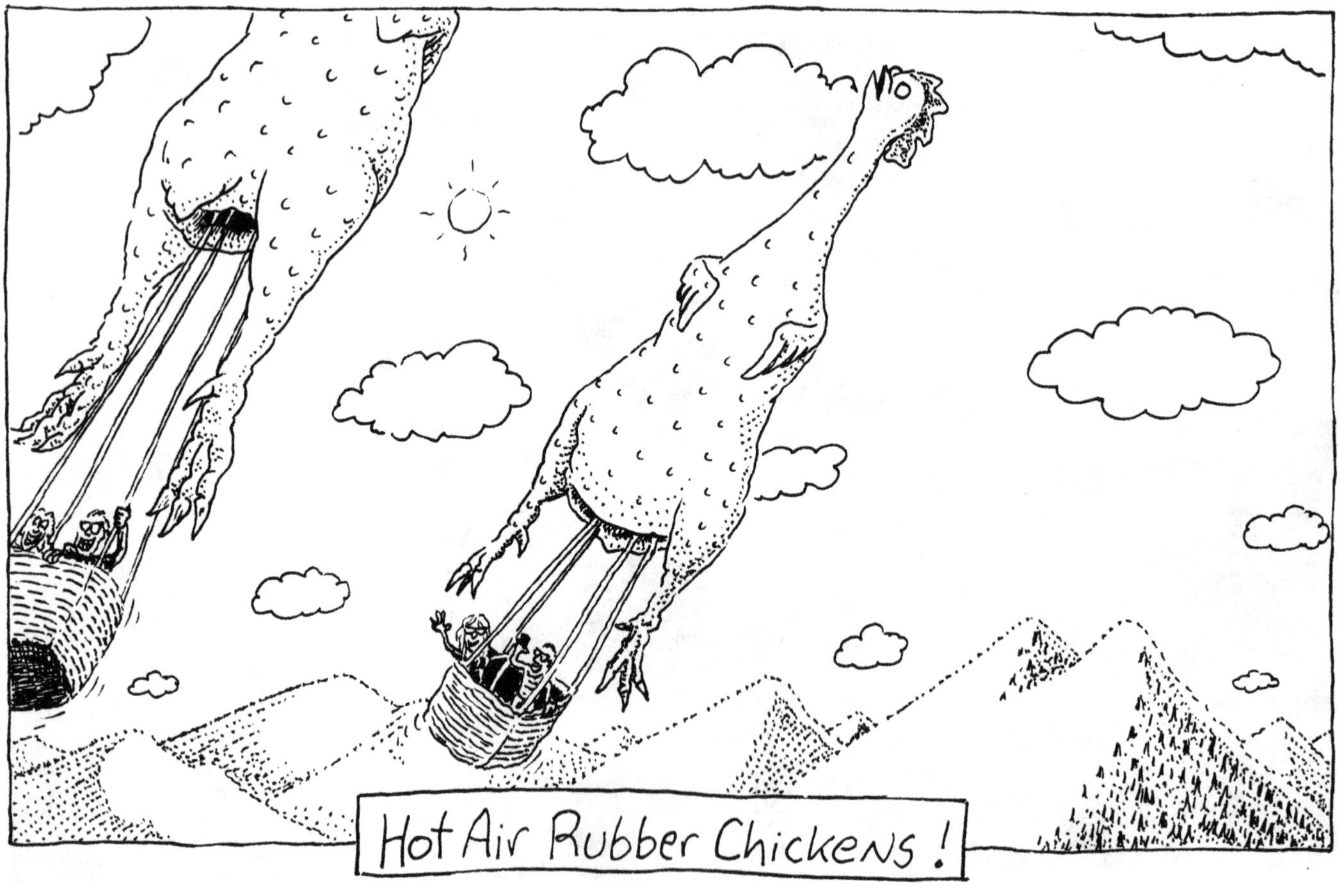
Hot Air Rubber Chickens!

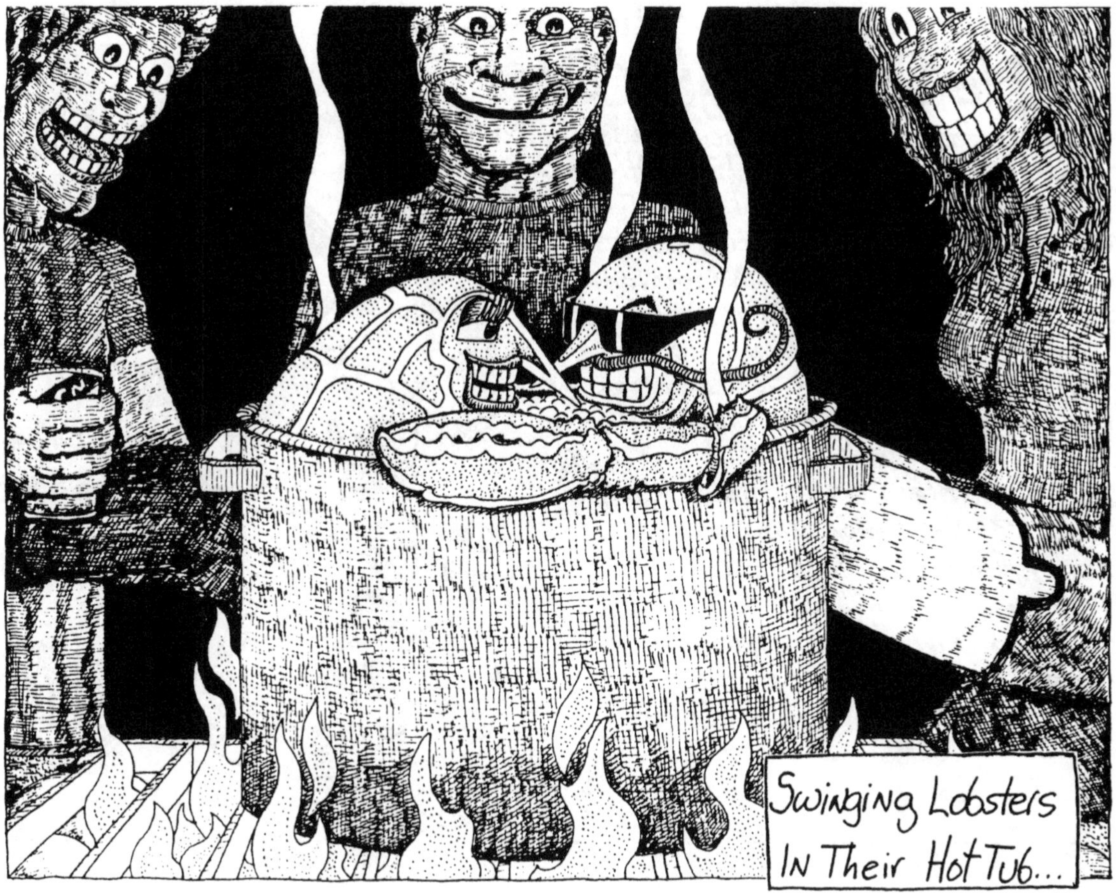
Swinging Lobsters In Their Hot Tub...

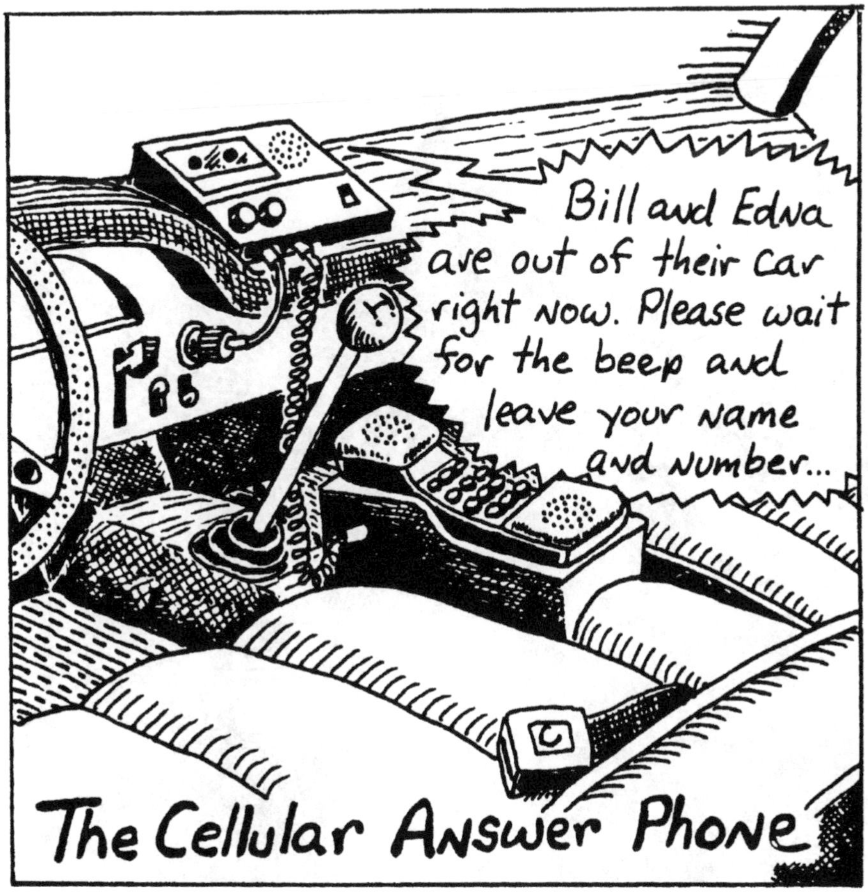
Bill and Edna are out of their car right now. Please wait for the beep and leave your name and number...
The Cellular Answer Phone

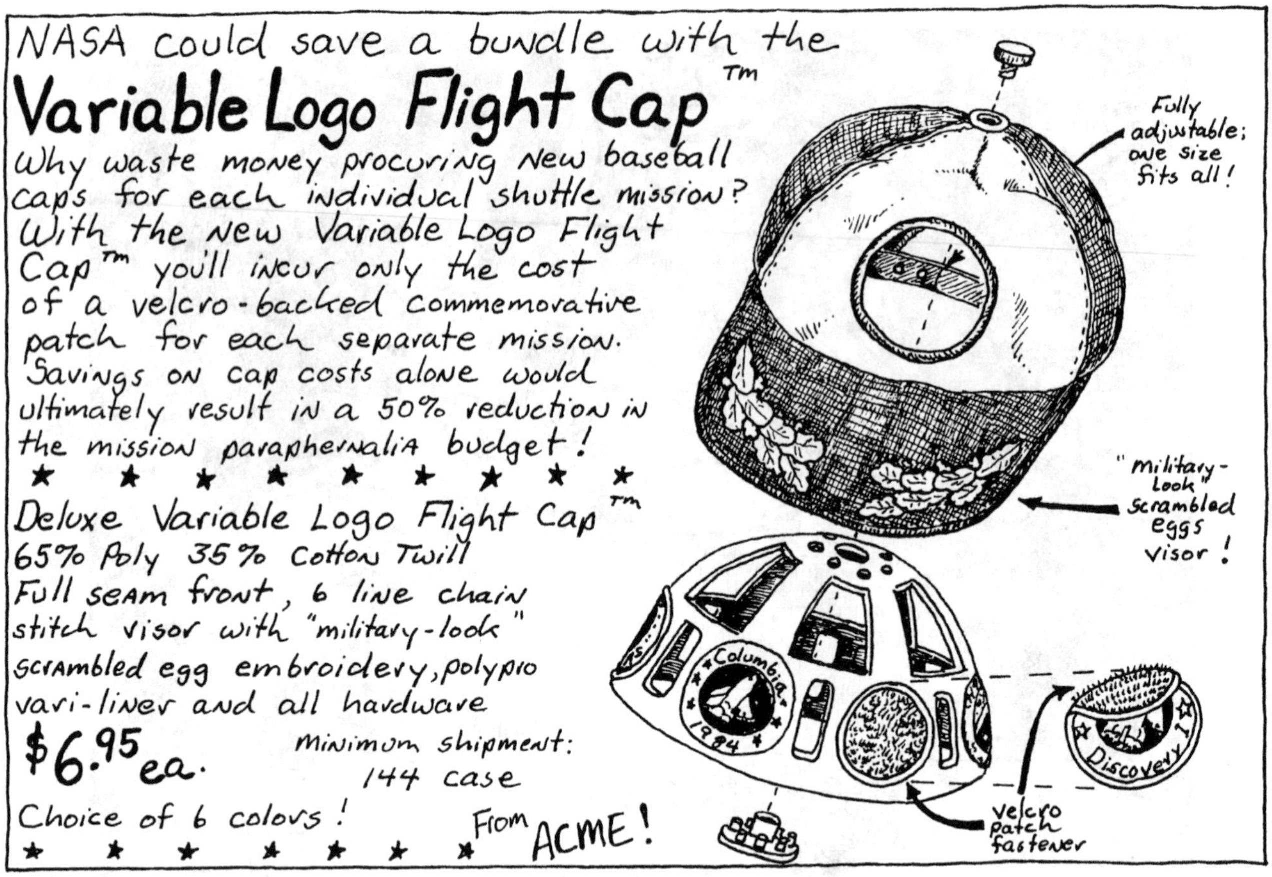
NASA could save a bundle with the
Variable Logo Flight Cap™
Why waste money procuring new baseball caps for each individual shuttle mission? With the new Variable Logo Flight Cap™ you'll incur only the cost of a velcro-backed commemorative patch for each separate mission. Savings on cap costs alone would ultimately result in a 50% reduction in the mission paraphernalia budget!
Deluxe Variable Logo Flight Cap™
65% Poly 35% Cotton Twill
Full seam front, 6 line chain stitch visor with "military-look" scrambled egg embroidery, polypro vari-liner and all hardware
$6.95 ea.
Minimum shipment: 144 case
Choice of 6 colors!
From ACME!
Fully adjustable; one size fits all!
"military-look" scrambled eggs visor!
Columbia 1984
Discovery
velcro patch fastener

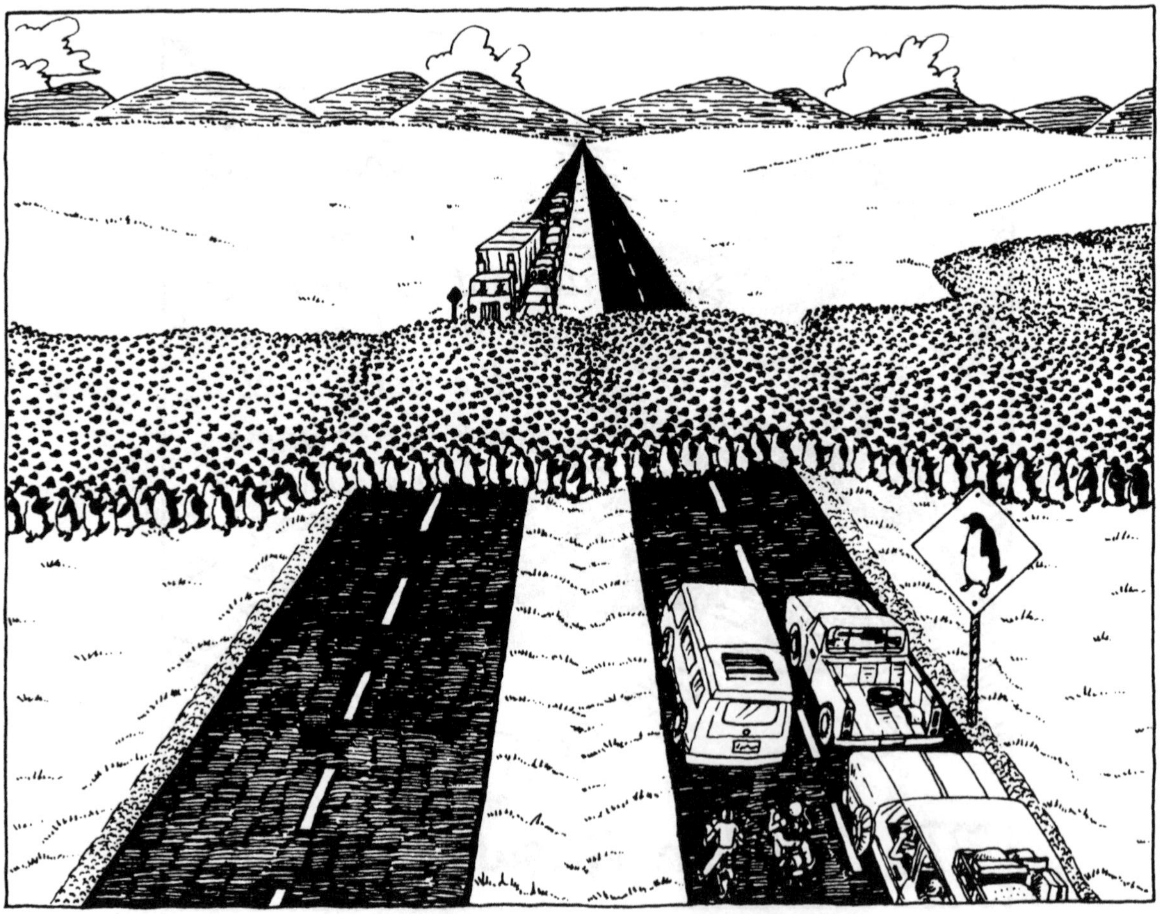

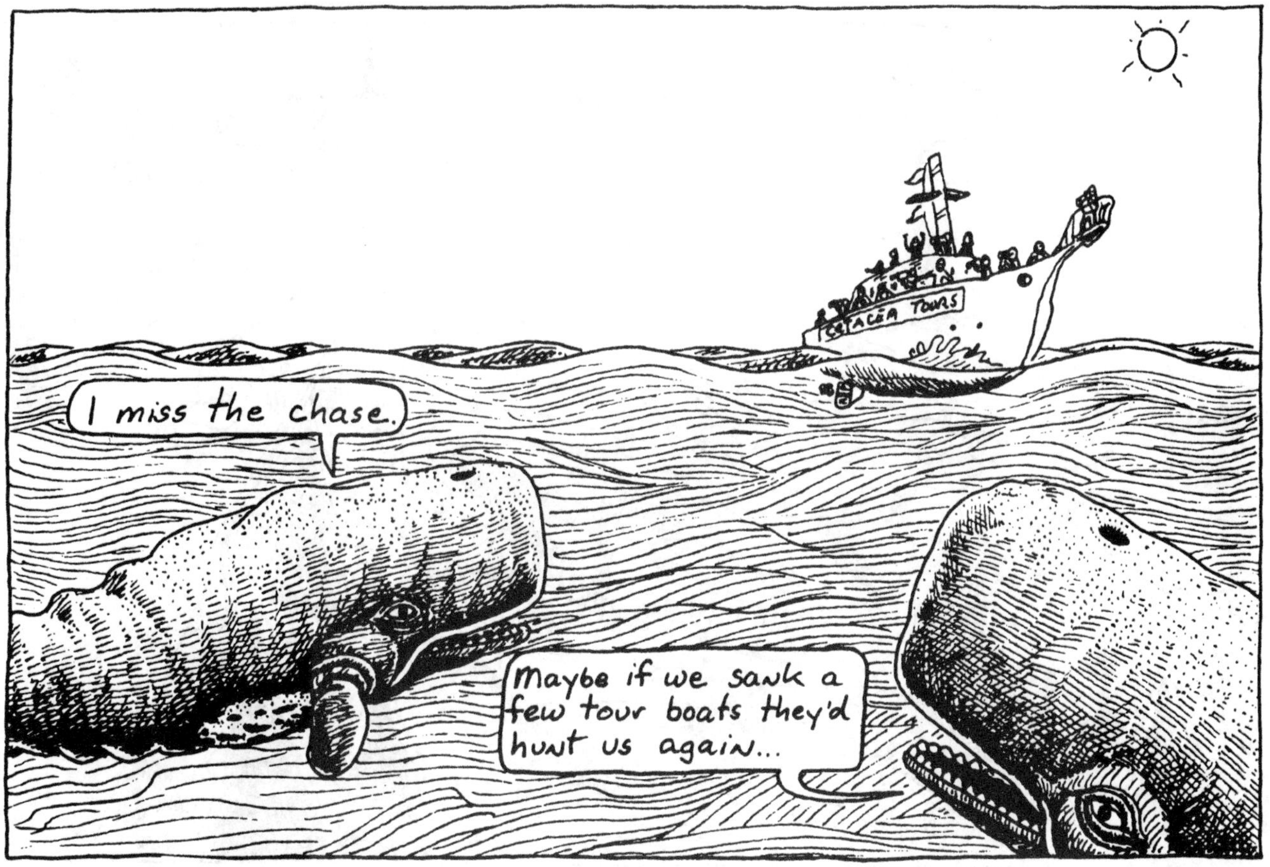
CETACEA TOURS
I miss the chase.
Maybe if we sank a few tour boats they'd hunt us again...

Granola (grân·ō·lâ) N. Radical vegetarian with New Ageist tendencies. Likes: earth colors, cross country resort touring, Volvo, Birkenstock, large crystals, Windham Hill hippie muzak, Sierra Club, and yoga. Dislikes: day-glo neon attire, snowboarders, gnarly mogul fields, radical mountainbikers, getting drunk and puking on your buddies, mohawks, bands with names like "B-52's" and "Anthrax", wines that come in bottles with screw-off caps, cigarettes/cigars, drunk Texans, and four wheel drive vehicles with jacked-up suspensions and gun racks full of assault rifles. Hates: sarcastic cartoonists, rap music, handguns, A-10 Warthogs, and Earth First.

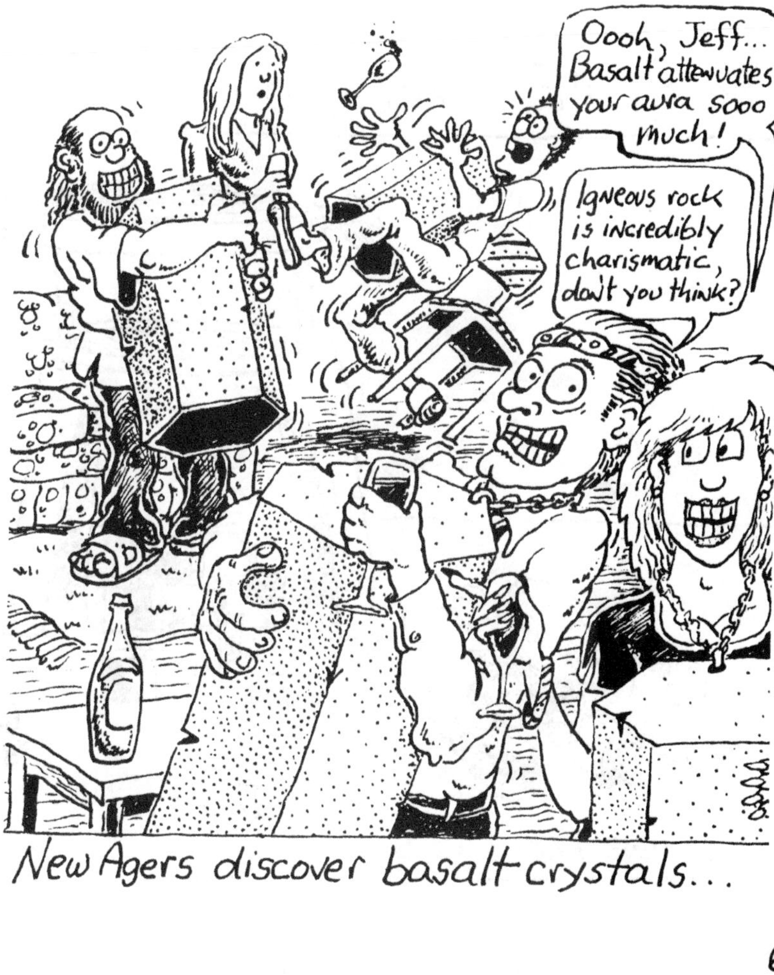
Oooh, Jeff... Basalt attenuates your aura sooo much!
Igneous rock is incredibly charismatic, don't you think?

New Agers discover basalt crystals...

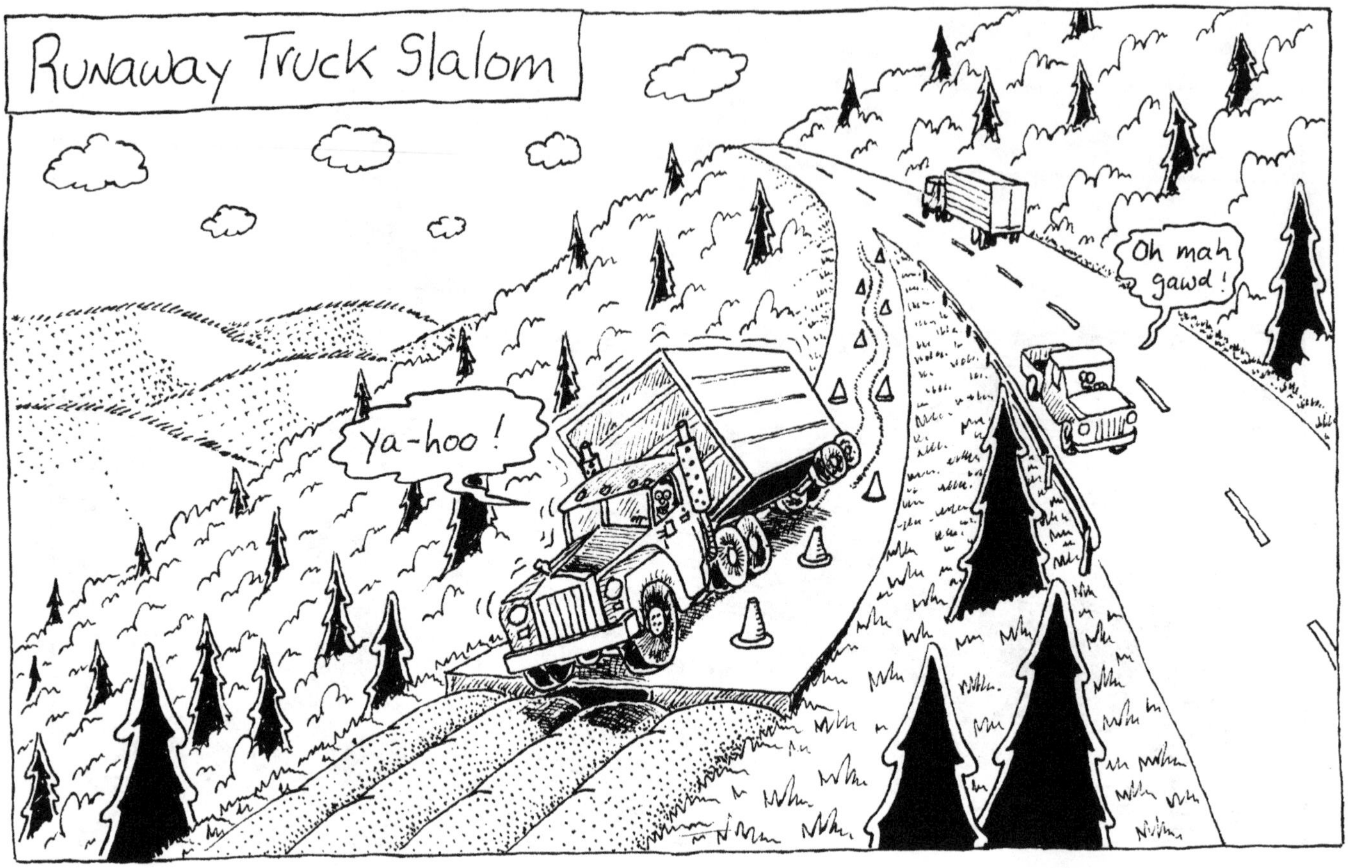
Runaway Truck Slalom
Ya-hoo!
Oh mah gawd!

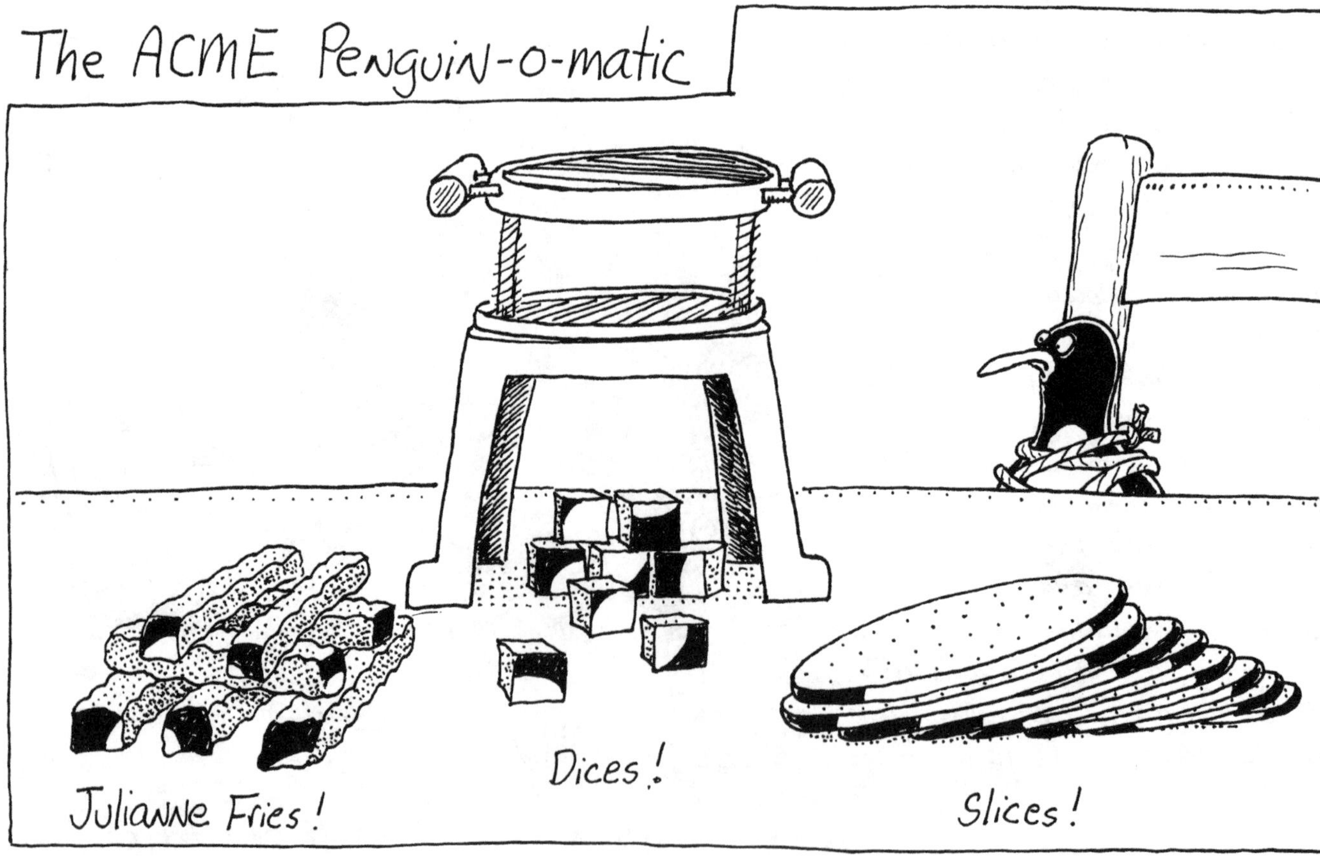
The ACME Penguin-o-matic
Julianne Fries!
Dices!
Slices!

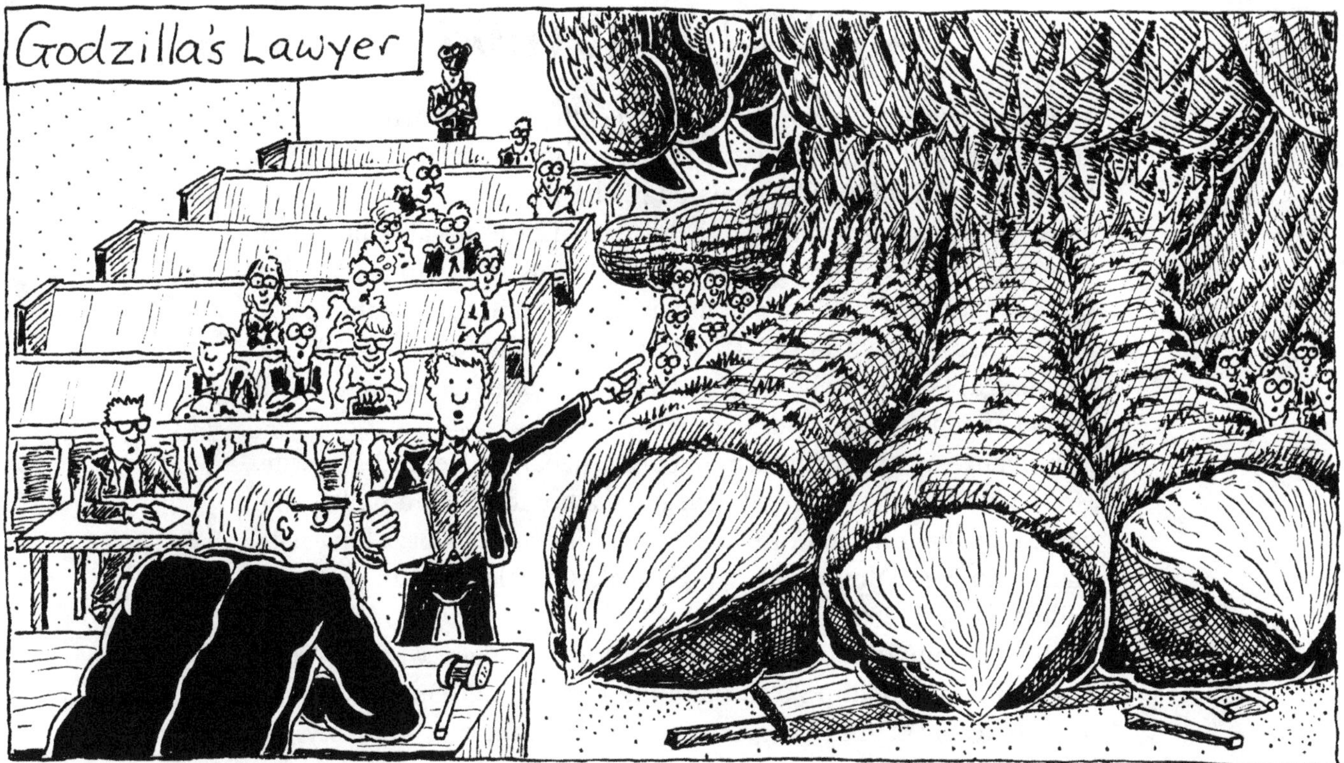
Godzilla's Lawyer

"...a fit of pique? Perhaps.... but the absolute destruction of an entire metropolitan area!? Your Honor... these charges against my client are utterly preposterous!"

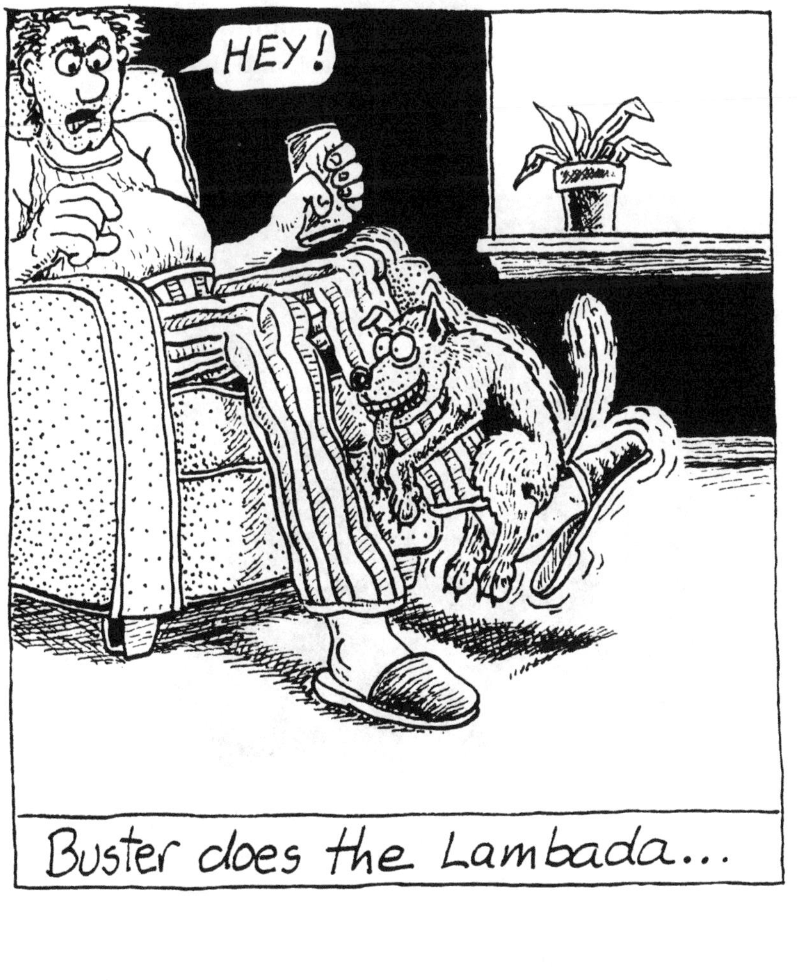
HEY!

Buster does the Lambada...

ABOUT THE AUTHOR

William "Not Bill" Nealy was a wild, gentle, brilliant artist and creator turned cult hero who wrote 10 books for Menasha Ridge Press from 1982 to 2000. William shared his hard-won "crash-and-learn" experiences through humorous hand-drawn cartoons and illustrated river maps that enabled generations to follow in his footsteps. His subjects included paddling, mountain biking, skiing, and inline skating. His hand-drawn, poster-size river maps of the Nantahala, Ocoee, Chattooga, Gauley, Youghiogheny, and several other rivers are still sought after and in use today.

William was born in Birmingham, Alabama. He and his wife, Holly Wallace, spent their adult years in a home William built in the woods on the outskirts of Chapel Hill, North Carolina, along with an assortment of dogs, lizards, pigs, snakes, turtles, and amphibians. William died in 2001.

His longtime friend and publisher, Bob Sehlinger, wrote: "When William Nealy died in 2001, paddling lost its poet laureate, one of its best teachers, and its greatest icon. William was arguably the best-known ambassador of whitewater sport, entertaining and instructing hundreds of thousands of paddlers through his illustrated books, including the classics: *Whitewater Home Companion Volumes I and II, Whitewater Tales of Terror, Kayaks to Hell,* and his best-known work, *Kayak,* which combined expert paddling instruction with artful caricatures and parodies of the whitewater community itself."

You can learn more about William, his art, and his many books at thewilliamnealy.com.

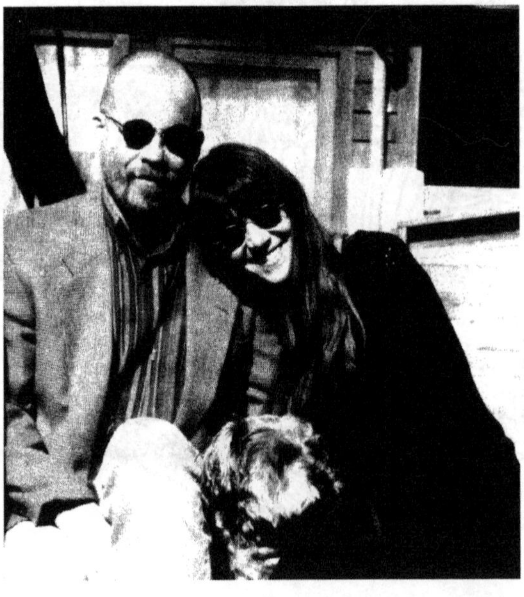

photo: MAGPIE

CPSIA information can be obtained
at www.ICGtesting.com
Printed in the USA
JSHW060333210423
40663JS00002B/5

9 781634 043700